Oriental Wells

Oriental Wells

The Early Romantic Poets and Their Eastern Muse

Md. Monirul Islam

BLOOMSBURY
NEW DELHI • LONDON • OXFORD • NEW YORK • SYDNEY

BLOOMSBURY INDIA
Bloomsbury Publishing India Pvt. Ltd
Second Floor, LSC Building No. 4, DDA Complex, Pocket C – 6 & 7,
Vasant Kunj, New Delhi 110070

BLOOMSBURY, BLOOMSBURY ACADEMIC INDIA and the Diana logo are trademarks of
Bloomsbury Publishing Plc

First published in India 2021
This edition published 2021

Bloomsbury Academic
An imprint of Bloomsbury Publishing Plc

ISBN: HB: 978-93-89165-19-7; eBook: 978-93-89165-21-0

2 4 6 8 10 9 7 5 3 1

Typeset in Minion Pro by Manipal Technologies Limited
Printed and bound in India by Replika Press Pvt. Ltd.

To my teacher Sri Shankar Chatterjee and my late father Md Hasen Ali

Contents

Acknowledgments ix

Introduction 1

I "Stick to the East": Understanding the Context 21

II Tales and Translations: Setting Tropes and Shaping of Genres 43

III "For the darkness of Asia was startled": Blake and the East 73

IV "Orientaliana": Landor and Southey 106

V The "damsel with a dulcimer": Coleridge, Wordsworth, and the Eastern Muse 155

Conclusion 222

Works Cited 229

Index 253

About the Author 278

Acknowledgments

The book is based on the research conducted since 2007 when I started working for my PhD degree on the Eastern connections of the British Romantic poets. In this long and arduous journey, my mentor Sri Shankar Chatterjee has been a great source of inspiration. He stood by me through thick and thin. I am also immensely indebted to my teacher Smt. Sharmila Majumdar for tirelessly going through the drafts and giving her valuable suggestions. I must mention Professor Ashok Sengupta for the support I have received from him. I would take this opportunity to express my gratitude to my colleagues at Presidency University and elsewhere. Dr Souvik Mukherjee first made the proposal that I should work on a monograph with Bloomsbury; Professor Sumit Chakrabarti has often helped me with his suggestions on different issues related to this book; Kalyan Kumar Das had always had the time to discuss the project, and Dr Chirantan Sarkar helped my ideas take shape with his sharp questions and critical observations.

I also owe a lot to different libraries and digital platforms for my research. I would like to thank the employees of the National Library, Kolkata, the Presidency University Arts Library, the British Library, London and the British Council Library, Kolkata for the cooperation I have received from them. Among the digital platforms, special mention must be made of The Blake Archive and Romantic Circles.

It has been a great experience to work with Mr Chandra Sekhar, Publisher: Academic Books, of the Bloomsbury group. Thanks, Mr Chandra Sekhar and the members of the editing team. You have been instrumental in bringing out this volume.

Most of all I am grateful to my beloved wife, Taslima Pervin, my little daughter, Moureen, and my mother, Fazilatunesha for their constant support, and for tolerating my long hours of absence from home and household duties. I owe everything to you.

Introduction

Raymond Schwab in his book *The Oriental Renaissance* argues that though the Roman and the Grecian wave ruled the European mind since the fifteenth century, Europe's entire landscape changed as the Asian influence poured in during the late-eighteenth and early-nineteenth centuries. This overpowering Eastern influence, according to Schwab, caused an Oriental Renaissance in Europe. A seismic effect of this was felt in European art, literature, and culture during the eighteenth and nineteenth centuries. To give an example, between 1776 and 1800, twenty-four plays or dramatic performances based on Eastern themes were staged in London theatres alone (Barfoot 73). Writing in the midst of the Oriental Renaissance, the Romantic poets generously borrowed from the East in their effort to re-orient the British poetic tradition. For the Romantic poets, the East with its antiquities, literature, religion, and mythology became a locus that inspired their creative imagination and an "essential" link was forged between Romanticism and the East (Schwab 482). Oriental Tales, translations of Persian, Arabic and Sanskrit literary, philosophical and religious works, tales of travels from the East, soldiers' diaries, reports, and testimonies of diplomats flooded the British print market. The amorphous body of materials affected the sensibilities of Romantic writers. These "foreign factors," as Andrew Warren defines them, also "played a role in creating a 'Romantic imagination' that forged the way for a new vision of British nationalism and imperialism" (9).[1] In other words, the Romantics' engagement with the East involved a process of negotiation as they were often concerned with 'self'-preservation—upholding the superiority of the British, the Christian, and the European tradition. This study, therefore, attempts to understand the place of the East in early Romantic poetry with a dual objective in place: firstly, understanding the nature and extent of Eastern influence on early Romantic poetry; and secondly, exploring the politics of their engagement with the East. The study mainly engages with the Romantic poets' creative negotiations with the Middle East and India and with the two Eastern religions—Islam and Hinduism.

Before proceeding any further into the act of analyzing the way the Romantic poets negotiated with an overpowering Eastern influence, it is essential to talk about certain terminological issues. Words like East, Eastern, Orient, Oriental, Near East, Far East will be employed throughout this book. Employing these terms in a twenty-first-century study is very problematic because their definitions, or what they designate, have changed over the ages and the terms are discursively loaded. However, they are unavoidable in any study of East–West encounter and, therefore, a clarification must come as to the possible senses in which these terms are used in this study. Ewan Anderson's explanation of the various parts of the East may be illuminating in this context:

> From the Great Age of Discovery in the fifteenth century it has increasingly become customary to distinguish between the Near East and the Far East. The Near East comprised essentially the Eastern Mediterranean and adjacent lands while the Far East was everything east of India. The Indian Subcontinent was in terms of trade and military strategic thought the centre of the British empire and was, other than its most northerly and westerly approaches, located in the East but not the Near East or the Far East. Thus the Area in the Middle, the Middle East, was almost by default that lying between the Indian Subcontinent and the Near East or Levant. (12)

Anderson accepts that the currency the term Middle East enjoys today owes to American geopolitical historian Alfred Mahan. However, he points out that the term was in currency in the British India Office during the mid-nineteenth century. Although Anderson's observations are very useful for the present study, the terms are cautiously used here, because the terms are very reductive as they share a close affinity to Western Orientalism and colonialism and were often conceived in opposition to the West. Moreover, the area of the Near East or the Levant, as defined by Anderson, is included within the broader idea of the Middle East. The label 'Near East,' therefore, is seldom used in this study in relation to the Romantic poets; however, it is sometimes used in relation to the Medieval or Early Modern period, when the idea of the Near East was more relevant.

In the current edition of the *Shorter Oxford English Dictionary,* one of the meanings of the term 'orient' is: "the countries east of the Mediterranean esp. those of eastern Asia." However, the notion of the East and the Orient in the nineteenth century can be better understood from the meaning of 'orient' as provided in the 1896 edition of the *Standard Dictionary of English Language*. The word 'orient' is explained as referring to "those countries collectively that begin with Islam on the Eastern Mediterranean and stretch through Asia." The East or the Orient for the Romantics was predominantly the Middle East and India, but China in the Far East also formed an important part of it. A clue to the Romantic conception of the East can be found in Robert Southey's *Commonplace Book*. The section entitled "Orientaliana, or Eastern and Mohammedan Collections" contains numerous references to the Islamic countries of the Middle East (Morocco, Egypt, Ethiopia, Turkey, Syria, Persia, etc.) and the Indian subcontinent; there are some references to China and Japan but these are limited in number.[2] The Romantics' notion of the East can also be estimated from Thomas De Quincey's (1785–1859) *Confessions of an English Opium Eater* (1821) where, in the section "Oriental Dreams," his dreams take him to "China and Indostan," and to Mesopotamia (Euphrates); he also dreams of Egypt, where he is kissed by the "cancerous Crocodiles" in the "Nilotic mud" (80–82).

The East, as it was understood by the Romantics, was a major source of poetic inspiration for them and the titular phrase, "Oriental

Wells" is indicative of this. The title is inspired by an entry in Robert Southey's *Commonplace Book* and Javed Majid's interpretation of the images of liquidity in Romantic poetry in *Ungoverned Imaginings: James Mill's The History of British India and Orientalism* (1992). It also draws on the long association of fountains, rills, and wells with poetic inspiration. In the section, "Orientaliana, or Eastern and Mohammedan Collections" of his *Commonplace Book*, Southey gathers different kinds of information on the East, beginning with the mundane to the literary–philosophical; it puts together extracts from other writers in addition to his commentaries. There is one excerpt here entitled "Oriental Wells." The passage from Captain Thomas Williamson's book *Oriental Field Sports* describes a well from where water can be sourced quite easily. A reading of the quoted passage shows that this water is used to increase the fertility of the land around it and nurture crops. Men bind earthen or iron pitchers in ropes and dip them into the well and when the pitcher is filled, the water is dropped into the channels that lead to the fertile fields. However, the wells that make the land fertile are also a source of danger:

> From the insecure manner in which these wells are generally finished, as well as from the looseness of the soil in many places, they rarely last long. In such cases the peasant digs others, without doing anything to those which have fallen in. This is productive of considerable danger, not only to hunters, but to foot passengers; many of whom are precipitated into them. (*Commonplace Book* 414)

The wells, therefore, watered the land making it fertile, but were also a source of peril and anxiety. The whole section "Orientaliana, or Eastern and Mohammedan Collections" characterizes the East as fertile and full of resources, but at the same time dangerous; it reflects a simultaneous presence of attraction and anxiety. So, the 'wells' becomes a signifier of the East itself—the East as a source of poetic inspiration but also a source of anxiety.

Images of liquidity, fountains, wells, rills, etc., are frequently employed by the Romantic poets and Javed Majid interprets such images in their Eastern poems in terms of Romantic creativity. Majid discovers in Southey's *Thalaba* and *The Curse of Kehama,* a preoccupation with images of "plumbing and probing depths" (49) and interprets them as indicating "a tentative exploration and probing of new sources of creativity and material made available by oriental renaissance" (50–51). The images of liquidity and flooding, according to Majid, reinforce the sense of tapping of new sources of creativity in Southey's epics. However, often a sense of chiaroscuro and refraction are evoked in these images of depth and this, according to Majid, "indicates the perilous nature of this tapping of new sources of creativity, as does the evocation of the overwhelming sense of flooding in the epics." As Majid explains, the Oriental Renaissance was not only a source of creative inspiration, but it also posed a threat to the superiority and uniqueness of the Greco-Roman heritage which was central to the definition of the European notion of cultural superiority (81–84). The title, therefore, conveys the main concern of the book, namely, the relation between the East and Romantic creativity. The Romantic poets, we will see, turned to the East for their poetic inspiration and they used the easily available materials on and from the East as their creative sources; but simultaneously, the East was also a source of anxiety for them. The anxiety was caused by a number of factors, such as the fear that the domestic space may be infected by the empire, the fear and anxiety over preserving the sacredness and primacy of Christianity, the anxiety over preserving the pre-eminence of the European as opposed to the Asian culture and the fear of being infected with Oriental corruption, vice and diseases. The plural, 'wells,' significantly captures the multiplicity of the sources that the Romantics drew their inspiration from.

This study centers on the first generation Romantic poets. The poets covered in this study started their poetic career in the last decade of the eighteenth century or before when British Orientalism was in its early phase of enthusiasm, and they continued to write deep into the nineteenth century when the initial phase of Orientalist fervor in Britain was over and the nature of the Orientalist discourse changed significantly. William Blake (1757–1827) began his poetic career in the 1780s, and William Wordsworth (1770–1850), Samuel Taylor Coleridge (1772–1834), Robert Southey (1774–1843), and Walter Savage Landor (1775–1864) in the 1790s. It is William Blake who is taken up for discussion before others, but this study does not follow any chronological pattern; Coleridge is discussed before Wordsworth or Landor before Southey because it makes better sense of the discourse presented in this study. By the end of the eighteenth century, significant traces of Eastern influence were notable in all these five poets and most of the poems examined here were either written or begun before 1810. Landor's *Gebir* was published in 1798; Southey's *Thalaba, The Destroyer* was completed at the beginning of the nineteenth century, and he started composing *The Curse of Kehama*; while Coleridge's *The Rime of the Ancient Mariner* was part of the *Lyrical Ballads,* his "Christabel" and "Kubla Khan" were composed during 1798–1799 and the collaborative, but aborted epic on the life of Muhammad was also conceived during this time; and a version of Wordsworth's *The Prelude* was published in 1799. The first generation Romantics were more frequently writing on Eastern themes in the early phase of their career and, therefore, their early works dominate this study, but their later compositions are also significant in terms of locating their changing perspective vis-à-vis the East.

The only Romantic poet who might appear to be an omission from this study is Thomas Moore (1779–1852). His *Lalla Rookh* constitutes an important example of Romantic Orientalism. In the *Edinburgh Review,* Francis Jeffrey lavishly praised it as a specimen of "finest orientalism" and wrote: "It is amazing, indeed, how much at home Mr Moore seems to be in India, Persia, and Arabia; and how purely and strictly Asiatic all the coloring and imagery of his book appears" (qtd in Wright, *Ireland, India* 98). The rationale behind excluding Moore is the late appearance of his poem, and discursively, it is closer to the Orientalist poems of the second generation Romantics. Moore's *Lalla Rookh* was written on Byron's suggestion and was published in1817.[3] Therefore, it is customary to consider Moore with Lord Byron (1788–1824), Percy Bysshe Shelley (1792–1822), and Thomas De Quincey (1785–1859) than with the early Romantics.[4]

Most of the poems introduced in this study, except those of Blake, can be classified as what Herman Fischer defines as the "Romantic verse narrative." Landor's *Gebir*, Southey's *Thalaba* and *The Curse of Kehama,* Wordsworth's *The Prelude*, and the two romances "The Armenian Lady's Love" and the "Egyptian Maid or The Romance of the Water Lily," Coleridge's "Christabel" and *The Rime of the Ancient Mariner*—all would fall under the category of the verse narrative.[5] Fischer mentions Sir Walter Scott (1771–1832) as a major contributor to the development of the Romantic verse narratives and he considers the *Lay of the Last Minstrel* as a landmark poem. Fischer, however, considers *Gebir* as a forerunner of Scott along with the *Lyrical Ballads* and Southey's narrative poems and moves on to Scott's later poems and to Thomas Moore, Byron, and others to illustrate the growth of the Romantic verse narrative to its maturity. With the advent of Byron and Moore on the scene of literary Orientalism, Fischer contends, the uncertainties of the genre of the Romantic verse narrative were over. According to him, the epic, the romance, and the ballad vastly contributed to the development of the Romantic verse narratives (11–35). He does not, however, grant any space to the large body of Oriental Tales in prose and verse which, as would be seen, had a major contribution to the development of the Romantic verse narrative.

Although Scott is considered an important figure in the development of the Romantic verse narrative, he is not included in this study. He produced a series of narrative poems such as *Marmion* (1808), *The Lady of the Lake* (1810), *Rockby* and

The Bridal of Trierman (1813), *The Lord of the Isles* (1815), etc., and chronologically, he began his career in the early phase of Romanticism, but his verse narratives do not have a distinct Eastern strain. In Scott's novels, however, Islam and the East often played a crucial role as many of his novels were set in the backdrop of the Crusades. *Count Robert of Paris* (1831), for instance, was set in Constantinople at the time of the First Crusade. Three other novels were set during the Third Crusade: *Ivanhoe* (1819) and *The Betrothed* (1825) were concerned with events on the home front, whereas the plot of *The Talisman* (1825) was set in Palestine and centered on the friendship between a Scottish knight and Saladin (Riley-Smith 65). Novels, however, are not within the purview of this study.

An enormous amount of literary texts was produced during the Romantic period in different forms and genres and it is not possible to include everything in this study. There are existing critical works on different dimensions of Romantic Orientalism. This study aims to address the areas which have not received adequate attention. A summary of the critical approaches to Romanticism and Orientalism is provided by Andrew Warren in *The Orient and the Young Romantics.* Warren identifies three categories that have become "a staple in nearly every key study of the era's relationship to Orientalism": "the Romantic imagination, the foreign or exotic, and the emergent nation state" (9). Critics like Schwab, Samar Attar, John Drew, J.J. Clarke, Michael J. Franklin and Mohammad Sharafuddin emphasized the link between the East and the Romantic imagination. The focus of these critics is on the cultural exchanges between the East and West. Except for Sharafuddin and Attar, who pay attention to the Middle East, other critics primarily concentrate on the relationship that was forged between India and the West in the Romantic period. Another interesting study that centers on the relationship between Romantic creativity and the Middle East is Emily Haddad's *Orientalist Poetics: The Islamic Middle East in the Nineteenth Century English and French Poetry*. Haddad argues that the Islamic Middle East was a fertile poetic source for almost all the poets in nineteenth-century England and France. The Orient in Romantic poetry, according to Haddad, functions as an alternative poetic space. Critics like Nigel Leask, Isaiah Berlin, Mary Louise Pratt, and Saree Makdisi focus on the relationship between empire, nationalism, and Romanticism. Fulford and Kitson in "Romanticism and Colonialism" argue that Romanticism is defined by its desire to rule the exotic (47). Leask argues that British "national culture was as much a product of imperial expansion, as imperialism was the 'expression' or exportation of that culture" (*British Romantic Writers* 86). Similarly, Isaiah Berlin calls Romanticism a type of homesickness, "the daydreams of exiles and colonists" (16). Mary Louise Pratt also claims that "Romanticism originated in the contact zones of America, North Africa, and the South Seas" (138).

The three categories of critical voices on Romantic Orientalism are interrelated and one category runs into the other. This study, therefore, aims to connect the critique of Romantic Orientalism, on the one hand, and the critics who have attempted to delineate the relation between Romantic poetics and the East, on the other. It follows the path laid down by critics like Samar Attar, Raymond Schwab, Garland Cannon, Emily Haddad, and long before them J.L. Lowes in studying the Eastern influence on Romantic poetry, but it does so without dissociating poetics from politics. Taking a stimulus from Schwab's observation that England, the hearth of the Oriental Renaissance, could not be its home because of Britain's imperial concerns, this study locates how the early Romantic poets' response to the East was enmeshed in the contemporary imperial, political, and religious discourses.

Most of the critics mentioned above have studied the Middle East and India in isolation, but the object of this study is put them together in the same frame. This does not mean that the East is considered a monolithic whole and that the Romantic reception and representation of India and the Middle East can be analyzed on similar lines. However, the Romantic engagement with the East can be best understood when they are studied together because, as Said notes, "Europe's involvement in the more distant parts" of Asia influenced their "interests in Near East, Islam, and the Arabs" (17). There was also a tendency among the Romantics to homogenize the East where one could easily connect an experience in Egypt to an experience in India. As Emily Haddad remarks, nineteenth-century poets and readers "could perceive the oriental virtually anywhere between Greece and the Pacific Ocean" (2). The endeavor is to unravel and critique the sweeping generalizations and stereotypes of the East in Romantic poetry not to consolidate them.

The tendency to homogenize the East is reflected in the way the Romantics unquestioningly associated geographical areas with religions. In Romantic imagination, India and Hinduism were inseparably connected and these two terms were sometimes used (as in the writings of Blake) synonymously. The 'discovery' and the scholarly translations of the ancient Indian texts led by Sir William Jones (1746–1794) were responsible for the growth of such ideas, as "Britons like Sir William Jones believed that one of their historical tasks was to liberate Hindus from the effects of centuries of Mughal misrule and restore the glories of a classical, Upanishadic golden age" (Leask, "Rev.").[6] Daniel Sanjib Roberts, explaining the growth of the idea of Hinduism and of a "Hindu India" during the Romantic period, notes that though the word 'Hindu' or 'Gentoo' was "largely geographical in origin," courtesy the British Orientalists and the imperialists by the end of the eighteenth century,

> the term had been codified into an "ism". "Hinduism," expressive of the actions or conduct of a class of persons, even if the precise nature of religious doctrine was hard to pin down, given the weltering array of religious practices and beliefs to be found in the region. (88)[7]

One reason behind this homogenization might lie in the fact that none of the early Romantic poets (and among the later Romantics, only Byron was the exception) did have any first-hand experience of the East and they were dependent upon the English or French Orientalists, travelers or administrators for their perception of India. Similarly, the Middle East for the Romantics was chiefly Islamic with some exception in the case of Egypt and Ethiopia. Egypt was often connected to paganism and Ethiopia to early Christianity. The rise of Islam in the Middle East followed by the Crusades and the powerful Turkish Empire under Muslim rulers consolidated the idea of the Middle East chiefly as the region of the Muslims or the 'Mahometans.' The identification of geographical areas with particular religions indicates that in Romantic discursive formations, religion became a major factor in the process of homogenization of the East; India and Hinduism, Middle East and Islam, China and Buddhism were often bracketed together ignoring the immense diversity of these bracketed units. It is only by the most reductive logic that India can be made synonymous with Hinduism and the Middle East with Islam or China with Buddhism. Moreover, the differences and diversities among the Hindus in the Indian subcontinent, the Muslims in the Middle East or the Buddhists in China also were mostly ignored in Romantic discourse. The sweeping generalizations constitute an important aspect of Romantic period Orientalism, which this study proposes to critique.

Europe, like the East, was not a monolithic unit either; the concept of a uniform European identity had always been a myth and it was more so during the early nineteenth century. The decline of Turkish power encouraged territorial war among the European superpowers, especially over the Balkans. There was also conflict and competition among the European colonizing nations vying for control over the colonies. In India, for example, the British fought the French and emerged victorious to become the dominant European power in the subcontinent. On another front, the North American British states fought and won their war of freedom with the aid of France. Similarly, Egypt became a battleground for the British and the French. The idea of a pan-European Christendom, that dominated European popular imagination since the Crusades, became a thing of the past.[8] The pan-European identity was replaced by a shared sense of national identity. Christianity remained important, although with the availability of more knowledge about other religions, traditionally familiar Islam, Zoroastrianism and Hinduism, there was a growing concern over the pre-eminence of Christianity. Faced with the new challenge posed by non-Christian theological belief systems, especially by Hinduism, the period saw the growth of religious syncretism. Christianity came to be compared, contrasted and measured against these religions, but it was retained as a measure for every other theology. This study, therefore, would engage with the East–West binary, but would be more concerned with its specific dimensions that relate to England and the early Romantic poets.

The early Romantic poets creatively employed theological ideas of Hinduism and Islam in the poems written in the early days of their career, and both, Islam and Hinduism played a vital role in shaping the spirit of Romanticism. Christianity, however, played a neutralizing role in containing and controlling the Eastern influence. The first generation Romantic poets sacrificed their early syncretism and sympathetic approach to other religions in favor of Christianity. The use of the myths and theological ideas of Hinduism and Islam in Blake, Coleridge, Wordsworth, and Southey, and their tendency to privilege Christianity creates a complex web and requires close examination. When it comes to the possible role of religion in defining the early Romantic poets' perspective on the East, there is a notable absence of critical works.

Another issue in studying the Romantic encounter with the East is the lack of necessary attention to the combined role of the Oriental Tale and the Gothic novel in molding Romanticism and its negotiation with the East. The relationship between the Gothic and the Oriental Tale and how the combined features of the Gothic and the Oriental Tale are incorporated into Romantic poetry are little discussed in critical circles.[9] Elements from the Oriental Tale migrated into Romantic poetry directly as the Romantics were avid readers of the collections of Oriental Tales, and also indirectly, mediated by the Gothic. Both, the Oriental Tale and the Gothic novel, had a liberating influence on Romanticism and it is imperative to examine how the Gothic Other and the Oriental Other is conflated in Romanticism—the dark fallen world of the Gothic and the degenerated East are woven together in the works of Blake, Coleridge, Southey, and Landor. The intimate connection between Romantic Gothicism and Romantic Orientalism remains to be explored. Similarly, the role of the scholarly writings, translations, and creative pieces of Jones shaping Wordsworth's poetic theory in the Preface to *Lyrical Ballads* requires greater attention. The impact of Wilkins's translation and publication of *The Bhagvat-Geeta* and its reception among the early Romantics also demands further critical attention.

Although the target of this study is to do a close and critical analysis of early Romantic poetry, an understanding of a wider context of the Romantic turn to the East is necessary. The chapter that follows this introduction, therefore, traces the developments in the domestic as well as the global stages that had close connections with the Romantics' turn to the East. The chapter locates how dissatisfaction with prevailing poetic principles and a search for a new poetics found a ground in Eastern literary practices. Along with literary dissent, the development of religious Nonconformity and political dissidence in the late eighteenth century posed a challenge to the British ruling class, especially in the aftermath of the French Revolution. The government responded by passing gagging acts, making writing and speech treasonable. The early Romantic poets were involved in the revolutionary politics of the day and to bypass the repressive laws, they set their radical narratives in the distant lands of Asia and Africa. However, it is contended that the Romantics' turn to the East was not merely an escapist move. The Romantics were genuinely engaged with the scores of materials made available by the Oriental Renaissance to re-orient British poetry. All this, of course, is closely linked to British colonial expansionism and imperialism and it indicates imbrication of the Romantics in the imperial politics and policies.

The second chapter of the book is a survey of the genres that led to the unprecedented impact of the East in English literature of the Romantic period. The Oriental Tale had been a major literary form of the pre-Romantic period and the Romantic poets were fascinated with the genre. The chapter traces the role of the Oriental Tale in the development of the Gothic, and how the Gothic and the Oriental Tale helped in the creation of an alternative aesthetic principle away from the neoclassical creeds. Secondly, it considers how the scholarly translations of poetic, religious, literary, and philosophical texts oriented the British writers and poets to think beyond the European tradition but simultaneously, created a sense of anxiety concerning their conception of the superiority of the Greco-Roman cultural heritage or Christianity. The study contends that this anxiety might be the cause behind the growth of syncretism during the early phase of Romanticism. Thirdly, the chapter tries to analyze the nature of Orientalism practiced in the eighteenth century and how the Romantic period saw the transition from the Jones era Orientalism to the comparatively rigid form of Orientalist discourse that emerged during the nineteenth century.

The third chapter explores the possible connections between Blake's poetry and the East. Traditionally, Blake has been regarded as the poet of the spiritual world beyond the grip of materiality. However, as the reading here reveals much of his spirituality was grounded on the concrete reality of the world around him and beyond. The East of the scholars, travelers, and painters was adapted by Blake to suit his creative design and poetic mythography. An examination of Blake's relationship with the East reveals that he was deeply influenced by the scholarly works of the Orientalists based on Calcutta, and for him India and Hinduism were synonymous. His approach to Hinduism was syncretic as he equated Hinduism with other religions including

Christianity. In his effort to criticize organized religion, he used Hinduism as the example of first institutionalized religion. He was inspired by scholars like William Jones who valorized Hinduism, but was also influenced by the negative image of Hinduism and India that was created during the Hastings trial or in the writings of Evangelicals like Charles Grant. Blake's engagement with Islam was very complex. He exploited the popular belief of the licentiousness of Islam to criticize the rigidity of monastic life and he uses a "wise tale" from the Qur'an to illustrate Christian morality. About Muhammad and Islam, Blake harbored an ambivalent attitude. The paintings and engravings of Muhammad, "The Vision of the Last Judgement," "The Visionary Head" and "The Schismatics and Sowers of Discord: Mohammed" reveal this ambivalence. This ambivalence, it is maintained, might be the result of the conflict between the residual and the emergent ideas on Islam. Although the traditional views of Islam and Muhammad still prevailed, the Romantic poets were inspired by some of the alternative and subversive writings that emerged during this period. However, in Blakean mythography, India, as well as the Middle East, are part of the world of 'Generation', the domain of Urizen awaiting regeneration. Blake envisions a resurrection of the world in *Jerusalem the Emanation of the Giant Albion*, the poem he composed through two decades. The problem with his vision, however, seems to be his Anglo-centric and Christo-centric conception of the world.

The fourth chapter begins with a discussion of Landor's *Gebir* which exercised its influence on Southey when he composed *Thalaba*. *Gebir* is the first long narrative poem that set the tone for the verse romances on the East that became very popular during the Romantic period. Landor claims in the preface to the poem that it is about the "folly of invading a peopled country." It is disputed whether the poem is anti-imperial in its outlook and the question is raised on the phrase "peopled country." Robert Southey made a scheme to write a poem on each of the mythological systems of the world. As part of his scheme, he wrote *Thalaba*, where he uses Islamic monotheism to explore his

Unitarian beliefs in the figure of the Bedouin hero. In *The Curse of Kehama*, the image of a degenerated Hindu society and despotic Hinduism serve an evangelical and nationalistic purpose. In Landor's tale, the conflict is between the Western Gebir and the Eastern Dalica. In Southey's poems, East is pitted against East. A monotheist, simple, working class Thalaba fights against the rich and polytheist magicians of the Domdaniel. *Thalaba* as a follower of Muhammad is presented as an iconoclastic warrior hero just as Coleridge would present Muhammad in the fragment, "Mahomet." Thalaba's valour and unwavering faith are celebrated in the poem, but Southey goes on condemning Islam, the people, the art, the architecture, and the literature of the East. In *The Curse of Kehama,* Kailayal and Ladurlad, the lower-caste father-and-daughter duo fight an unequal battle with the "man Almighty" Kehama. Like Thalaba, Kailyal and Ladurlad's confidence in goddess Maraitaly is unwavering and eventually, they achieve victory. However, this tale is used by Southey as a pretext to condemn Hinduism as evil and priest-ridden; it is presented as a religion exploiting women and lower-caste Hindus. The poem marks his movement away from Jonesean syncretism to the Anglican criticism of Hindu society. However, the poem produced confusion among contemporary readers, who often mistook Southey's denigration of Hinduism as an act of glorification. The confusion of contemporary readers is indicative of a public paranoia regarding Hinduism. It is also suggestive of the fact that Southey could not efface his syncretism, even though he was guided by the Evangelical rhetoric of the Clapham sect and the British nationalistic ideals.

The final chapter opens with the argument that Coleridge's negotiation with the East presents a spectacle different from that of Southey's. Southey made little effort to assimilate the Eastern elements; he maintained a distance from his subjects. Coleridge's assimilation of the theological ideas of Hinduism and Islam or elements from the Oriental Tales into his poetry was exceptional and unequalled by any of the early Romantics. His *Osorio* is perhaps the best example of the Romantic reception of Hindu philosophy, and he was equally inspired by Islamic monotheism. However, some of the strongest criticism of Hinduism and Islam also came from him. There is a strong contrast between the early and the late Coleridge. Once he rejected Unitarianism, he criticized Prophet Muhammad as a "trickster." He overruled his early belief in "pantheism" and "Oneness" as he moved toward Fichte's idealism from Spinozan materialism. This movement, as it is argued, cannot be dissociated from Coleridge's growing nationalism and conservatism—the Anglo-centric and Christian-centric turn in his career. However, the East was all-pervasive in the most creative phase of his career; the more insular he grew, the more the "oriental wells" dried up and he became less creative. Two distinct phases of Wordsworth's engagement with the East is traced in this study: his early negotiations with Eastern poetic customs and literature from the East as seen in the Preface to *Lyrical Ballads* and *The Prelude* and a few poems he produced late into his career. The later poems are marked by a distinct hostility toward the East. Even though Wordsworth was influenced by the Perso-Arabic poetry and the works of William Jones, he revised Jones's ideas and replaced the East of Jones with the English countryside and desperately criticized the Eastern landscapes and nature, which inspired the kind of poetry he valorises in the Preface to *Lyrical Ballads*.

The chapter on Wordsworth and Coleridge is followed by some conclusive remarks. The early Romantic poets wrote at a time, which witnessed major changes in the world around them and beyond. It was a time when conflicting and opposing forces co-existed. The Orientalist discourse remained quite flexible. However, by the 1820s one could locate the free-floating nature of the Orientalist discourse undergoing some durable changes. Concerned with consolidating its position in the growing empire in India, there was a large-scale policy makeover and it affected the Romantic representation of India. In respect to the Middle East, the commencement of the Greek War of Independence encouraged philhellenism among the British and it shaped a new rhetoric of hostility in some of the Romantic poets. The new tendencies find reflections in the works of Thomas De Quincey (1785–1859), Percy Bysshe Shelley (1792–1822), and Lord Byron (1788–1824). However, it is very difficult to straightjacket the later Romantics' approach to the East. For example, Shelley who wrote *Hellas* favoring the Greek cause, also wrote *Prometheus Unbound* locating the force of liberation in Asia.

Notes

1 The phrase "foreign Factors" is used by Warren to define the influence of "non-Western cultures, such as translations from philosophical and poetic works in Sanskrit, Farsi, and Arabic, or scientific studies conducted across Africa, Asia, and the Americas" on Romantic poetry (9).

2 See Peter J. Kitson's *Forging Romantic China: Sino-British Cultural Exchange 1760–1840* (2013). For the Western encounter with Buddhism, one may also see Mark S. Lussier's *Romantic Dharma: The Emergence of Buddhism into Nineteenth-Century Europe* (10–20). Lussier's is the most detailed treatment of the relationship between Buddhist tradition and Romanticism. The chapter "Coleridge: 'Kubla Khan' and the Rise of Tantric Budhhism" in John Drew's *India and the Romantic Imagination* (183–226) is also very relevant in this respect.

3 Byron wrote to Moore in May, 1813: "Stick to the East. . . . The North, South and West have all been exhausted; but from the East we have nothing but [Southey's] unsalables. . . . The little I have done in that way is merely a 'voice in the wilderness' for you; and if it has any success, that will also prove that the public are orientalizing, and pave the path for you." See *Byron's Letters and Journals* III (101).

4 See Makdisi's essay "Romantic Cultural Imperialism" in *The Cambridge History of English Romantic Literature* (601–620); and Diego Saglia's "Orientalism" in *A Companion to European Romanticism* (467–487).

5 The poems referred to here are of different lengths, but as Fischer observes, "[T]he length of a romantic tale in verse has hardly any influence on its qualification for the genre, which includes both poems of a few hundred lines to tales running to thousands of verses" (3).

6 For the relation between the growth of the concept of India as a Hindu land and Orientalism, see Richard King's *Orientalism and Religion: Postcolonial Theory, India and The Mystic East* (96–117). See also Daniel Sanjiv Roberts's essay "Orientalism and Hindu Nation: Robert Southey's Palimpsest of Kehama, 1800–1810" in *Nation in Imagination: Essays on Nationalism, Sub-nationalisms, and Narration* (88–99); and Neil Gray's "Orientalism Inverted: The Rise of 'Hindu Nation.'" *Mute* 2.10 (2008).

7 Roberts traces the earliest use of the term "Hindooism" to Michael Symes's *An Account of an Embassy to the Kingdom of Ava* (1800), "[T]he Shaster prescribes the whole world, and denies the cord of Hindooism to all mankind" (88).

8 It is necessary to remember, however, that literary writers often employed this trope. Walter Scott plays with this trope in his historical novels and some of the later poems of Wordsworth replicate the crusading spirit of the medieval romances.

9 Though there have been studies on the influence of *The Arabian Nights* on English literature, there is a lack of critical works focusing on the Oriental Tale in general: How the popularity of the Oriental Tale with its boundless imagination laid down the foundation for Romantic revolt against neoclassicism.

I

"Stick to the East": Understanding the Context

Byron wrote to Moore in May 1813, "Stick to the East. . . . The North, South and West have all been exhausted; but from the East we have nothing but [Southey's] unsalables [sic], . . . The little I have done in that way is merely 'a voice in the wilderness' for you; and if it has any success, that will also prove that the public are orientalizing, and pave the path for you" (*Byron's Letters and Journals* III 101). Almost half a century before Byron, William Jones made a similar plea, but in a much deeper vein. Commenting on the beauty and felicity of the poetry of the Eastern nations, Jones advocated for the dissemination and study of the "principal writings of the Asiaticks, which are reposited in our publick libraries" (Pachori 144). This would provide the European scholars and poets with "a more extensive insight into the history of the human mind," and the European mind would be "furnished with a new set of images and similitudes, and a number of excellent compositions would be brought to light, which future scholars might explain, and future poets might imitate" (Pachori 144). Byron's letter indicates that it was necessary to orientalize to gain popularity and commercial success as a poet; for Jones, the primary objective of turning to the East was to introduce a freshness of spirit into British poetry. Jones was writing at a time when poetic Orientalism was in a nascent state and Byron after poetic Orientalism had gained considerable ground. A customary look at Orientalist poetry from the Romantic period, whether it is of the first generation Romantics or the later Romantics, reveals that they turned to the East not merely for salability or for aesthetic reasons. The politics of the time, whether it was the domestic political scenario or the colonial politics abroad, had a crucial role to play in shaping the Romantic turn to the East. In other words, there is a broader context of Romantic period Orientalism that demands attention. Therefore, an attempt will be made in this chapter to understand the intellectual climate and the sociopolitical scenario—both domestic and international—to contextualize the Romantic turn to the East.

Neoclassicism dominated eighteenth-century literary culture. However, a large body of literature produced during the time deviated from the accepted norms of neoclassicism and followed alternative aesthetic principles.[1] It was symptomatic of a growing sense of tedium and disagreement with the prevailing mode of Augustanism. Jones pointed to this sense of tedium when he wrote about the failing inspiration for European poetry and its subsistence for too long "on the perpetual repetition of the same images and incessant allusions to the same fables" (Pachori 144). At several places in his writings, and especially in the essays, "Essay on Arts Commonly Called Imitative" and "An Essay on the Poetry of the Eastern Nations," Jones argued in favor of injecting a new spirit into European poetry, which has been dominated for too long by the spirit of neoclassicism. He was pleading in favor "of expressing passions in verse, and on enforcing that expression by melody" that was characteristic of the Asiatic poetry, rather than continuing with the imitative poetry of the Neoclassicals (Pachori 131). The Augustan principles of literature as imitation, its dual objective of providing instruction and delight, imitating civil life centered on cities, replicating the Greco-Roman classical authors created a kind of shackle which Jones felt European poetry must do away with by following the Eastern poetic mode. This search for alternative aesthetic principles becomes manifest in the second half of the eighteenth century with the advent of the Gothic, the development of the cult of sentimentality, the revival of the ballads and Pre-Romantic medievalism. As Roger Lonsdale puts it, "characteristics condemned by neo-classical critics were becoming attractive to the immediately post-Augustan generation" (371).

The French were literary gurus of the English neoclassicism, and it is not surprising that the French neoclassical critic, Boileau, played the role of a catalyst in the revival of the Gothic in England in the eighteenth century. Boileau translated and interpreted Longinus' treatise on the sublime (Ned O'Gorman 71). Boileau's translation and the numerous commentaries on it made the readers aware that "the terrible, the incomprehensible and the limitless exceeding human reason could be more attractive than the regular, beautiful and picturesque" (Lessenich 165). Two important English treatises on the sublime were Edmund Burke's *Philosophical Enquiries into the Origin of the Ideas of Sublime and Beautiful* that came out in 1757 and "On the Pleasure Derived from Objects of Terror; with Sir Bertrand, A Fragment" jointly produced by Barbauld and John Aikin in 1773. Like Boileau, Burke and the Aikins also helped the Gothic taste to grow in eighteenth-century England. In an atmosphere of Gothicism, the Gothic style architecture gained popularity replacing the neoclassical Palladian buildings. Horace Walpole, who was to write the first Gothic novel in 1764, started building his Strawberry Hill in 1749 and toward the end of the century, William Beckford constructed the Foothill Abbey. The Gothic interest in the dark world also found expression in the graveyard poetry of Thomas Gray, William Collins, William Cowper, James Thompson, Christopher Smart, and others. Just like the Gothic, graveyard poetry also posed a challenge to the principle of rationality as it involved death and suffering, and was characterized by an extremity of feelings. Exploration of the human passions, however, found its most elaborate expression in the cult of sentiment, especially the sentimental novels, for it investigated "into the strength of those feelings which the rationalists tried to suppress" and "balance and reason of the Enlightenment" were "crushed beneath the weight of feeling and passion" (Punter 29). Along with the growth of the Gothic novels and the cult of sentimentality, literary medievalism of the late eighteenth century also helped to subvert the principles of Augustanism by creating an interest in the native northern European past and certain medieval literary forms. Bishop Percy's (1729–1811) collection, *Reliques of Ancient English Poetry* (1765) fostered an interest in the native English past by reviving the ballad form.[2] Macpherson's (1736–1796) Ossian poems (*The Works of Ossian* 1765), though later proved to be forged, created an interest in the Gaelic tradition.

An interest in the Orient, whether Biblical or contemporary, ran alongside these developments. It was the Biblical Orientalism of Robert Lowth (1710–1787)[3] in *De sacra poesi Hebraeorum* (1753), translated into English in the year 1787 as *Lectures on the Sacred Poetry of the Hebrews* and his elevation of the "irregular sublime poetry of the Hebrew Old Testament as high ranking literature" "led to European interest in Old Arabic, Persian, Indian and Chinese literatures" (Rolf Lessenich 166). In his Biblical commentaries, Lowth spoke of an alternative form of poetry whose home was the East. The popularity of the Oriental Tales since the first Grub street version of *The Arabian Nights* started appearing in the first decade of the eighteenth century was a part of this anti-Augustanism and like the other developments, it put the neoclassical doctrines under pressure. Writing about the popularity of the Oriental Tales in eighteenth-century France, Martha Conant Pike remarks that "the popularity of these fantastic and marvellous stories, restless in plot and exuberant in colour, had testified to the truant desire to escape from the artistic rules and classical ideals of masters like Boileau" (243). Pike's observation equally applies to eighteenth-century England. The tendency to move away from the dominant literary mode of neoclassicism, therefore, had two major avenues: if one route against the prevailing literary codes led the writers and poets to the native past in the form of Gothicism, medievalism or Ossianism, the other led outward to the East in the form of Orientalism.

It is interesting to note that literary dissent in the eighteenth century coincided with religious Nonconformity and political dissent. In post-French Revolution Britain, the radical dissenters "sought to change the 'radix,' or 'root' of society" the way literary artists wanted to transform the literary aesthetics (Lessenich 167). Eighteenth-century religious life in Britain saw the spectacular rise of the Nonconformists or religious dissenters. Scientific rationalism, the rise of discourses on natural rights, the failure of the established Church to adapt to the changing conditions of life and changes in the demographic pattern in the wake of the Industrial Revolution have been identified as some of the possible reasons behind the rise of Nonconformity (Jarvis 126). This dissenting tradition, however, was deeply rooted in the English Reformation. Religious reformation in the sixteenth century was followed by an intense religious/political conflict in the seventeenth leading to political events like the dethroning of Charles I and his beheading, formation of the Puritan government under Cromwell and finally, the Glorious Revolution of 1688–1689. In post-Revolution Britain, the dominance of the Anglican Church was ensured, but some concessions were granted to the Dissenters in the form of The Toleration Act of 1689 that allowed freedom of worship to the Dissenting Protestants. However, as the Corporations Act (1661) and the Tests Acts (1673, and 1678) were still in force, their freedom was very limited and the Dissenters were denied certain vital rights. They could not, for instance, occupy public office and were not allowed to get an education at Oxford or Cambridge unless they vowed their allegiance to the Church of England. Notwithstanding this, religious Nonconformity was on the rise as dissenting groups like Presbyterians, Congregationalists, Baptists and Quakers increased their followings. These dissenting groups got divided into different factions like Unitarians, Evangelicals, Methodists, Deists, and Atheists, etc.

The Dissenters saw a great opportunity to undo religious inequalities in England with the revolutionary call for liberty and equality in France. They sought to change England from a "confessional state" to a liberal state ending discrimination on religious grounds. After a long struggle, their efforts for equal rights bore fruit with the repeal of the Test and Corporation Acts in 1828 and the Catholic Emancipation Act of 1829. Many of the dissenting religious leaders connected the French Revolution to the Biblical prophecy of Christ's second coming encouraging millenarian radicalism. Presbyterian minister Richard Price, Unitarian Joseph Priestly, and the mystic preacher Emanuel Swedenborg interpreted the contemporary events in apocalyptic terms with reference to the Book of Revelation that foretells Christ's rule over a regenerated Earth before the final destruction of the world and the Last Judgment. Dissenters took a leading role in spreading the revolutionary principles and social historians have claimed that English radicalism in the late eighteenth century was predominantly motivated by religious heterodoxy (Clark, *English Society* 239–256).

In fact, one of the first reactions to the Revolution came from the Nonconformist preacher Richard Price, who saw the French Revolution as the true heir to the English Revolution of 1688 announcing a new dawn for humanity:

> After sharing in the benefits of one Revolution, I have been spared to be a witness to two other Revolutions, both glorious. —And now, methinks, I see the ardor for liberty catching and spreading; a general amendment beginning in human affairs; the dominion of kings changed for the dominion of laws, and the dominion of priests giving way to the dominion of reason and conscience. (18)

As religious leaders spoke and wrote in support of political liberty, political leaders pitched for religious rights. In his letter to Burke, Charles Stanhope, the third Earl of Shaftsbury praised the policy of religious tolerance adopted by revolutionary France where the non-Catholics were allowed to hold offices, religious or civil. He compared French liberal policy to the restrictions imposed on non-Anglicans in England under the Test and Corporations Acts and hailed the Revolution as the harbinger of religious, civil, and political liberty.[4] The discourses on civil and political rights, therefore, were closely allied to the question of religious belief and rights in the eighteenth and early nineteenth centuries.

Central to the radical political or religious discourse was the question of "natural rights" in post-1789 Britain. The immediate ignition to the rights issues was provided by the French Constituent Assembly's adoption of Declaration of the Rights of Man and of the Citizen (*Déclaration des droits de l'homme et du citoyen de 1789*). The impetus for this rights movement, however, came primarily from the native and continental philosophical and religious discourses. John Locke in his *Two Treatises on Government* (1689) emphasized the dual necessities of securing individual liberty and the protection of individual property rights. He argued that in the "State of Society," the government existed on the trust of the citizens and the citizens had the right authority to withdraw their confidence from their rulers. In the "State of Society," the government was formed when humans relinquished some of their "natural rights," which they enjoyed in the "State of Nature," but an incursion into the remaining rights on part of the government would warrant a change. Thomas Paine's *Rights of Man* (1791–1792) made a considerable impact with its argument in favor of "equal natural rights" based on the premise that all men are "born equal" (Paine 66). Another important development in the 1780s and 1790s England centering on the question of rights was the Abolitionist movement that highlighted the human rights of the slaves and condemned slavery and slave trade as inhuman and anti-Christian. Apart from Paine, Mary Wollstonecraft and William Godwin emphatically argued against injustice and in favor of universal rights. Wollstonecraft's pamphlet, *A Vindication of the Rights of Men* (1790) is at once a critique of Burke's conservative defense of the ruling classes in his *Reflections on the Revolutions in France* and a moral argument against an exploitative aristocracy among other things. In her more famous *A Vindication of the Rights of Woman* (1792), she devotes her attention to her sex only because she felt that the discourses on man's rights excluded women. In *Enquiry Concerning Political Justice* (1793), Godwin pitched for rational anarchy to wipe out injustice against humanity. The American War of Independence and the French Revolution created an atmosphere of republicanism in England and in its early days, people across the political spectrum welcomed the developments in France. Even William Pitt, the Prime Minister of England hoped that that revolutionary fervor in France would ultimately lead to "general harmony and regular order" (qtd. in Jarvis 4). Like many of the leading intellectuals of the time, the first generation Romantic poets were euphoric in their support for the revolution in the 1790s and fought for civil and political rights. Blake wrote a series of revolutionary prophecies. Wordsworth, who was in France immediately after the revolution, recounted in *The Prelude*, "Bliss was it in that dawn to be alive, / But to be young was very heaven!" (Book XI, 108–109) and it is definitive of the early reactions of the first generation Romantics to the events in France. One may also recall Wordsworth's poems like "Michael" (1800) and "Guilt and Sorrow" conceived after his return from France in 1792 for their humanitarianism and focus on the common man. The humanitarianism and the democratic tendency in the Romantic theory of poetry and their praxis had an obvious connection with the revolutionary ideals of equality and fraternity. Coleridge's "Fire, Famine and Slaughter" (1798) is very critical of Pitt's policy and welcomes liberty, "Liberty the soul of Life shall reign;" and in "Ode to the Departing Year," he is critical of the undesirable forces of reaction against France. Coleridge and Southey planned the pantisocracy, the establishment of an egalitarian community based on the principles of aspheterism (common ownership of property) and pantisocracy (equal government for all).[5] They also joined the Abolitionist movement and worked for the rights of the slaves. Coleridge lectured on the evils of slavery in Bristol. In 1797,

Southey published his *Poems on the Slave Trade.* Apart from the poems on slavery, Southey's early radicalism is also reflected in *Wat Tyler* (1794).

The revolution gave impetus to radical politics and poetics in England, but it also encouraged counter-revolutionary forces. Therefore, if one characteristic of post-French Revolution-period Britain was the development of radical politics, ethics, and aesthetics, the other was the development of a strong reactionary conservatism asserting itself in an organized form that vehemently opposed the moral, political and aesthetic freedom that the radicals sought after. The initial British enthusiasm with the Revolution gave way to doubts and questioning of the revolutionary ideals, especially after the September Massacres (1792). The violence unleashed on the so-called opponents of the republican cause followed by the Reign of Terror (1793–1794) and France's declaration of war with England (February 1793) turned the tide against British radicalism. These developments created a crisis within the Republican ranks and a large faction of the Whigs sided with the government in quelling Jacobinism in England. The earliest reactionary response to the Revolution in the form of Burke's *Reflections,* however, came out in 1790. Burke saw the Revolution and its republican spirit as a threat to the established order of the society and argued in favor of the old order and sought to maintain status quo, because the new order, he thought, would bring anarchy. This Burkean fear of the new order as anarchic got consolidated with revolutionary excesses and commencing of the Franco-British war (1793–1815). The government became more authoritarian trying to quash every radical activity; any kind of dissent, including in the form of writing and speech, was suppressed by the Seditious Meetings Act and Treasonable Practices Act of 1795. The Habeas Corpus was suspended between 1794 and 1801. An extensive spy network was created by the Pitt government and England became a kind of surveillance state. Many of the radical writers and leaders were arrested and tried for treason and others fled England to escape the Treason Trials. In 1795, Thomas Hardy, John Thelwall, Horne Tooke, and many others were tried for treason. Among the early Romantics, William Blake was indicted for sedition, and Coleridge and Wordsworth were spied upon (Bygrave 44).

Under the political pressure, various dissenting religious groups and their leaders changed their stand. Robert Hall, for example, published *Christianity Consistent with a Love of Freedom* in 1791, but in 1801 he wrote *Modern Infidelity* comparing French Revolution to infidelity (Jarvis 132). In the wake of anticlericalism in France and the de-Christianization campaign of 1793–1794, the conservatives concluded that "revolutionary France was a post-Christian country" (Ryan 88). This anti-religious turn in France created an atmosphere of religious insularity in Britain and atheism came to be equated to anarchism. Religious groups whether, Anglicans or Dissenters, had an increased social concern and the role of religion in maintaining social order was highlighted (Hole, 131–132). This change was reflected in the writings of William Wilberforce, the leader of the Clapham sect of Evangelicals. In his *Practical View* (1797), he criticized both Jacobinism and the modernizing trends in Christianity (Jarvis 139). As summed up by Gerard Cohen-Vrignaud, "Evangelicals and the moralists . . . felt the need to become more assertive in the wake of the French Revolution and the moral threats it seemed to represent to the conventional society" (4). Moreover, the Anglo-French war created a nationalist fervor and it exercised pressure on the writers to support the British regime and conform. The creation of a political frontline also "entailed aesthetic frontline formation." There was an increasing demand for literary conformity. "Supporters of the ancien regime, . . . constructed the . . . many discordant voices of literary dissent into heretical 'schools': the Satanic School, the Lake School, the Cockney School, the Jacobinical School etc., meaning multiplicity of heresies opposed to the one true school of Augustan neoclassical tradition of rule and reason" (Lessenich 167). Interpreting literary implication of the situation, C.C. Barfoot has observed that by the end of the eighteenth century, the aesthetic principles of Augustinism eased out, but political and moral Augustinism created pressure on the writers (71). In the ambience of suppression of speech, censorship of the press and demand for conformity, the Romantic poets took recourse to an oblique language and created a spatio-temporal distance in their poetic texts to mask their republican views. They often set their narratives in some distant time and place and the East proved a favorite ground for such distancing. As Barfoot observes, "the exotic and the oriental offered writers means of escape and an opportunity to revolt against the assertive social and moral restraints" (72). So, what started primarily as a means to escape from the overbearing rules of neoclassicism in the early eighteenth century, becomes a means to evade the "repressive governance at home" and "the moral regulations of normativity" in the Romantic period (Cohen-Vrignaud 4).

However, it would be an oversimplification to consider the Romantic turn to the East in terms of domestic politics alone or merely as a form of escape from pressures at home. Their Eastern poems might have a Western core, but the Eastern exterior is equally significant. In other words, the interior/exterior binary does not always hold good when it comes to the Eastern poems, because the narratives are not mere allegories for domestic situations, but are about the "contact zones"[6] where the East and West meet. Moreover, the location of the Romantics in the political spectrum of the age was never fixed. Almost all the early Romantic poets, except for Blake, distanced themselves from their early radicalism and their political views underwent major transformations by the second decade of the nineteenth century. Similarly, their perception of the East also kept changing and the transformation of their positionality concerning the East swayed with the British colonial politics and policies. And very significantly, their understanding of and relationship with Christianity also played a crucial role in shaping their engagement with the East. Therefore, if the domestic context is important for understanding the Occidental core of the Orientalist poems of the early Romantics, it is equally important to have an overview of the global or more specifically, the Eastern context for a fair appreciation of these poems.

Though Europe had familiarity with the countries of Asia and Africa since ancient times, the Early Modern period saw a great widening of the horizon for the West, chiefly as a result of successful European navigational enterprises.[7] Like other seafaring countries, England eagerly participated in contemporary adventures of exploration and trade. The first activities of Elizabethan commerce were confined to countries such as Persia, Turkey, and Morocco but soon, England succeeded in creating its trading posts in the Asian and African countries and established considerable presence in the Americas. Several trading companies were established during this time. The Muscovy Company was established in 1555 for trade with Russia and Persia; the Cathay Company (1576) for trade with Asia via Canada; the Levant Company (1592) for trade in the Near East. The Levant and the North African trades were followed by the establishment of the East India Company (1599). The East India Company was granted a monopoly in trade in the East Indies with the formal restriction that it might not contest the prior trading right of any Christian prince. As the geographical horizon expanded, the idea of the East was no longer confined to the familiar Ottoman East and very significantly the Indian subcontinent and China became crucial locations for Europe from the eighteenth century onward.

Together with the geographical extension, certain geopolitical developments brought the East closer to the West during the seventeenth and eighteenth centuries. With regard to the Ottoman East, a significant change accrued from the decline of the Turkish power. During Soliman I's reign, Europeans achieved their first victory in the sea battle of Lepanto in 1571, almost marking an end to Turkish incursions into Europe. About a century later the siege of

Vienna (1683) was thwarted by John Sobieski and the Peace Treaty of Karlowitz (1699) was signed marking the end of Turkish expansion in this part. The loss of the Ottomans was the gain for European powerhouses. Austria, Russia, France, and England all had stakes in the decadent Ottoman Empire. Russia, under the Czars, had the aim to annex some part of the Balkans and the rest of Europe feared that Russia may occupy the whole of the Ottoman territory. The Habsburgs of Austria were the first to taste victory over the Turks and they wanted to increase their hold over the Black Sea, and so did Russia. England was more concerned with the growing empire in Asia, where it became the unrivalled European power after the defeat of the French in the Seven Years War (1756–1763). England's policy toward the Middle East was directed by its concern with safe passage to its growing empire in the Indian subcontinent, which was continually under the French threat. The rise of Napoleon and the fear of being invaded by his army put most of the European countries on tenterhooks. England had multiple problems with the French Revolution and the rise of Napoleon—the fear of being invaded, the fear of their access to the colonies being blocked, the fear of losing dominance in India, and the fear of revolutionary forces rising within Britain, to mention a few. The geopolitical situation led England to strengthen its ties with the Turkish rulers in the Middle East. These developments had a larger implication for European and British reception and representation of the Middle East and Islam.

Firstly, the partial decrement of the traditional enmity with the Islamic rulers and the increasing competition and conflict among the European nations helped in interrogating the notion of monolithic Christendom. This partial loss of the pan-European Christian identity also helped in the consolidation of national identity. Despite the intra-national religious, political and ideological divisions within England, there was a consolidation of the British identity during the Romantic period. Non-Europeans and even Europeans were compared and contrasted with the British. It was often the English or British who stood in opposition to the East. Christianity and British nationalism, therefore, would play a very crucial role in defining the engagement of the early Romantics with the East. Timothy Webb in "Romantic Hellenism" argues that the early Romantics like "Wordsworth, Coleridge and Southey . . . preferred a northern and the Christian to a phenomenon they regarded as southern and pagan [the Hellenic]" (149). According to him, "those who subscribed to the values of the patriotic and the English," Hellenism provided a challenge to them (149). Webb perhaps overstates the case when he says that the early Romantics resisted Hellenism, but it is undeniable that Christianity and British nationalism played a decisive part in shaping the early Romantics' response to the East.

Secondly, with the improved relationship with the Islamic East, cross-cultural negotiations with the Middle East became easier. Impact of this improved relationship can be gauged from the growing body of works on the Middle and Near East. Europe's fascination with Islam persisted; biographical works on Prophet Muhammad were published and translations of the Qur'an were made during the period. Alexander Ross's version of the Qur'an was published in 1649 as *Alcoran of Mahomet* (translated from Arabic into French by Sieur der Ryer) and George Sale's translation of the Qur'an as *The Koran, Commonly Called the Alcoran of Mohammed* in 1734. Lancelot Addison published *The Life and Death of Mahumed* in 1679. Humprey Prideaux brought out his *The True Nature of Imposter fully displayed in the Life of Mahomet* (1697). Sir Paul Rycaut's *The Present State of the Ottoman Empire Containing the Maximum of the Turkish Politic, The Most Material Points of the Mahometan Religion* (1668), and Henry Stubbe's *The Rise and Progress of Mahometanism* (1674) were two other important works on Islam. These works do have conflicting opinions about Islam and the East, but Stubbe's book is considered as the beginning of what Humberto Garcia, in *Islam and the English Enlightenment, 1670–1840,* defines as the tradition of "Islamic republicanism" in Europe. These works made their impact on the literary scene of their age. Paul Rycaut's *History of the Turks* was used as a source by many of the seventeenth- and early-eighteenth-century dramatists. The examples include Mary Pix's play called *Ibrahim the Thirteenth Emperor of the Turks* (1696), Eliza Haywood's *The Fair Captive, A Tragedy* (1721), and Edward Young's *The Revenge* (1721). The conflict between the residual traces and a more 'enlightened' emergent notion of Islam and its followers created an ambivalence toward Islam in the imagination of the eighteenth-century authors. This uncertainty in interpreting and representing Islam also finds its way into Romantic poetry. Some of the early Romantic poets had Unitarian sensibility at the beginning of their career, which brought them closer to Islamic theology.

Along with the translations and texts on Muhammad and Islam, several histories of the 'Islamic East' made their appearance during this period: Simon Ockley's *History of the Saracens*, Pierre Bayle's *A General Dictionary, Historical and Critical* (1737–1741), Richard Peacocke's *A Description of the East* (1743–1745) and Alexander Russell's *A Natural History of Aleppo* (1756) are some examples of this genre. With the English ambassadors taking residence in Constantinople, travelers flocked to Egypt, Persia, Turkey, and other countries of the Middle East and many of them wrote about their experience (Makdisi, *Romantic Imperialism* 113). W.C. Brown in his article, "The Popularity of English Travel Books about the Near East, 1775–1825" notes that there had been at least seventy travel books on the Near East during the years 1775–1825. Lady Mary Wortley Montagu (1689–1762) wrote an account of her experience of Eastern life in her *Turkish Embassy Letters* (1776). James Bruce (1730–1794) published his *Travels to Discover the Source of the Nile, In the Years 1768, 1769, 1770, 1771, 1772 and 1773* in 1790. His Ethiopian travel accounts are praised for their accuracy, and it is acknowledged that he made a real addition to the geographical knowledge of his day. Other significant travel accounts included James Dalloway's *Constantinople, Ancient and Modern* (1797), William George

Browne's *Travels in Africa, Egypt and Syria from the Years 1792 to 1798* (1799), and Edward Daniel Clarke's *Travels in Various Countries of Europe, Africa and Asia* (1810). Many of these travelers shared their tales of justice, hospitality, and tolerance that they experienced among the Eastern people. However, most influential of the travelers was Volney whose *Travels in Syria and Egypt, During the Years 1783, 1784, & 1785* (in two volumes, 1788) and *Les Ruins* (1791), which was translated into English as *The Ruins: or a Survey of Revolutions of Empire* in 1792, made a considerable impact on the radical thinkers of the day. Volney's critique of empire and organized religion in *The Ruins* appealed to the Romantics and they often followed Volney's argument in their treatment of these subjects. The travel accounts, along with the histories and translations of theological texts, played the role of mediators between the East and the writers who never crossed the confines of Europe.

Along with the Near and the Middle East, Europe's incursion into India during the seventeenth and the eighteenth centuries immensely contributed to European knowledge of the East and made considerable additions to the existing repertoire of poetic images. Within a century and a half after Thomas Roe's success in arranging a commercial treaty with the Mughal Emperor Jahangir in the early years of the seventeenth century, the East India Company became the most powerful European agency in India with their double victory—they won the Seven Years War (1756–1763) against France and they came victorious in the Battle of Plassey (1557) against the Nawab of Bengal. After 1764, when they were granted rights to collect taxes, the Company became the de facto ruler in the provinces of Bengal, Bihar and a part of Orissa. The vast expansion of the Company's power was seminally brought under the purview of the English government by the Regulating Act of 1773 (also known as the East India Company Act) and Warren Hastings was made the first Governor-General of Bengal. British attention to India increased further when they lost their American colonies with the American War of Independence (1775–1783).

In the initial days of its conquest, the Company faced hostile challenges from the Indian rulers and the hostilities had their impact in the early histories of India produced by the British soldiers. The earliest English works on India came from the East India Company soldiers John Z. Holwell and Alexander Dow, who wrote respectively, *Interesting Historical Events, Relative to the Provinces of Bengal* (1765–1768, 3 volumes) and *The History of Hindostan* (3 volumes: 1768, 1 & 2; 1772, 3). Dow extensively commented on different aspects of the "Hindoo" society and the History included three dissertations: *A Dissertation concerning the customs, manners, language, religion and philosophy of the Hindoos*, *A Dissertation on the origin and nature of despotism in Hindostan*, and *An Enquiry into the State of Bengal with a plan for restoring that kingdom to its former prosperity and splendour*. Holwell demonizes the Bengal Nawab Siraj-ud-Daulah, who defeated them in the battle of Alinagar in 1756. As the East India Company strengthened its hold over Indian territories, travelers, scholars, and painters became interested in India and a large body of travel narratives also started pouring in from British travelers to India. For instance, in 1793, William Hodges published an illustrated book, *Travels in India*. Hodges is very critical of Mysore rulers, who posed a major threat to the Company in the late eighteenth century. Lord Valentia's *Voyages and Travels to India* was published in 1809 and Sir John Barrow's *Travels in China* in 1804. James Forbes's *Oriental Memoirs* was published in two volumes beginning in 1813. Many of these travelogues directly influenced the Romantic poets. William Hodges, for example, influenced the early Romantics like Southey and Coleridge as Wortley Montagu's writings would color the imagination of Byron.

A significant moment about the eighteenth-century British knowledge formation about India was the arrival of William Jones to Calcutta and the subsequent establishment of the Asiatic Society of Bengal in 1784. Under Warren Hastings's patronage and William Jones's curatorship, important works of translations of the ancient Indian literary, philosophical, and religious texts were made.

The Orientalists were overawed and overwhelmed by the discoveries from the Indian antiquity, and there was great enthusiasm for Hindu theological texts in Europe. However, the introduction of knowledge of Hinduism[8] to Europe posed a fresh challenge for Christianity. The challenge was to deal with a religion that was much older. The ancientness of the Mosaic religion was challenged by the European discovery of the ancient Hindu religious texts. The West responded to the challenge initially by recourse to syncretism, as one Romantic poet would write, "All Religions are One."[9] Another response was to dismiss Hinduism altogether. The conflicting views led to a debate between the Orientalists and the Anglicists. The Orientalists valorized the ancient Indian philosophy and religion but they condemned contemporary Hinduism and Hindu society as decadent, degenerated, priest-ridden, and despotic. The Anglicists used this degenerated state of the Hindu society to claim that Hinduism was the source of the social evils prevalent among Hindus. Therefore, to the equation of the Muslim East and Christian West was added a new equation of the degenerated Hindu India as opposed to an enlightened Christian Britain. With the Hastings trial (1788–1795) the Anglicist-Orientalist debate escalated resulting in the ultimate victory of the Anglicists with the inclusion of the "pious clause" in the Charter Act of 1813. The whole debate is proof that Christianity played a defining role in the politics of the time and the reception, representation or the rejection of the Eastern religions and philosophies during the Romantic period. Another significant point to consider at this stage is: The valorization of Hinduism by the Orientalists during the East India Company's rule under Warren Hastings was not merely a scholarly move; it was a trenchantly political gesture. The transfer of power in India was chiefly from the Muslim rulers to the British. So, there was a move to demonize the Mughals and the Muslims, who posed a threat to the growing power of the East India Company and to valorize Hinduism. As Leask indicates, it was a part of the imperial strategy of the British in the 1780s (Rev).[10] The early Romantic poets initially responded to

Hinduism following the track of Jonesean syncretism, and there was a tendency to valorize philosophical Hinduism, but things changed very quickly for them with the rise of the Anglicist Clapham sect under the leadership of William Wilberforce and Charles Grant.

Together with India, the Western inroads into China brought the Far East under Western purview. Although Europe played with the idea of a sea route to the East as far back as 1300, it was not until three centuries later that this dream was brought to fulfillment. In 1488, Bartolomeu Dias rounded the Cape of Good Hope. Ten years later, Vasco da Gama reached Calicut in India. A Portuguese ship reached China from Malacca in 1514. Although China did not allow foreigners into its territory, Jesuits in the sixteenth and seventeenth centuries tried to infiltrate Chinese territories and gathered certain ideas about Chinese civilization. Finally, the Chinese government expelled the missionaries in 1724. The Jesuits were Europe's main source of knowledge of China. They found China akin to what they considered an ideal state, and they reported so to Europe. The dissolution of the Jesuits in Europe destroyed the main carrier of Chinese thought and ended the era of appreciation of China in Europe. Whereas at the beginning of the eighteenth century, the polite society in Europe spoke of the Chinese art and culture in a familiar tone, by the end of the century, China ceased to influence European art and philosophy (Clyde and Beers 66). England's hostility toward China increased after the failure of the British Macartney embassy of 1792–1794. However, it brought China to the forefront and descriptions of Chinese gardens and landscapes flooded the British literary scene. According to Clyde and Beers, the symbolism of the Chinese garden influenced Europe's 'Back to Nature' movement and the "sentimental nature-worship" (66). The emergence of this new attitude toward and the interest in China is analyzed by the historians in relation to the new developments in Europe, particularly to the formation of the nation-state in the early nineteenth century (Clyde and Beers).

The seventeenth- and eighteenth-centuries Europe saw an unprecedented expansion of the horizon of knowledge and by the time the Romantics came to the scene, there had developed certain literary styles, forms and themes in response to the importations of a large body of "cultural goods" from the East. These forms, genres, and styles were available to be consumed, imitated, emulated, and polished by the Romantics. Secondly, the effulgence of the Eastern elements in Romantic literature grew out of the tendencies seen in the eighteenth-century literary dissent against neoclassicism. The following chapter, therefore, is devoted to the dissenting genres, be it Oriental Tales in prose and verse, translations, or the Gothic novels that helped in the development of Romantic sensibilities and shaped the Romantic turn to the East.

Notes

1 This section provides a bare outline of the forms of literary dissent during the eighteenth century. An analysis of some of the genres and their connection with the Romantic interest in the East is considered in detail in the second chapter of the book.

2 It is interesting to note that Percy translated the first Chinese novel into English from the Portuguese *Hau Kiou Choaan* (1761). His medievalism went hand in hand in with his Orientalism.

3 *De sacra poesi Hebraeorum* (1753; Eng. trans. *Lectures on Hebrew Poetry,* 1787).

4 Earl Charles Stanhope. *A Letter from Earl Stanhope, to the Right Honourable Edmund Burke: Containing a Short Answer to His Late Speech on the French* Revolution. George Stafford, 1790. In the last part of his response (30–35), Stanhope writes about religious tolerance.

5 What the scheme would be like is clear from a letter Southey wrote to Horace Walpole Bedford on 24 August and 3 September of 1794:

> that state of society be happy where every man laboured two hours a day at some useful employment. where all were equally educated—

where the common ground was cultivated by common toil, & its produce laid in common granaries. where none were rich because none should be poor. where every motive for vice should be annihilated & every motive for virtue strengthened? such a system we go to establish in America ... by this day twelve months the Pantisocratic society of Aspheterists will be settled on the banks of the Susquehannah.

The scheme did not materialize, but it reflects the radical sentiments of the poets in the early 1790s.

6 The term was coined by Mary Louis Pratt in *Imperial Eyes: Travel Writing and Transculturation* (1992). Pratt defines contact zones as "the space of colonial encounters, the space which peoples geographically and historically separated come into contact with each other and establish ongoing relations, usually involving conditions of coercion, radical inequality and intractable conflict" (6).

7 The influence of Eastern thought and the presence of Eastern elements in European literary and philosophical writings have been traced back to the time of Plato and the Neo-Platonists, and even before. Raymond Schwab, who considers the translation of the *Zend-Avesta* in 1771 by Anquetil-Duperron as the first major breakthrough (7), quotes from Sylvain Levi to make the point that the East-West interaction begun long before that: "Plotinus, Porphyry and the entire school of Neoplatonists reflect the metaphysics of Kapila and Patanjali. Mani and the Gnostics introduced the Brahman and the Buddhist spirit into Christianity, while a colony of Nestorians brought the gospels to India" (qtd. in Schwab 3). John Drew's study of the subject looks back at the "history of the metaphorical or metaphysical passage to India begun by the Greeks" (vii); for Drew, India has been an inspiration for the Western mind since ancient times. Edward Said traces the origin of the Western politics of representation back to the time of Aeschylus. He writes, "as early as Aeschylus's play *The Persians* the Orient is transformed from a very far distant and often threatening Otherness into figures that are relatively familiar (in Aeschylus's case the grieving Asiatic women)" (21).

8 The term Hinduism and the history of its coinage is provided by Daniel Sanjib Roberts. Roberts traces the earliest use of the term "Hindooism"

to Michael Symes's *An Account of an Embassy to the Kingdom of Ava* (1800): "[T]he Shaster prescribes the whole world, and denies the cord of Hindooism to all mankind" (88).

9 See "All Religions are One" (1788) in *The Complete Poetry & Prose of William Blake*, edited by David V. Erdman, Electronic edition, Virginia: Institute for Advanced Technology in the Humanities, 2001. The aphorism reflects Blake's religious syncretism. Blake's syncretic approach is taken up for discussion in the third chapter of this book.

10 A very interesting document in this regard is William Hodges's *Travels in India: During the Years 1780, 1781, 1782, & 1783* (1793). Hodges came to India in 1780 and lived under the patronage of Hastings, traveled widely and painted various aspects of life in India. He went back to England and wrote his book. The core of Hodges's rhetoric is formed by a strong condemnation of the Mughals and the Muslims and a valorization of Hinduism and portrayal of the Hindus as feminine, domesticable, and docile.

II

Tales and Translations: Setting Tropes and Shaping of Genres

The genre that inundated the eighteenth-century literary market was the Oriental Tale. However, Oriental Tale was not a new phenomenon, as it already had a long history of its presence in Europe. Martha Conant Pike, for instance, refers to four great collections of Oriental Tales that came to Europe in Latin translations in the medieval age: *Sendebar*, *Kalila and Dimna* or *The Fables of Bidpai*, *Discplina Clericalis*, and *Barlaam and Josaphat*. Some of the stories also came to England and appeared as metrical romances, apologues, legends and tales of adventure (xix–xx). *The Fableau of Dame Siriz*, *The Proces of Sevyn Sages*, Mandeville's *Travels* and Chaucer's *The Squire's Tale*, and possibly several other Canterbury Tales, according to Pike, owe their origin to the Eastern sources (xix–xx). However, it was only in the eighteenth century that the literary market was flooded with Oriental Tales. Some important preludes to the great era of Oriental Tale in the eighteenth century included L'strange's version of *The Fables of Bidpai* and eight volumes of Marana's *Letters Writ by a Turkish Spy*, published toward the end of the seventeenth century. The magical moment, however, came just at the beginning of the eighteenth century with the French translation of *Alf Layla wa Layla* by Antoine Galland. The first part of his twelve-volume *Les mille et une nuits* (*The Thousand and One Nights*) appeared in 1704. Its English version appeared between 1704 and 1717 marking the beginning of an explosion of Oriental Tales in prose and verse.

This large oeuvre of the Oriental Tales available in the eighteenth century has been analyzed in detail by Martha Conant Pike.

Pike sub-divides them into four different groups: the imaginative group, the moralistic group, the philosophic group, and the satiric group (xxvi). The division is made based on the subject matter and mode of discourse in the tales. The imaginative group includes *The Arabian Nights, The Persian Tales, The Turkish Tales, New Arabian Nights,* Collins's *Persian Eclogues, African Eclogues* by Chatterton, *Oriental Eclogues* of James Scott, *Vathek* by Beckford, and *Charoba* by Clara Reeve, to mention some of them. Some of the tales in the moralistic group are *The Hermit* by Thomas Pernell, *Murad the Unlucky* by Maria Edgeworth. Works like *Vision of Mirza* by Addison and *Rasselas* (1759) by Dr Johnson form part of the philosophic group. In the satiric group, there are tales like *The Persian Letters* of Montesquieu, *The Citizen of the World* by Goldsmith, Defoe's *System of Magic*, and Horace Walpole's *Hieroglyphic Tale*. This study does not have the scope for a detailed discussion of these tales. Therefore, a brief analysis of some of the tales will be attempted here by dividing them into two categories—the translations and the pseudo-translations or the imitations. In the category of translations, only those tales will be considered which were translated from original Oriental manuscripts by Western writers. Most of these tales were translated into English via their French versions. The tales that will be considered under the category of pseudo-translations were originals by Western writers, but those were passed off as translations from some Oriental source. However, some writers produced Oriental Tales without pretending that they are translations and these tales are categorized as imitations. The difference between the pseudo-translations and the imitations is only external. The pseudo-translations are acts of literary disguise, and it is interesting to note that these literary disguises prefigured some of the (in)famous poetic forgeries by Macpherson, Chatterton and Ireland in the latter part of the eighteenth century.[1]

Identifying the reasons behind the incidents of forgery during the Romantic period, Debbie Lee observes, "One of the things imposters and forgers make strikingly clear is the period's idolatrous worship of authenticity and truth" ("Forgeries" 521). It was the same "idolatrous worship of authenticity and truth" of the East that led writers to forge authenticity for their tales and add additional notes to give an aura of verisimilitude to their description of the East. Beckford's *Vathek*, for example, is presented to the readers as a translation and extensive notes are appended to the text (App. I. 163). Beckford had to take recourse to the notes because he wanted to achieve the effect of truthfulness. The notes also reveal the inability of the author to deal with an alien world. The narrative alone becomes inadequate to delineate the incidents depicted and, therefore, notes are added. In the same manner, Elizabeth Hamilton in *Translations of the Letters of a Hindoo Rajah* (1796) included a hundred-page explanatory essay with a glossary to familiarize her readers with the history and cultures of India.[2] This method of using notes appended to the tales became a standard feature of the Romantic verse narratives dealing with the East. The pseudo-translators by their disguise achieved a dual purpose: Firstly, they were able to produce the effect of realism in their description of the East; and secondly, as the readers were ready to devour anything Eastern, the disguise helped the writers gain commercial success.

Although the Oriental Tales were very popular, they were not well accepted by the literati, because the eighteenth-century aesthetics based on the Enlightenment principles of reason and restraint went against the imaginative and moral freedom that characterized these tales. This attitude of the intelligentsia is reflected in the fact that the Oriental Tales came to be mocked in parodies. Caylus' *The Oriental Tales* (1745) and Horace Walpole's *Hieroglyphic Tales* (1785) are two well-known parodies. It was, perhaps, the same apprehension of getting rejected by the pundits that led Horace Walpole to project the first Gothic novel as a translation from an Italian manuscript. In the preface to the first edition of *The Castle of Otranto,* Walpole forged an extensive history of the origin of the text. When the novel was well accepted, he lamented it in the preface to the second edition, and apologized to the readers "for having offered his work to them under the borrowed personage of a translator" (xv). Similarly, Elizabeth Hamilton did not acknowledge her authorship for *Translations of the Letters of a Hindoo Rajah* until after the work's initial success.[3] The writers of the Gothic novel and the Oriental Tale, therefore, had a similar concern regarding the reception of their stories, as both these forms aesthetically challenged the neoclassical literary taste. The journey from denial to acceptance of authorship indicates an interesting difference between the pseudo-translations and imitations: The imitations mark a change in the attitude of the authors; gradually, they became courageous enough to acknowledge their authorship.

Any discussion on the Oriental Tale must begin with *The Arabian Nights*[4] which is considered a landmark in the history of the genre. Though the tales in the *Nights* are traditionally associated with medieval Arabic culture, they are rooted in several oral traditions, containing motifs from a variety of geographic areas and historical periods, including ancient Mesopotamia, India, early medieval Persia, Iraq and Egypt of the Middle Ages. Scholars agree that the frame story is most likely of Indian origin. The first identifiable written version of the *Nights* is a book of Persian tales called *Hazar Afsanah* (*A Thousand Legends,* written between 225 and 250 CE), translated into Arabic around 850 CE. Although the tenth-century Arab writer Al-Mas'oodi referred to this Arabic text, noting that it was known as *Alf Layla* (*A Thousand Nights*), it is now lost. The stories underwent considerable modification between the tenth and the sixteenth centuries, kept alive by professional storytellers, who would perform them in coffee houses all over the Middle East.[5] The title, "Thousand and One Nights" was known in the twelfth century and likely to have originated from the Turkish expression '*bin-bir*' (thousand and one), which, like the Arabic '*alf*,' simply indicates a very large number. There is no definitive Arabic textual source of the work, but there are several surviving manuscripts containing many of the stories.[6]

The *Nights* was very popular in the Middle East but was never a part of the Eastern literary canon. However, when it reached Europe, it became a representative Eastern literary text and an important document on Eastern life. Kabbani Rana, therefore, rightly observes that Galland is not a "mere translator of these Arabic stories; he is the inventor of a western phenomenon, a circular narrative that portrayed an imaginary space of a thousand and one reveries" (24–25).

The Arabian Nights has a frame. The frame story concerns a Persian king and his new bride. King Shahryar is shocked to know that his brother's wife is unfaithful and later on discovers the infidelity of his own wife. He is shocked and sad. In his bitterness and grief, he has his wife executed and he concludes that all women are the same. Subsequently, the king begins to marry a succession of virgins only to execute each one the next morning before she has a chance to dishonor him. Eventually, the vizier, whose duty it is to provide the king with maidens, cannot find any more virgins. Shahrazad, the vizier's daughter, offers herself as the next bride and her father reluctantly agrees to it. On the night of their marriage, Shahrazad starts telling the king a story only to leave it unfinished. The king is forced to postpone her execution to hear the conclusion of the story. The next night, as soon as she finishes the tale, she begins a new one, and the king, eager to hear it out, postpones her execution once again. In her storytelling, Shahrazad is helped by her sister Dinerzad. It goes on for 1,001 nights and with Shahrazad, the lives of thousands of other women are saved. Shahrazad's narrative, therefore, becomes her life and the lives of other women.

The tales have fascinated generations of European readers. The immediate impact of the *Nights* upon the readers can be gauged from the fact that it underwent nineteen editions by 1798. The influence of the *Nights* and other Oriental Tales upon English literature in general, and on Romantic poetry, in particular, had been immense.[7] Pike defines the "history of the Oriental Tale in England in the eighteenth century" as "an episode in the development of English

Romanticism" (vii). She observes that "the strand of interest in the Orient is interwoven with other Romantic threads" (246). Almost all the Romantic poets—Wordsworth, Coleridge, Shelley, Byron, Keats—were avid readers of the *Nights* and other collections of Oriental Tales. Apart from the poets, the novelists and the essayists also borrowed from the *Nights*. Pike describes the *Nights* as "the fairy godmother of the English novel" (241). Similarly, Ross Ballaster in his essay "Narrative Transmigrations: The Oriental Tale and the Novel in Eighteenth-Century Britain," traces the relationship between the Oriental Tale and the English novel. With reference to *Nourjahad* (1767) by Frances Sheridan and *Charoba* (1785) by Clara Reeve, Ballaster shows how Oriental fiction was domesticated by these writers. The eighteenth-century novel, he argues, depicts the struggle between the pleasures of reading and the mission to ensure that it provides a vehicle for the transmission of virtue and *The Arabian Nights* is a "model in this struggle" (75).

Another important book that came to be translated into English at the beginning of the eighteenth century was *The Persian Tales or Thousand and One Days* (1714). The frame tale here, as in the *Nights,* introduces and completes the collection, but here we find a female equivalent of King Shahryar. The central figure is the princess of Kashmir, who in her dream sees an ungrateful stag abandoning a hind. After this dream, she loses her faith in men and decides not to marry. She is very beautiful and is followed by multiple suitors. Her father is disappointed with her for her refusal to tie the knot. The old nurse comes to the rescue deciding to tell her stories of faithful lovers to change her thoughts on marriage. The tales are continued to be told for thousand and one days but the princess remains obdurate. At last, she is moved to marry the prince of Persia under the magical power and religious authority of a holy dervish. Just like the *Nights*, one important theme of the collection is the power of narrative to bring about a change in the real world. The nurse's narrative transforms the princess as Shahrazad's narratives transform the king. A similar emphasis on the power of narrative to transform the world becomes Coleridge's concern in "Kubla Khan" and "Christabel."

Another collection with similar structure and thematic concern is *The Turkish Tales,* which was translated into English via its French version in the first decade of the eighteenth century. The collection has the alternative title, *Malice of Woman,* and is concerned with the malicious passion of Queen Canzade for her stepson who turns down the proposal of love from her and thwarts her scheme to murder the king. After being rejected, the queen persuades the king to decree the death of the prince. Meanwhile, the prince goes to a cave to observe forty days' silence to avoid a calamity predicted by the tutor. Forty viziers successively plead for the prince by telling the king stories of wicked wives and virtuous sons. The queen, on the other hand, tries to win the king by telling him stories with opposite themes. Finally, the prince is saved. "The Santon Barsisa," one of the tales in this collection, was a major source of *The Monk* by Gregory Lewis. Lewis, of course, was a major influence on the Romantics, especially Coleridge.

Another very influential work of translation, but a different genre, was *Hayy Ibn Yaqzan*. It was translated from Arabic by Simon Ockley in 1708. Ibn Tufyal's (1110–1185 CE) philosophical novel tells the story of a child who is raised by a gazelle. The child (Hayy) lives alone on a desert island in the Indian Ocean. Without any contact with other human beings, Hayy discovers the ultimate truth of life through a systematic process of reasoned inquiry. Later in the novel, he comes into contact with civilization and religion when he meets a castaway named Absal. He determines that certain trappings of religion and civilization, namely imagery and dependence on material goods, are necessary for the multitude in order that they might have decent lives. However, he believes that imagery and material goods are distractions from the truth and ought to be abandoned by those whose reason recognizes that they are distractions. Ibn Tufyal derived his ideas from earlier works by the eleventh-century philosopher, Ibn Sina

(980–1037). This novel (it is said to be the first novel in the Arabic language) influenced many European writers and philosophers. Johnson's *Rasselas* (1759) follows Tufyal's narrative pattern. *Robinson Crusoe* (1719) with its marooned hero also resembles it. It is also imitated by Rousseau in *Emile: or, On Education* (1762), which is a treatise on the nature of education and the nature of man written in the manner of Ibn Tufyal. Here, we find a similar celebration of "natural man." The emphasis on natural education as opposed to the nurturing of civilization, a shift from urban to the rural, from nurture to nature that form the core of the Romantic movement are integral to Tufyal's novel.

These major translations of Oriental Tales in the eighteenth century were accompanied by numerous pseudo-translations as there was an overwhelming response to these original translations. One of the first pseudo-translations, *Serendipity and the Three Princes, from the Peregrinaggio*, which came to England in the second decade of the seventeenth century was a translation from the French of De Mailli, who translated it from the Italian *Peregrinaggio.* The frame tale recounts the stories of three gifted princes who in their various enterprises achieve success. The events of their adventure were used by Voltaire in his philosophical tale *Zadig*. It also possibly influenced Johnson's *Rasselas.* This very tale was included in the first collection of tales, *The Soirées Bretonnes* (*Breton Nights* 1712) by Thomas Simon Gueullette. Four other pseudo-translations by Gueullette were translated into English as *Chinese Tales or the Wonderful Adventures of Mandarin Fum-Hoam* (1725), *Mogul Tales or The Dreams of Men Awake, Tartarian Tales or a Thousand and One Quarters of Hours* and *Peruvian Tales Related in One Thousand and One Hours*. From the *Mogul Tales*, Beckford got the episode of the flaming heart of the sinners. Beckford, however, was more indebted to another pseudo-translation, *The Adventures of Abdalla, son of Hanif* translated into English by William Hatchett from its French version by Jean-Paul Bignon. Another important pseudo-translation was *The New Arabian*

Nights, which came via its French version made by Dom Chavis and M. Cazotte. It is presented to the readers as if it is a continuation of *The Arabian Nights*. The tale of "Maugrabby, the Magician," which is the source of Southey's *Thalaba, the Destroyer* comes from this collection.

Another group of writings that must be included within the category of pseudo-translations are the volumes of letters written by Western hands but purported to be original writings by an Oriental traveler. These volumes of epistolary literature involve elaborate fictional invention for creating a semblance of reality. On the one hand, the fictional narrators could comment upon the European society and its customs, and on the other hand, they had the capacity to give an authentic description of the Eastern customs and manners as they originally belong there. There was no necessity to provide extensive additional notes. This tradition started with *Letters Writ by a Turkish Spy*, which is considered to be only next in importance to *The Arabian Nights* in the history of the Oriental Tales. It is agreed that the first volume of this work was written by Giovanni Paolo Marana, a Genoese political refugee to the French court of Louis XIV. The first volume (102 letters) was published in several parts between 1684 and 1686 in both Italian and in French. They were translated by W. Bradshaw into English in 1687 under the supervision of Robert Midgley who owned the copyright of the work. The remaining seven volumes appeared first in English between 1691 and 1694. The letters are supposed to be written by Mahmut, the Turkish spy. The fictional narrator is sent by Sultan Amurath (Murat IV) as a spy to report European affairs from Paris, where he takes the disguise of an expert in Oriental languages as "Titus, the Maldovian." *The Turkish Spy* is regarded as the pioneer of the genre of spy fiction and its influence is wide-ranging upon the literature of the time.[8] The use of the ethnographic observer in *The Turkish Spy* is imitated by Montesquieu in his *Letters Persanes* or *The Persian Letters*, which appeared in French in 1721 and was translated into English in 1730. Here, two fictional Persian noblemen, Uzbek and Rica are shown traveling through France recounting their experiences to people back home. The first English imitation of this form was by Lord Lyttenton's *The Persian Letters* (1735). Horace Walpole published *Letters from Xo-Ho* in 1757. Here Xo-Ho is the fictional narrator writing letters to his friend, Lien Chi. This is probably one of the influences upon Goldsmith's *Citizen of the World* or *Letters from a Chinese Philosopher Residing in London to His Friends in the East. The Turkish Spy* is also regarded as an influence on the genre of the periodical essay. Srinivas Aravamudan sums up the influence of Marana upon the literature of the eighteenth century, "Marana can . . . be cited as a common source for the Oriental Tale and the Spectator papers; for epistolary satire and the periodical essay; for fiction and social commentary" ("Fiction/Translation/Transnation" 62). Interestingly, the method of introducing an Eastern character to criticize contemporary society from a distance would prove to be a model for the Romantics, who often commented on different aspects of domestic life by situating their narratives in some parts of the distant East.

The pseudo-translations and imitations were not confined to prose literature alone. Oriental Tales were also imitated in verse. These imitations are very significant in terms of prefiguring the Romantic verse narratives on the East. The narratives are thematically simple and do not have much sophistication, but they started the custom of weaving a tale in verse with the Eastern setting and characters. These narratives adopted the method of indirectly criticizing issues at home from a distance. One of the first pseudo-translations in verse was done by William Collins. He wrote the four-part *Persian Eclogues* (1742): "Selim or the Shepherd's Moral," "Hassan or The Camel Driver," "Abra or the Georgian Sultana" and "Agib and Secander, or the Fugitives." Collins invented a long history of their origin:

> I received them at the Hands of a Merchant who had made it his business to enrich himself with Learning, as well as the silks and Carpets

> of the Persians. The little information I could gather concerning their Author, was, That his Name was Abdallah, and that he was a native of Tauris ... the Time of the Writing them was probably in the Beginning of Shah Sultan Hosseyn's Reign, the successor of the Sefi or Solyman, the Second. (Lonsdale, *Poems* 371–372)[9]

The first of these eclogues is a celebration of virtue rather than the beauty of the Persian maids. The second eclogue shows the conflict between pleasure and peace at home and the desire for wealth that drives men to undertake long and arduous journeys. Hasan leaves his beautiful beloved and peace of home and begins his travel through the desert. The hardships and the dangers on the way make him repent his decision of setting on such a journey: "Cursed be the Gold and Silver which persuade / Weak men to follow far-fatiguing Trade" (378, 131–132). The third eclogue celebrates the love between a simple shepherd girl, Abra and the king, Abbas. The fourth eclogue is a lamentation for the lost happiness and peace as Agib and Secander fly from the ravaging Tarter:

> Still as I haste, the Tartar shouts behind,
> And shrieks and Sorrows load the sadd'ning wind:
> In rage of Heart, with Ruin in his Hand,
> He blasts our Harvests, and deforms our Land. (384, 23–26)

It is a kind of war pastoral, and it came to be imitated by Chatterton in his eclogues. Certain tropes used by Collins in the eclogue migrated into the Romantic verse narratives. For instance, the trope of the desert journey described by Collins in the second eclogue foreshadows some of the passages in *Thalaba, the Destroyer* or the journey of Arab Bedouin in *The Prelude*.

Collins's eclogues, however, are characterized by a kind of artificiality and have no involvement of the author, nor are they capable of arousing much interest in the reader. Chatterton's first of the *African Eclogues*, "Heccar and Gaira" (written in January 1770) is a war pastoral like the last eclogue of Collins. Chatterton uses the form to express an anti-colonial and anti-slavery attitude in the poem and there is an emotional involvement of the author in the poem.[10] Chatterton's eclogues employ the exotic setting of Africa to pursue the themes of doomed love and martial glory. The dramatic backdrop is formed by the exotic nomenclature, the desert, and the jungle. Although "Heccar and Gaira" "conforms to the late eighteenth-century stereotypes of African cultural misrepresentation, it is unusual in its construction of the Atlantic slave trade" (Wood 72–73). The eclogue shows Heccar, an African chief and his warrior, Gaira, reposing on the sand following a furious battle with the European slave-masters. Heccar advises Gaira to talk about their desire for vengeance against the White slavers:

> The Children of the Wave, whose pallid race,
> Views the faint sun display a languid face,
> From the red fury of thy justice fled,
> Swifter than torrents from their rocky bed. (118)[11]

Gaira's wife and children have been kidnapped by the slavers: "The pallid shadows of the azure waves / Had made my Cawna and my children slaves" (120). Heccar and Gaira vow unceasing vengeance on the slave traders:

> When the loud shriekings of the hostile cry
> Roughly salute my ear, enrag'd I'll fly;
> Send the sharp arrow quivering thro' the heart
> Chill the hot vitals with the venom'd dart;
> Nor heed the shining steel or noisy smoke,
> Gaira and Vengeance shall inspire the stroke. (121)

Chatterton strongly anticipates the republicanism and anti-slavery sentiments that characterize the poetry of William Blake and the other Romantics.

This radical outlook of Chatterton and his anti-imperialism is echoed in John Scott's *Oriental Eclogues* (1782), particularly in "Oriental Eclogues II. Serim; or, the Artificial Famine: An East-Indian Eclogue."

The eclogue condemns the British for the famine that ravaged the provinces of Bengal, Bihar, and Orissa between 1769 and 1773. The Hindu sage, Serim is shown bemoaning the fate of his countrymen by the banks of the Ganges. The peace and happiness of the people are lost in satisfying the lust and avarice of the British: "'Bring gold, bring gems,' the insatiate plunderers cry; / 'Who hoards his wealth by Hunger's rage shall die.'" (15–16). Serim surveys the damage caused by the ravenous Europeans, who have confronted the oppressed with a harrowing choice between famine and sacrilege. People suffer as "tenfold tax the farmer forc'd to yield / Despairs, and leaves unoccupied the field" (49–50). The farmers "Quit their sad homes, and mourn along the land, /A pensive, pallid, self-disabled band!" (57–58). Serim denounces the invaders and feels that the wrongly acquired wealth and luxury will bring a curse upon them: "Sad sounds shall issue from your guilty walls, / The widow'd wife's, the sonless mother's calls" (160–162). While Serim goes on cursing the British, a "British ruffian" tumbles him headlong into the river. Through this final incident, Scott depicts the extreme cruelty and inhumanity of the British. However, there is a difference between Chatterton and Scott in the matter of their treatment of the indigenous people's opposition to the colonizers. Scott's Serim is dependent upon the retribution of God for the punishment of the colonizers as it is seen only as "God's prerogative," but "Chatterton's Africans do not require such divine retribution and are capable of bringing about their own violent justice" (Wood 73). Toward the beginning of the poem, Serim invokes the "Guardian Genius" of the "sacred wave" to save the people from the cruelty of the Europeans: "Europe's fell race controul the wide domain, / Engross the harvest, and enslave the swain" (9–10). Even the advice from God to Serim is that of tolerance and forgiveness: "Forbear, rash man! nor curse thy country's foes; / Frail man to man forgiveness ever owes" (137–138). The poem is remarkable for criticizing the British and drawing our attention to the plight of the Indians. However, the poem also creates stereotypes of Indians as passive sufferers and fatalists incapable of fighting back.

Robert Southey repeats many of these tropes representing India in *The Curse of Kehama.*

In the headnote to the poem, Scott points out that it is based on a real "account of British conduct and its consequences, in Bengal and the adjacent provinces, some years ago" (*Poetical Works* 145). Some contemporary reviewers appreciated the poem for its originality. In the *Critical Review*, it was remarked that "amongst the Eclogues, of which there are five, Serim, or the Artificial Famine, is the best written. . . . There is great poetical merit in the whole of this Oriental Eclogue, which paints in the warmest colours the various scenes of misery and distress brought on the natives of India by their cruel English task-masters: there is too much truth, we fear, in this narrative" (Smollet 47). The description of the cruelty of the British rulers in India, as the review betrays, proved quite disturbing to the British. It is evident in John Hoole's analysis of the poem:

> The Eclogue of Serim, or the Artificial Famine, has much poetical merit; but perhaps it were to be wished, that the philanthropy of the author had not led him to make choice of a story so apparently disgraceful to the British name in India, the circumstances of which have been, doubtless, greatly exaggerated, while the enormities of a few individuals have been swelled, by designing men, into a general and universal spirit of rapine, avarice, and cruelty. (*Critical Essays* lxx)

Scott's third and final eclogue, "Li-Po; or, The Good Governor: a Chinese Eclogue" is set in China and begins with a fantastic piece of landscape description, obviously modeled on Chinese porcelain, and the poem praises the good authority and governance of the Chinese. English rulers of the second eclogue stand in strong contrast to the rulers in China. The first eclogue by Scott is entitled "Zerad; or The Absent Lover: An Arabian Eclogue." Its subject matter, as is evident from the title, is the lamentation (and deplorable condition) of the lover due to the absence of his beloved. In the headnote provided by the poet, a reference is made to William Jones's "Essay on the Poetry of the Eastern Nations" to show how Arabian love poetry is marked by the presence of the figure of the absent lover (126). One notable aspect of the eclogues is the author's effort to familiarize the readers to the events presented in them by adding explanatory notes. These rather short annotated eclogues contributed to the development of the annotated verse narratives in the Romantic period.

Before turning to the relationship between the Oriental Tale and the Gothic, it would be relevant to have a brief discussion on *Rasselas* (1759). Here is a case of a classicist turning into an Orientalist. *Rasselas* was written to raise a substantial sum of money within a week against Johnson's own principle of writing for money (Schmidt 104). He exploited the fashion for Oriental Tales to meet his economic ends, just as some of the Romantics would do a few years later. *Rasselas* is very important in the history of the Oriental Tale because many of the preoccupations of these tales are combined in this philosophical novel. The novel begins with a travel account provided by Imlac, who describes people and places as far as the Mughals and Surat. The narrative is followed by a journey by Rasselas, Imlac and the princess. In the course of their travel, the readers meet many exotic places and peoples—the merchants, the hermit, the robbers and the mummies. The pleasure of the Oriental Tale, as Ross Ballaster states, is "a game of fictional metamorphosis . . . where s/he [reader] can test out a series of 'exotic' roles, male and female, safely distanced by being placed in a historically and geographically remote 'East' in order to adjust her or his own mental horizons" ("Narrative Transmigrations" 80). No other tale gives greater opportunity for experiencing this pleasure than *The Arabian Nights*. Similarly, Johnson's *Rasselas* with its exotic setting provides the reader with the opportunity of encountering myriad groups of people and characters and thereby allowing the readers to enjoy the pleasure of role-playing. In *Rasselas*, Johnson also hints at the anxiety of the British trading class through the character of Imlac. Imlac was appointed by his father for making a profit by trade, but neglecting the assigned duty, he follows his desire for knowledge.

British trading companies might have experienced a similar sense of anxiety as the conflict between the scholar and administrator could be seen in the case of William Jones and his colleagues in Calcutta. The East India Company (EIC) officials, who took an extra interest in the Indian civilization, was a cause of worry because there was also the possibility of them going native. The trial of Warren Hastings reflected these issues.

Imperial anxiety left a greater imprint on the Gothic novels. However, it is necessary to remember that the Gothic was closely connected to the Oriental Tale during the early years of its development. David Punter and Glennis Byron recognize the fact that the Oriental Tale helped in fashioning the eighteenth-century taste for the Gothic resulting in an "effulgence of Gothic" in the last two decades (181–184).[12] One of the earliest Gothic tales, *Vathek* (1786) forms an intersection between the Gothic novel and the Oriental Tale. Edith Birkhead in *The Tale of Terror: A Study of the Gothic Romance* classifies the numerous Oriental Tales as Anglo-Oriental tales and observes that Beckford was extremely bored by the moral overweight of these tales. He reacted against the superficiality of these tales by writing *Vathek,* an "Eastern tale of horrors" (95). The phrases, "Eastern tale of horror" or "Oriental Gothic" are very important because by using these terms, critics try to underscore the hybridity of *Vathek* and differentiate it from other Gothic fictions. *Vathek* is similar to many of the Oriental Tales, particularly to the "Adventures of Abdalla, the son of Hanif," but *Vathek* is more than an Oriental Tale. Pike finds in *Vathek* many passages similar to *Mystries of Udolpho* and other "tales of terror" (67). Comparing the element of horror in *Vathek* with that of the tales of *The Arabian Nights*, Pike observes "in the latter it is more objective and lacks the psychological, uncanny quality found in *Vathek* and others [other Gothic tales]." She defines *Vathek* as "a thoroughly Oriental tale of terror" (67). However, as Fredrick S. Frank points out that it will be wrong to dismiss *Vathek* as an Oriental Tale only and he relates Mrs Barbauld's concept of the pleasure of the terror to Beckford's novel ("The Gothic *Vathek*" 157–172). Massimiliano Demata identifies in *Vathek* many of the elements that would become stereotypical features of the Gothic novel: "Beckford often uses dark, enclosed and claustrophobic spaces, while his attention to magic and necromancy would soon become stereotypes of the novel of horror." With reference to Beckford's novel as well as to the extensive notes provided by Henley and edited by Beckford, Demata argues that in *Vathek*, the author attempts to create "a narrative space" in which the "tale" is intruded upon by the elements of "reality," a narrative space which discloses to the readers the dangers and proximity of the alien presence of the Oriental Other: "The East resurfaces in the West in shapes which are the domain of the uncanny." Demata's analysis is not confined only to *Vathek*. He uses the same argument to show that like Beckford, Maturin in *Melmoth, the Wanderer* "leads the reader to view the 'fiction' of the tales within a disturbing and tangible aura of reality" and concludes that both Beckford and Maturin express their "anxiety of imperial conquest and oppression" through the Gothic form ("Discovering Eastern Horrors" 20–25). It is interesting to note that the use of Gothic images in Romantic poetry often reveals a similar sense of imperial anxiety.

Whatever *Vathek*'s position may be within the tradition of the Gothic novel, it is undoubtedly clear that *Vathek* and other Oriental Tales in the eighteenth century was a major impetus for the growth and development of Gothic conventions. Eve Kosofsky Sedgewick in *The Coherence of the Gothic Conventions* claims that the Gothic text is pervasively conventional: "Once you know that a novel is of the Gothic kind (and you can tell from the title), you can predict its contents with an unnerving certainty"(9). The important features are an oppressive ruin, a wild landscape, a catholic or feudal society, a heroine with trembling sensibility, the impetuous lover, the tyrannical old man with a piercing glance. Formally, "it is likely to be discontinuous and involuted, perhaps, incorporating tales within tales, changes of narrators, or as such framing devices as found in manuscripts or interpolated histories." It involves priesthood and monastic institutions; sleep-like and death-like states; subterranean spaces; unintelligible writings; the poisonous effects of guilt and shame; nocturnal landscapes and dreams; apparitions from the past; Faust-like or wandering Jew-like figures; charnel house and madhouse (9–10). If the most common features of the Oriental Tale are placed beside these conventions of the Gothic, it will become obvious that the Gothic tradition begun by Horace Walpole drank deep of the Oriental Tales. There are certain recurring features of these tales which were incorporated within the Gothic tradition. Almost every collection of the Oriental Tales involves the following features: a frame story, a tyrannous ruler with fierce anger, a wandering journey often into an abyss, an opulence of wealth and luxury, excessive violence and lust—the harem being the embodiment of it, magic and supernaturalism, horrible sinning and equally horrible punishment. *Vathek* fulfills almost all the characteristic features of the Gothic novel pointed out by Sedgewick, as well as of the Oriental Tales: we have a violent tyrannical ruler with a fierce gaze in *Vathek*; he is a Faust-like figure who will do anything to satisfy his want—when the Giaour demands, he sacrifices fifty children; he has a magician mother. Vathek lives in extreme luxury with "five wings, or rather palaces," destined for the "gratification of each of the senses"—the last of the five palaces is designed to gratify his sexual desire: "The fifth palace, denominated *The Retreat of Mirth*, or *The Dangerous*, was frequented by troops of young females beautiful as the Houris, and not less seducing; who never failed to receive with caresses, all whom the Caliph allowed to approach them, and enjoy a few hours of their company" (1–3). He is also obsessed with gaining knowledge. When the grotesque Giaour visits Samarah, he excites the curiosity of Vathek with the strangely inscribed sabre he leaves behind. Vathek does all he can for the inscriptions to be deciphered, but he does not succeed. Soon, his curiosity leads to the return of the Giaour, who requests the blood of fifty children in return for an even greater knowledge that would allow him entry to the Palace of the Subterranean Fire beneath ancient Istakhar, where he will find the treasures of the pre-Adamite kings and the talismans that control the world. For this, he will have to renounce his religion and his faith in God. Vathek accepts this with ease, and the story progresses to his journey to Istakhar. On the way, he breaks the orders of Eblis and stops at a village, where he finds the beautiful Nouronihar, who joins him in his journey. Vathek commits countless acts of violence in the course of his journey. Once they reach the Palace of the Subterranean Fire, Eblis betrays them and they discover

> a vast multitude was incessantly passing; who severally kept their right hands on their hearts; without once regarding any thing around them. They had all, the livid paleness of death. Their eyes, deep sunk in their sockets, resembled those of phosphoric meteors . . . some shrieked in agony . . . whilst others, grinding their teeth in rage, foamed along more frantic than the wildest maniac. (109–110)

The Faustian Vathek faces the same fate with Nournihar and her evil mother, Carathis: "[T]heir hearts immediately took fire, and they, at once, lost the most precious gift of heaven: —HOPE" (119). Violence, lust, guilt, sin, magic, ambition, supernatural horror, and wandering—all the motifs of Gothic novels are present here.

Although *Vathek* has all the features of a Gothic novel, it is not regarded as the trendsetter of the Gothic genre, since it appeared nearly two decades after *The Castle of Otranto*. However, while writing *The Castle of Otranto* (1764) and his Gothic tragedy, *The Mysterious Mother* (1768), Walpole's taste for the Gothic was certainly molded by the Oriental Tales, and it is not a coincidence that Walpole had an interest in the Oriental Tales and produced *Heiroglyphic Tales* structuring his stories on a firm "fairy tale" foundation (Christensen). Kenneth Gross calls the tales representatives of a tradition of "oriental fables" that also found expression in such works of the period as

Voltaire's *Zadig*, and Johnson's *Rasselas* (Intro. x). It is a parody of the genre of the Oriental Tales, and doing a parody involves a deep knowledge and interest in the subject involved. Walpole used this repertoire of knowledge in producing the first Gothic novel.

There are a number of similarities between the "oriental gothic" *Vathek* and the first Gothic novel, *The Castle of Otranto*: Both the heroes are driven by their ambition and desire for wealth—Manfred wants to retain the wrongly possessed title for the family and Vathek wants to possess the wealth of the pre-Adamite sultans. They are villain heroes and not entirely detestable because they are sublimely wicked. Both have anti-religious tendencies: Vathek joins hands with the satanic forces to fulfill his Faustian ambition; Manfred tries to violate and defile the Christian morality by attempting to rape Isabella. Both the authors incorporate the element of irony and humor and the darkness of evil looms large over both the narratives. Both novels share most of the elements of Gothic pointed out by Sedgewick, and perhaps, not a single characteristic feature of the Gothic is left outside when we take the two novels together, except the tale-within-the-tale, for which the Gothic writers were indebted to the Oriental Tales. When the element of horror is added to the existing structure of the Oriental Tale, it becomes the Oriental Tale of terror and when the Eastern setting with mosques and palaces of the Oriental Tale of terror is replaced with some medieval monasteries and haunted castles with claustrophobic spaces we get the formula for the Gothic novel. This becomes evident if we have a look at *The Monk* (1796), one of the representative Gothic novels where M.G. Lewis combines the elements from the Oriental Tales, *Vathek*, and *The Castle of Otranto*.

In the advertisement to the novel, Lewis acknowledges the fact that the "idea of this romance was suggested by the story of Santon Barsisa related in the Guardian" (xxi). The tale "The History of Santon Barsisa" was published in the Guardian, No. 148, Monday, August 31, 1713. It is introduced by Richard Steele to the readers as having a moral "entirely Christian and is so obvious that I shall leave every reader the pleasure of picking out for himself. I shall only premise, to obviate any offence that may be taken, that a great many notions in the Mahometan religion are borrowed from the Holy Scriptures" (295). It is a story about Santon Barsisa who has been leading a pious life for 100 years but succumbs to his sexual passion when the beautiful daughter of the king is taken to his cave for treatment. He is tempted by the devil to violate the chastity of the lady and to kill her. His actions are discovered, and he is to be punished by hanging until death. Moments before he is to be hanged, he is once more tempted by the devil, who offers to rescue him if he submits his soul to the satanic forces. Barsisa agrees only to be betrayed by the devil.

Ambrosio's story in *The Monk* is almost similar. Ambrosia is a paragon of virtue like Barsisa. His closest mate in the abbey is Rozario, who is revealed to be a woman, Matilda. Rozario/Matilda seduces Ambrosio releasing his confined sexual passions. Dissatisfied with Matilda after a while, he seeks new object to quench his lust in an innocent teenager Antonia, who is, in fact, his sister. With Matilda's assistance, he is able to seduce the girl. When the scheme goes wrong, Antonia's mother is murdered by Ambrosio and Antonia is carried to a crypt and raped repeatedly on her awakening. Later on, she is murdered and her murder is discovered during anti-clerical violence. Ambrosio is captured and brought before the Inquisition, but Matilda tempts him to sell his soul to the devil in exchange for freedom only to be betrayed by Satan. There is, of course, a subplot that tells the story of Don Raymond and Agnes. Here, the motif of lust and violence run parallel, though on a lower pitch.

Unlike *Vathek, The Monk* is not set in the East but in Spain, and the backdrop is formed by church, monastery, and abbey. The hero of the novel is modeled upon the character of Vathek. Ambrosio transgresses the laws of Christianity as Vathek transgresses the laws of Islam. The source story of *The Monk*, of course, shows the transgression against Islam. In *The Monk,* there is no harem, but

Ambrosio creates his own harem in the crypt by kidnapping Antonia and continuously raping her. Lust and violence of the Oriental Tales are concentrated in the character of Amborsio. The theme of incest is suggested in *The Castle Otranto* in the form of Manfred's desire for Isabella and Frederic's for Matilda and in *Vathek*, through the relationship between Carathis and her son Vathek. Lewis leaves no space for suggestion as Antonia is discovered to be Ambrosio's sister. Whereas Antonia seems to belong to the breed of Matilda and Isabella, the innocent sensitive heroines of the Gothic novel, Matilda of *The Monk* is a combination of Gulshenroz and Carathis, the mistress and the mother of Vathek, respectively. Carathis, who has magical power, leads Vathek to the satanic world of the Giaour. In the same way, Matilda is the instrument of transformation of Ambrosio from a pious monk to a devilish sinner. Moreover, the temptation of the devil in Lewis's source story and the role played by Giaour in *Vathek* are also condensed into the character of Matilda.

A close look at the Gothic novels reveals that apart from the weak and innocent heroines, we find a second category of strong female characters that often help in the transgression of the Gothic heroes or become their accomplice. Carathis, Matilda, or Gulshenroz would fall into this second category. In fact, Carathis in *Vathek* or Matilda in *The Monk* look back, albeit with certain changes, upon the Eastern heroines of the Middle English romances[13]—beautiful but violent, cunning and lustful—and look forward to the various manifestations of the demonic female and female magicians in Romantic poetry, beginning with Landor's Dalica and Myrther in *Gebir* to Maimuna and Khawla in Southey's *Thalaba, the Destroyer*, Coleridge's Geraldine, Shelley's Queene Mab and Byron's Gulnare in *Lara* or the mysterious lady in Keats's "La Belle Dame Sans Merci."

Two other features that bind nearly all the novels in the Gothic tradition and the Oriental Tales and go on to influence the Romantic poets are the element of journey or wandering and the villain-hero. The element of wandering transmigrates into Romantic poetry in its various manifestations. Southey's Oriental epic *Thalaba, the Destroyer*, Landor's *Gebir*, Shelley's *Revolt of Islam, Prometheus Unbound, Alastor, Queene Mab, The Witch of Atlas*, Moore's *Lalla Rookh*, Byron's *Childe Harold's Pilgrimage* and the Turkish Tales, Wordsworth's *The Prelude,* Coleridge's *The Rime of the Ancient Mariner* and *Christabel*, to mention a few of the Romantic poems that contain the trope of wandering and journey. The Byronic heroes are constructed around the figure of the Gothic villain-heroes: somber, brooding, haughty, scheming, an outcast, ambitious and demonic, suffering from a secret sense of guilt. Apart from the Byronic hero, two other iconic Romantic heroes have affinities to the Gothic villain-hero, namely, the Satanic and the Promethean. One of the first satanic villain-heroes in Romantic poetry is Oswald/Rivers in Wordsworth's *The Borderers* (written in 1796–1797); Coleridge's Osorio is another such figure.

Apart from certain themes, motifs, narrative structures that are assimilated into Romantic poetry, another significant role played by the Gothic narratives and Oriental Tales was in terms of freeing literature from the shackles of neoclassicism. Andrew Smith and William Hughes in the introduction to *Empire and Gothic: the Politics of Genre,* remark that in the Gothic, as in Romanticism in general, there is a challenge to the post-Enlightenment notions of rationality and "this challenge was developed through an exploration of the feelings, desires and passions which compromised the Enlightenment project of rationality calibrating all forms of knowledge and behaviours"(1). The releasing of passions that Smith and Hughes speak of began with the advent of Oriental Tales in the eighteenth century. Therefore, Gothicism, Orientalism and Romanticism share close affinities. As pointed out in the *Norton Anthology of English Literature,* the Oriental Tales and the Gothic novels are but two strands of Romanticism: "Pleasurable terror and pleasurable exoticism are kindred experiences, with unreality and strangeness at the root of both" ("Romantic Orientalism: Overview," par. 3).

Another factor that enormously contributed to the Romantics' interest in the East was the growing body of scholarly translations. European efforts seeking new trading posts undoubtedly produced commercial and economic benefits, but it also bore fruits in terms of accumulating knowledge of the East. Raymond Schwab identifies d' Herbelot's *Bibliotheque Orientale* (1697) as the point of beginning for Oriental scholarship and the translation of the *Zend-Avesta* (trans. 1759) by Duperron (1731–1805) as a major breakthrough. Duperron also translated the *Upanishads* in 1786 from the Persian version of the Sanskrit texts done by the Mughal prince Dârâ Shukoh. Commenting on the impact of Duperron's contribution to the European knowledge of the Orient, Schwab remarks, "he interjected a vision of innumerable civilizations from ages past, of an infinity of literatures" to the European schools, whose knowledge was "limited to the narrow Greco-Roman heritage of the Renaissance" (6). It was primarily the result of the French endeavor to know the East. The French effort to gather knowledge on the Orient culminated with Napoleon's Egyptian expedition (1798–1801), which is considered a turning point for modern Orientalism by Edward Said for its systematic attempt to study Egypt (*Orientalism*, Chapter 1: Projects). One of the outputs of Napoleon's project was the massive twenty-three volume *Description de l'Égypte*, which came out between 1809 and 1828. The expedition created great interest among the Romantics in Egypt and North Africa: Landor set his *Gebir* in ancient Egypt to comment on the contemporary European political scene; Southey's *Thalaba* borrowed much from Landor's *Gebir*; Wordsworth wrote "The Egyptian Maid or The Romance of the Water Lily"; in "Kubla Khan," Coleridge employed Egyptian and North African myths.

However, during the second half of the eighteenth century, it was the English-speaking Orientalists who achieved breakthroughs in the 'discovery' of the East, particularly in relation to the Indian subcontinent and China. After the establishment of the Asiatic Society in Calcutta in 1784, a series of translations, as well as some creative writings, started appearing in English. Schwab gives a chronological list of works published between 1784 and 1794 to show the eruption in Oriental scholarship after the Asiatic Society of Bengal was established (51–52).[14] Of all the important figures from this period, the name of William Jones comes first and foremost. Jones's interest in the East, however, began long before his arrival in India in 1783. In 1771, he published *Grammar of Persian Language*, which contained the often reprinted translation of "A Persian Song by Hafiz" and his *Poems; Consisting Chiefly of Translations from Asiatick Languages. To Which are Added Two Essays* came out in 1772. "A Persian Song by Hafiz" was reprinted in this volume. The poem is viewed as the third most important English translation from Persian, surpassed only by the *Rubaiyat* and *Sohrab and Rustom* (Pachori 13). The year 1774 marked the appearance of *Commentaries on Asiatic Poetry* (in Latin *Poeseos Asiaticae Commentariorum* in six volumes), which provides Jones's critical views on Middle-Eastern metrics, imagery, subject matter, diction and his opinion of a few individual poets (Pachori 4). In 1783, he produced "a dissertation On the Manners of the Arabians before the time of Mahomet, illustrated by seven poems, which were written in letters of gold, suspended in the temple of Mecca, about the beginning of the sixth century" (Pachori 5). He introduced Arabic poetry to Europe with the publication of *The Mollakat,* a translation of the Arabic poet Imr-al-Qais. In his Indian phase, Jones translated the legal and religious treatises from Persian and Sanskrit. Simultaneously, his efforts were directed in translating Sanskrit literary texts into English and authoring his own creative pieces in imitation of the works he translated. Among the literary translations, *Hitopodesa,* Jayadeva's *Gita Govinda* (1789), and Kalidasa's *Shakuntala* (1790) have remained most influential. Along with *Shakuntala,* Jones published his nine hymns addressed to the nine deities of Hindu mythology. The *Hymns* anticipated the extent of impact Indian mythology was going to have on Romantic poetry. Jones was also the editor of the journal *Asiatick Researches,* where the findings of the Society were put forward for the European metropolitan audience; information gathered in Calcutta was disseminated throughout Europe through this journal.

The scholarly works of the Orientalists had immense impact on the European mind. As Schwab puts it: "The writings deciphered by the Orientalists made the world, for the first time in human history, a whole" (Schwab 4). Schwab argues that the Orient "served as alter ego to the Occident," and the two complemented each other, rather than competed with—or controlled—the other: India, he argues, "had worked to reunite the human with a divine that is the Universe," thereby locating Romanticism's penchant for the mystic and pantheistic in the writers' fascination with the subcontinent. It is beyond dispute that scholarly translations from the East had a major impact upon the Western conception of the world. However, Schwab ignores the political implications of Oriental scholarship, the issue of how Orientalist knowledge aided the imperial cause. Therefore, it is germane to probe the ideological location of the Orientalists and their attitude to the East keeping in mind the relationship between power and knowledge.

To consider the nature and purpose of the Orientalist knowledge of the East is to fall back on Said's pioneering study. Said's theory makes it impossible to see any representation and cultivation of knowledge as disinterested. However, the issue is fraught with complications as Said himself points out:

> I doubt that it is controversial, for example, to say that an Englishman in India or Egypt in the later nineteenth century took an interest in those countries that was never far from their status in his mind as British colonies. To say this may seem quite different from saying that all academic knowledge about India and Egypt is somewhat tinged and impressed with, violated by the gross political fact –and yet this I am saying in this study of Orientalism. (11)

The complication indicated by Said has relevance to the analysis of Jones and his colleagues. The academic Orientalism practiced by Jones and his friends in Calcutta cannot be simply condemned and dismissed as an imperial project, although it is undeniable that their work helped the British colonial agency, and the Orientalists were primarily administrators of the EIC. Richard Allen makes the point that Jones's and Hastings's position in the history of Orientalism may be different: "to a considerable degree, both felt that the colonized society had a separate and autonomous tradition which was to be valued alongside that of the European colonizers rather than simply cast aside." It is "just an accident of history—Jones and Hastings were part of an early period of colonization whose ideas were superseded" (38).

Concerning the representation of India in the West, Kejariwal observes that there were three distinct phases of the development of Western scholarly interest in India, and a new phase was reached with the translation of *The Bhagvat-Geeta* (1785):

> From a series of travellers' tales, and attempts to decry Indian customs and manners, a stage was reached when the west began not only to make efforts to understand, but value India and her culture. In the first stage scholarship was of little importance; the emphasis was on the exotic, the mysterious, the fantastic. In the second there was no lack of scholarship, it was scholarship with a purpose, and vested interest. But now the western scholars approached India with the desire to learn. (21)

The "desire to learn" often coexisted with the desire to govern. Hastings, for example, is often praised for his encouragement of the curatorial[15] policy in India. However, what he wrote to the Chairman of the East India Company defending the utilitarian value of publishing Wilkins' translation of *The Bhagvat-Geeta* betrayed his magisterial outlook. Hastings wrote: "Every accumulation of knowledge and especially such as is obtained by social communication with people over whom we exercise a dominion founded on the right of conquest, is useful to the state" (qtd. in Kejariwal 24). The Western approach to India during this period was dominantly curatorial. Jones projected India as a culturally rich territory and he had a "sunny" view of Hinduism. The colonial policy under Hastings "sought the preservation rather than the transformation of otherness," but the irony is that this preservation of otherness also involved "the ruthless annihilation of anything that impeded its intensive exploitation" (Makdisi, *Romantic Imperialism* 109).

The Orientalist discourse in the eighteenth century was relatively free and, therefore, the image of the East in eighteenth-century literature was free-floating; conflicting currents of thought coexisted. It is this openness that characterizes the early works of the first generation Romantic poets. In the early phase of their career, they were drawn to Jones or Volney and their syncretic or universalizing approach. They tried to assimilate philosophical and religious ideas from the East; they combined genres and brought together elements from disparate sources in their poetic compositions, giving new dimensions to the existing forms and genres of British poetry. The Oriental Tales, Gothic novels and scholarly translations, along with innumerable tales of travel and histories supplied the Romantics with a great diversity of materials they could work with. These genres shaped the forms and themes of early Romantic poetry and often played a decisive role in determining the Orientalist tropes therein.

Notes

1 Macpherson's *Ossian Ballads* was published in 1760; Chatterton invented Thomas Rowley (1753–1770) and William Henry Ireland committed Shakespearean forgery during the 1790s.

2 Hamilton's brother Charles went to India as a cadet for East India Company. In 1786, Charles returned to England with a commission to translate a commentary on Islamic laws, the *Hedaya,* into English. Hamilton assisted him in this, thereby becoming familiar with the manners and customs of India.

3 By 1813, Elizabeth Hamilton's novel underwent five editions.

4 Henceforth may be referred to as *Nights.*

5 For detailed discussion of the coffee houses and the tradition of storytelling in the Middle East, see Robert Irwin's *The Arabian Nights: A Companion* (110–112).

6 For a history of the origin of the *Nights*, see Ulrich Marzolph and Richard van Leeuwen's *The Arabian Nights: An Encyclopedia*, Vol. 1 (713–720).

7 Some of these studies are: *The Arabian Nights in English Literature: Studies in the Reception of The Thousand and One Nights into British Culture* by Caracclio Peter; *The Arabian Nights: a Companion* by Robert Irwin; *The Arabian Nights and Orientalism: Perspectives from East & West* edited by Yuriko Yamanaka Tetsuo Nishio; *The Arabian Nights in Historical Context Between East and West* by Saree Makdisi and Felicity Nussbaum; *Scheherazade in England: A Study of Nineteenth Century English Criticism of the "Arabian Nights"* by Muhsin Jassim Ali.

8 It was so popular that in its own genre, it was immediately followed by works like Edward Ward's *The London Spy* (1698–1700); Charles Gildon's *The Golden Spy* (1709); Captain Bland's *The Northern Atlantis or York Spy* (1713); the anonymous *The German Spy* (1738); *The Jewish Spy* (1755). Together with this, we should remember, by 1776, there had accumulated at least twenty-six different editions of *The Turkish Spy* (Aravamudan, "Fiction/Translation/ Transnation" 59). Daniel Defoe was so attracted by it that he wrote *Continuation of Turkish Letters Writ by a Turkish Spy in Paris* (1718) and extended the narrator's account from 1687 to 1693.

9 All references to Collins's poems are to Roger Lonsdale, editor. *The Poems of Gray, Collins and Goldsmith*. London and Harlow: Longmans, Green and Co. LTD, 1969.

10 The difference between Collins's eclogues and those by Chatterton is well documented in the anthology, *The Poetry of Slavery: An Anglo-American Anthology*, which contains "Heccar and Gaira."

11 Unless otherwise stated, all citations of Chatterton's poems are from *The Works of Thomas Chatterton*, Vol. I. London: Longman and Cottle, 1803.

12 The phrase "effulgence of Gothic" is taken from the title of Robert Miles's essay "The 1790s: the effulgence of Gothic."

13 In medieval literature, the Eastern woman was often (mis-)represented as beautiful, but lustful and cruel. Josian in *Sir Bevis of Hampton* forms

an example of this. Chaucer's characterization of Dido and Cleopatra in *The Legend of Good Women* follows a similar pattern. Presentation of Dido harps upon this point: "This fresshe lady" (1035), this queen "So yong, so lusty, with hire eyen glade"(1038), living in the epicurean splendour of Carthaginian court. This image of the Eastern woman with her lascivious beauty and unparalleled cruelty continuously haunted the Western imagination, including that of the Romantics.

14 See also the first chapter of O.P. Kejariwal's book, *The Asiatic Society of Bengal and the Discovery of India's Past, 1784–1838*, entitled "The Background," which analyzes the modern Western effort to know and discover India.

15 A triad is developed by Amartya Sen to frame outsiders in their attempts to "understand and interpret" India. He defines them as "the *exoticist* approaches, the *magisterial* approaches and the *curatorial* approaches." The exoticist approach "concentrates on the wondrous aspect of India"; the magisterial approach "sees India as a subject territory from the point of view of its British governors"; the third category "includes various attempts at noting, classifying and exhibiting diverse aspects of Indian culture" (141–142).

III

"For the darkness of Asia was startled": Blake and the East

In one of the chapters of *The Arabian Nights: A Companion* (1994), Robert Irwin, a prolific critic and an authority on the Western reception of *The Arabian Nights* observed that its influence upon European literature is so pervasive that "it might have been an easier, shorter chapter if I had discussed those writers who were not influenced by the *Nights*. A discussion of the lack of influence on, say, William Blake, Evelyn Waugh and Vladimir Nabokov might have been just as rewarding" (291). Later on, when Irwin discovered that Nabokov's family library had a copy of the *Nights*, he wrote in the preface to *The Arabian Nights and Orientalism: Perspectives from East and West* (2006): "[P]erhaps it is now time to reconsider the possible influence of the *Arabian Nights* on the poetry of William Blake and the fiction of Evelyn Waugh. . ." (ix–x). The statements indicate the fact that Blake is the most elusive poet among the Romantics in his relationship with the East. It is indeed surprising that though there is clear evidence on the other Romantics' familiarity with the *Nights,* no such proof has been discovered in the case of Blake, although he began his poetic career during the heyday of the *Nights*.

However, Blake's familiarity with the East, in general, has remained in critical vogue since the1920s. Efforts to trace the Eastern elements in Blake had begun as early as 1924 with the attempt made by S. Foster Damon, who claimed that Blake's mythography was in harmony with the Eastern spiritual tradition. Damon pointed to some interesting parallels between Blake and the Hindu theological tradition. He gave equivalent for Blake's four Zoas from the ancient Indian spiritual tradition. For him, "Urthona is Dharma [ordained duty]; Urizen, Karma [the practice of Dharma]; while both Tharmas and Luvah are included in Maya [illusion]" (145). In 1929, Denis Saurat explored certain parallelisms between Blakean myth and Hindu mythology arguing that

> essential elements of the Blakean myth [are] common also to Indian religion: the primitive hermaphrodite, or giant containing all the world, his separation into beings and especially his separation into Male and Female, the refusal of the female, her flight, the pursuit by the male, his conquest of the female, and the origin of all species from their union. (109)

Similarly, Charu Sheel Singh attempted to show how Blake benefitted from the Indian mythological and philosophical sources available to him in translations made by the eighteenth-century Indologists—Sir William Jones, Charles Wilkins, N.B. Halhed, J.H. Holwell, A.J. Arberry, and others. Another early critical voice, Northrop Frye observed that "Blake was among the first of European idealists to link his own tradition of thought with *Bhagavadgita*" (173).

In recent times, there has been a plethora of critical writings on Blake's relationship with the East. In *William Blake and the Impossible History of the 1790s* (2003), Saree Makdisi appreciates Blake's ability to remain outside the dominant ideological constructions by remaining free of the orientalizing tendency of his time: "Blake was basically the only major poet of the late eighteenth and early nineteenth centuries, who categorically refused to dabble in the recognizably oriental themes and motifs" (209). David Weir in *Brahma in the West: William Blake and the Oriental Renaissance* (2003), however, contends that Blake's thought and philosophy were steeped in Oriental elements, though he might not have the tendency toward exoticism. Weir divides his book into three parts for the convenience of reading Blake's relationship with the East—"Politics," "Mythography" and "Theology," respectively. To use Weir's own words, the chapters show "first how Blake would have been drawn to Hinduism for political reasons; second, how the parallels between the poet's myth and the Hindu system provide evidence of actual influence; and, third, how this influence played out in theological terms, as certain Christian interpretations of Hinduism found their way into Blake's composite mythology" (17). Although he concedes that it is extremely difficult to determine sources that were available to Blake, he identifies certain possible sources "that can be connected to Blake using the double criteria of personal affiliation and textual comparison" (52). The list of the sources given by him is worth quoting here:

> *The Ruins; or, a Survey of the Revolutions of Empires* (1791), by Comte de Volney; "On the Gods of Greece, Italy, and India" (1788), by Sir William Jones; *The History of Hindostan* (1796–98), by Thomas Maurice; "Enquiry into the Religious Tenets and Philosophy of the Brahmins" (3d ed., 1798), by William Julius Mickle; *A Comparison of the Institutions of Moses with those of the Hindoos and other Ancient Nations* (1799), by Joseph Priestley; and, finally, *The Hindu Pantheon* (1810), by Edward Moor. (52)

Weir suggests that Blake could have conceivably met Wilkins, who moved in the same circle as Blake's friend and publisher, Joseph Johnson (21–22). Johnson was also the main publisher of the periodical, *The Analytical Review*, which was one of the most important sources of information about the new scholarship on Indian culture produced by the Asiatic Society of Bengal. Weir contends that The Asiatic Society "founded and led by Jones" provided Blake with "an extraordinary profusion of mythic material" "in the form of various mythographic representations of Hinduism as he formed and reformed his own mythic system" (36). Davies Keri's article "Rebekah Bliss: Collector of William Blake and Oriental Books" in *The Reception of Blake in the Orient* (2006) takes Weir's attempt forward. Keri tries to trace the influences on Blake through his reading, particularly of the collection of books by Rebekah Bliss.

He locates distinct influences and assimilations of Eastern images, mythology, art forms in Blake's poetry and designs.[1] *The Reception of Blake in the Orient* is divided into two parts. The essays in the first part study how Blake was influenced by the Orientalism of his day and how he assimilated Oriental elements in the total design of his poetic archetype. Most of the essays highlight the engravings made by Blake that accompany the poems. The focus, in other words, is on the poet–engraver Blake rather than on the poet Blake alone. The second part of the book concentrates, as the title indicates, on the reception of Blake in the Orient.

The recent spate of critical views on Blake's relationship with the East, and its influence upon him has primarily concentrated on three issues: Firstly, Blake's relationship with India and Hinduism; secondly, Blake's representation of Egypt and Africa, together with his treatment of the slave-issue; and thirdly, Blake's conception of Islam and its representation. A small amount of criticism has shown Blake in relation to China. "Blake and the Chinamen," an essay by Mei-Ying Sung, for example, has in focus Britain's Chinese fashion in the mid-eighteenth century—the popularity of the ceramics and its relation to printmaking. The present chapter would take into account the existing critical debate on Blake's position vis-à-vis India and other countries in the East, but it will take religion as a coordinate and focus on the centrality of Christ, if not Christianity in Blake's vision of a liberated world.

Blake started publishing his works in the 1780s, almost a decade earlier than the other early Romantics. His formative years belongs to the eighteenth century than the nineteenth. This is the reason, perhaps, some tendencies of eighteenth-century Orientalism is evident in his works. In *Orientalism*, Said identifies four distinct developments in the late eighteenth century that, according to him, had helped in the formation of "modern Orientalism." The four phases are: expansion, historical confrontation, sympathy, and classification. The century saw the expansion of the Orient further East than the traditional

Islamic Orient, though "such widening of horizon," Said claims, "had Europe firmly in the privileged center." The capacity to deal with non-European and non-Judeo-Christian culture was strengthened, as there was a new conception of human history: "[T]he notions of human association and human possibility acquired a very wide general—as opposed to the parochial—legitimacy" (117–118). There was a change of policy in dealing with the Orient. Said observes: "Whereas the renaissance Historians judged the Orient inflexibly as an enemy, those of the eighteenth century confronted the Orient's peculiarities with some detachment and with some attempt at dealing directly with oriental source material, perhaps because such technique helped a European to know himself better" (117). The eighteenth-century mind, according to Said, "could breach the doctrinal walls erected between the West and Islam and see the hidden elements of kinship between himself and the Orient." "There was a tendency among the thinkers to exceed comparative study, and its judicious survey of mankind from 'China to Peru,' by sympathetic identification" (118). Blake's poetry constitutes an important example of the way the eighteenth-century mind broke the doctrinal walls by adopting a syncretic approach. Blake could easily connect all the continents and all forms of religious practices in his sweeping critique of organized religion and condemn all forms of evil cramping the human mind. One of the four elements identified by Said as an important component of eighteenth-century Orientalism is "historical confrontation." Most challenging of these historical confrontations was the revelation of the Indian antiquity. The European mind was baffled confronted with the ancientness of Hinduism because it challenged the primacy of Christianity. Blake devised his own method of dealing with this. He saw the world through the prism of his spiritualism, developed his own mythography, and Hinduism became a part of his mythological world. Blake's approach fits into Said's definition that "the major part of the spiritual and intellectual project of the late eighteenth century was a reconstituted theology" (114).

Blake considered Hinduism as the most ancient form of organized religion. This is seen in his first explicit reference to Hinduism in *Song of Los: Africa* (1795). In the context of his criticism of institutionalized religions, Blake mentions Brahma as the begetter of the most ancient of them. With the inception of Hinduism, evil breaks upon humanity: "Adam shudderd! Noah faded! black grew the sunny African / When Rintrah gave Abstract Philosophy to Brama in the East." Human 'hypocrisy' was born and so were other forms of social evils like slavery and war: "Night spoke to the Cloud! / Lo these Human form'd spirits in smiling hipocrisy. War Against one another; so let them War on; slaves to the eternal Elements." Blake goes on criticizing other forms of "abstract philosophy": "Palamabron gave an abstract Law: / To Pythagoras Socrates & Plato, [a]nd to Mahomet a loose Bible gave. . . . Till a Philosophy of Five Senses was complete/ Urizen wept & gave it into the hands of Newton & Locke." With this proliferation of the institution of religion, social institutions are born. "These were the Churches: Hospitals: Castles: Palaces" (Plates 3, 4, and 5, E 67–68).[2]

The reference to Hinduism in *The Song of Los* (1795) proves that Blake was familiar with the writings of William Jones and his fellow scholars, but there had been questions on the exact nature of his sources. The journal *Asiatick Researches* might be one of the primary sources of Blake's knowledge of Hindu theology. The transactions of the Asiatic Society were first published in 1788 in the *Asiatick Researches* and the subsequent four volumes came out in 1790, 1793, 1795, and 1797, respectively. Commenting on Brahma's connection with the rationally philosophical, Cathleen Raine refers to the 1794 edition of the *Asiatick Researches*, where Jones attributes a "technical system of logick" to Brahma (351). As suggested by David Weir, Blake might also have been familiar with *The Analytical Review* that was published by his friend Joseph Johnson. The periodical was established in 1788 and was the most important source of information on the new scholarship on India (Weir 21–22). Another suggestion is that Blake might have had access to Jones through his friend, the sculptor John Flaxman, who had links with Jones (Johnson, A.K. 93). Yet, another source of his knowledge might be Charles Wilkins. Blake made a painting of Wilkins translating *The Bhagvat-Geeta.* A description of the now-lost painting, *The Bramins* is found in the catalogue to Blake's exhibition of paintings in 1809:

> The subject is, Mr. Wilkin, translating the Geeta; an ideal design, suggested by the first publication of that part of the Hindoo Scriptures, translated by Mr. Wilkin. I understand that my Costume is incorrect, but in this I plead the authority of the ancients, who often deviated from the Habits, to preserve the Manners, as in the instance of Laocoon, who, though a priest, is represented naked.
>
> (E 548, NUMBER X., "The Bramins—A Drawing.")

The title of the painting is misleading since it shows Wilkins as the 'Bramin' translating *The Bhagvat-Geeta,* not the Hindu 'Pundits' as we would expect. After Wilkins's return to England in 1786, he moved in a circle very close to Blake. Men like Fuseli and Moses Haughton were members of this circle and, as Weir points out, they would later ask for Wilkins's assistance with the Devnagari script for Sanskrit text while engraving Edward Moor's *The Hindu Pantheon* (1810). Wilkins was the first person to discover and to use (in 1778) the methods of engraving, casting and setting Bengali characters. He was also the first man to produce Sanskrit letters for type printing, "making it possible to print Sanskrit for a wider audience" (Schwab 37). There was enough reason for Blake, an engraving artist and poet, to have had an interest in Wilkins. Connolly finds in Blake's representation of Wilkins an attempt to deny complicity in an imperialistic relationship between knowledge, power and profit. Blake, in his opinion, tried to create his distance from the Evangelical and intolerant Orientalism of 1809 by embracing the syncretism of the late eighteenth century. Nevertheless, he could not escape from the colonial discourse of knowledge construction ("The Authority"

146–148). While recommending the translation of *The Bhagvat-Geeta* to Nathaniel Smith, the Chairman of the East India Company in1784, Hastings wrote: "Every accumulation of knowledge and especially such as is obtained by social communication with people over whom we exercise a dominion founded on the right of conquest, is useful to the state (qtd. in Kejariwal 24)." By painting Wilkins in the task of deciphering knowledge with the help of the Brahmins (knowledge "obtained by social communication" with them), Blake ends up celebrating that knowledge construction in the aid of imperialism.

Blake's familiarity with Wilkins's translation of *The Bhagvat-Geeta* is also suggested by his reference to "the darkness of Asia" in *The Song of Los II: Asia*. Asia celebrates the coming of revolution; the journey of the revolution is from the West to the East having begun in America. The kings of Asia shudder at the prospect of this:

> The Kings of Asia heard
> The howl rise up from Europe!
> And each ran out from his Web;
> From his ancient woven Den;
> For the darkness of Asia was startled
> At the thick-flaming, thought-creating fires of Orc. (Plate 6, E 68)

The description of "the darkness of Asia" contains several layers of discourse. It seems to echo the preface to Wilkins's translation by Hastings where he describes the "dark rules" of the Mughal emperors in contrast to the enlightening British to whom the Brahmins open up their secret. It is also noteworthy that Hinduism was not uniformly praised by the Westerners at this point of time. There had been two opposed perspectives on Hinduism in the eighteenth century. Whereas Hinduism, as it was practiced then, was conceived as evil, priest-ridden and ritualistic, the philosophical Hinduism (evidenced by such text as the Gita) was idealized. Wilkins's translation of *The Bhagvat-Geeta* might have produced a favorable view of the philosophical and esoteric Hinduism, but the two prefaces added before the text comment on the degenerated priest-ridden state of contemporary Hindu society (*The Bhagvat-Geeta* 24).[3] Therefore, it was not unusual for Blake to present Hinduism as the first Urezenic religion. Blake produced the *Song of Los* in 1795, and he must have known about the dramatic trial of Hastings (1788–1795). The event became so popular that it was impossible for a Londoner to miss it. The trial highlighted the corrupt ways of Hastings, but it also narrated the prevailing evils of Indian society in lurid detail.[4] The trial led to the victory of the Anglicists who wanted to Christianize the natives and introduce English education among Indians, contrary to the Orientalist belief that Indians should be governed by their own law and according to their own custom and religion. Missionaries like Charles Grant saw Indian society as heathen, corrupt and uncivilized. He was appalled by such native customs as exposing the sick, burning lepers and the sati. He believed that Britain's duty was not simply to expand its rule in India and exploit the subcontinent for its commercial interests but to civilize and Christianize Indians. In 1792, Grant wrote the tract "Observations on the State of Society among the Asiatic Subjects of Great Britain." He pleaded for English education and argued that Christian missions should be allowed in India alongside the East India Company's traditional commercial activity. India, to Grant, became the classic example of a despotic country and the "'cruel genius' pervading Indian despotism was the ethos of Hinduism" (Butler, "Orientalism" 409). Thus, the reference to Brahma in the context of fallen humanity is comprehensible.

Blake condemns Hinduism as the most ancient form of organized religion. However, for that purpose, it may be said he condemns all religions. Hinduism is given the first place in this list of the religions he condemns because, during his time, the discoveries of the members of the Asiatic Society made this theory acceptable among the Europeans. Ezekiel in "The Marriage of Heaven and Hell" speaks on the subject:

> [T]he philosophy of the east taught the first principles of human perception: some nations held one principle for the origin & some another, we of Israel taught that the Poetic Genius (as you now call it) was the first principle and all the others merely derivative, which was the cause of our despising the Priests & Philosophers of other countries, and prophecying that all Gods would at last be proved to originate in ours & to be the tributaries of the Poetic Genius.
>
> (plate 12 and 13, E 39)

Here, an illustration is given as to how the principles of institutionalized religion create a divisive tendency leading to evils, such as war and slavery. All religions are manifestations of the same "Poetic Genius," "the tributaries," but as the priests and kings institutionalize them the conflict of interest arises. In his "religio-mythological radicalism" (Johnson, A.K. 94), Blake attempts to condemn all the religions in the manner of Volney, whose book *The Ruins* was one of his favorites. In Chapter XXIII of *The Ruins,* Volney condemns all religions as being equally responsible for the moral and social evils: "Thus by mutual reproaches the doctors [the religious leaders] of the different sects began to reveal all the crimes of their ministry—all the vices of their craft; and it was found that among all nations the spirit of the priesthood, their system of conduct, their actions, their morals, were absolutely the same" (269). The chapter is significantly entitled "ALL RELIGIONS HAVE THE SAME OBJECT." Blake's "All Religions are One" undoubtedly echoes Volney.

Volney's *Les Ruins* (1791) is scathingly critical of all religions. There is a passage in Volney where the members of other religions accuse the Christians of duping vulnerable people to conquer nations,

> 'Yes' cried they, 'these men are robbers and hypocrites, who preach simplicity, to surprise confidence; humility, to enslave with more ease; poverty, to appropriate all riches to themselves. They promise another world, the better to usurp the present; and while they speak to you of tolerance and charity, they burn, in the name of God, the men who do not worship him in their manner.' (267)

Marilyn Butler identifies Tom Paine, Alexander Geddes, and Volney as the "mediators through whom [Blake] locked up the vision of a world history that inspires his two great series of epics of the French revolutionary years"(407).[5] In the series of prophecies—*America*, *Europe*, and the *Song of Los* (*Asia* and *Africa*), Blake celebrates the coming of revolution to all the four continents of the world. "The old world is conceived in Volneyean lines as an evil empire maintained by 'priest-craft'" ("Orientalism" 407–408). By the time Blake was writing his prophecies, the idea of Hinduism as the "sunny" religion of the East gave way to a conception that deemed Hinduism and the state of India as "priest-ridden, cruel and despotic" and thus asking for Western conquest ("Orientalism" 411). Therefore, he could condemn Hinduism as the most ancient form of evil, but unlike the Anglicists, he is not contrasting despotic Hinduism with enlightened Christianity. On the contrary, along the chain of despotic practices, Christianity is equally condemnable because, for Blake, "All religions are One." Thinking in universalist terms provided Blake with the tool to criticize the Christian institution of the church. Blake's universalism, however, has its problems because, despite his censure of all the organized religions, Christ remains the privileged center to his vision of a regenerated world. Poetic Genius, Imagination—the Divine Vision in Blake's writings become synonymous with Jesus Christ. This association of the creative inspiration with Jesus shows that Blake places the origin of art and mythology inside the Judeo–Christian tradition (Connolly "The Authority" 154). In the Descriptive Catalogue, Blake wrote:

> The antiquities of every Nation Under Heaven, is no less sacred than that of the Jews. They are the same thing as Jacob Bryant, and all antiquaries have proved. How other antiquities came to be neglected and disbelieved, while those of the Jews are collected and arranged, is an enquiry, worthy of both the Antiquarian and the Divine. All had originally one language, and one religion, this was the religion of Jesus, the everlasting Gospel. Antiquity preaches the Gospel of Jesus.

> The reasoning historian, turner and twister of causes and consequences, such as Hume, Gibbon and Voltaire; cannot with all their artifice, turn or twist one fact or disarrange self evident action. (E 543)

Tristanne J. Connolly argues that Blake begins by asserting the equal sacredness of all cultural traditions, but he ultimately asserts that their "sacredness relies on their similarity not to each other but to Christianity." "If it is worthy of enquiry why the Jewish antiquities are collected and others neglected, it is also worth enquiring why Blake neglects them here by not naming them" ("The Authority"153–154). Blake rejects the classical to court the Biblical. In the Preface to *Milton*, Blake strongly criticizes the Greco–Roman tradition, but he does so comparing it to the 'sublime' Bible: "The Stolen and Perverted Writings of Homer & Ovid: of Plato & Cicero which all Men ought to contemn: are set up by artifice against the Sublime of the Bible" (E. 95).

In describing the picture of Nelson and Pitt in the "Descriptive Catalogue," Blake compares the figures, "to those Apotheoses of Persian, Hindoo, and Egyptian Antiquity, which are still preserved on rude monuments, being copies from some stupendous originals now lost or perhaps buried till some happier age." The visionary poet envisions the "stupendous originals":

> The Artist having been taken in vision into the ancient republics, monarchies, and patriarchates of Asia, has seen those wonderful originals called in the Sacred Scriptures the Cherubim, which were sculptured and painted on walls of Temples, Towers, Cities, Palaces, and erected in the highly cultivated states of Egypt, Moab, Edom, Aram, among the Rivers of Paradise, being originals from which the Greeks and Hetrurians copied Hercules, Farnese, Venus of Medicis, Apollo Belvidere, and all the grand works of ancient art. (DC, plate 6, E 531)

Blake imitates these grand "originals" seen in a vision in his paintings. After this, Blake makes his intriguing statement that the classical Greek artists were imitators of the "Asiatic Patriarchs":

> No man can believe that either Homer's Mythology, or Ovid's, were the production of Greece, or of Latium; neither will any believe, that the Greek statues, as they are called, were the invention of Greek Artists; perhaps the Torso is the only original work remaining; all the rest are evidently copies, though fine ones, from greater works of the Asiatic Patriarchs. The Greek Muses are daughters of Mnemosyne, or Memory, and not of Inspiration or Imagination, therefore not authors of such sublime conceptions. (DC, 6, E 531)

The statement apparently "stress[es] the Afro-Asiatic origins of European culture," but Blake places them in the Biblical Near East: "[T]hey are done by 'Patriarchs,' they are called 'Cherubim,' and they are 'erected in' Biblical lands connected to Eden. The origin of art and mythology is placed inside Judeo-Christian tradition" (Connolly, "The Authority" 154).

Two different aspects of Blake's approach to India and Hinduism, therefore, become recognizable: firstly, his approach to India and Hinduism follows his brand of universalist critique of organized religion; secondly, his universalism leads him to anachronism. In other words, Blake, it can be assumed, ignores the temporal dimension while equating all religions to give priority to Christianity or to criticize it; he becomes deliberately anachronistic. Connolly points to the anachronism in Blake as well as to the universalism, but he does not explain as to why Blake became anachronistic in dealing with a civilization and a religion far more ancient than Christianity or Christian civilization. The clue to the answer is there in E.S. Shaffer's argument in *'Kubla Khan' and the Fall of Jerusalem* which shows how in the eighteenth century, the view that Bible is mythological rather than historical was acknowledged.[6] This was very crucial for writers like Blake who used it to defend the Bible and make it equal to other ancient religious texts by considering them mythological as well. The discovery of Indian antiquity created anxiety for Christianity if not a crisis and the authenticity of the Bible stood challenged. Jones expressed this fear in the following terms: "Either the first eleven chapters of the Genesis, all due allowance made to the figurative, Eastern style, are true or the whole fabric of our national religion is false; a conclusion, none of us, I trust, would wish to be drawn" (Pachori 189–192). Mythological syncretism was, therefore, a refuge for writers like Blake. This vantage point assisted them to safely protect their Christ from falseness. Even a dissenter like William Blake had to use this defense mechanism because even when he was a dissenter his world was centered around Christ.

There are other references to India and Hinduism in Blake. India is referred to by alternate names like 'Hindu' or 'Hindustan' and in one of these places, India is described by plural 'nations' rather than by singular 'nation.'[7] In most of the places, India is mentioned as a part of a catalog of 'nations' where it serves to represent the East, or the whole world in its vast extent. There is not much illustration, but India is mentioned just as a place name that is part of the Generation awaiting regeneration, the coming of the New Jerusalem. In Blake's cosmology as developed in *Milton* and *Jerusalem*, Eden is the place for the eternal, infinite, truly human. Around Eden is Beulah, a place of rest for the weaker spirits from the fiery exhilaration of Eden. Beyond Beulah is abyss. Furthest from Eden is Ulro, the chaos, the place for the formlessness and non-entity. Los in Ulro is constantly building and rebuilding the beautiful city of Golgonooza which guards against chaos and is a refuge for souls escaping from chaos. Generation is between Ulro and Beulah. The four-fold pattern Eden–Beulah–Generation–Ulro fully emerges in *Jerusalem* (*A Blake Dictionary*). Blake mentions India or Hinduism six times in *Jerusalem: The Emanation of Giant Albion* and thrice in *Milton*. In plate 14, Blake's 'Hindostan' is part of the world of "Generation": "Albion trembled to Italy Greece & Egypt / To Tartary & Hindostan & China & to Great America (*Milton,* plate 14, E. 108). In plate 31, we find India weeping with other nations at the vision of the "Lord coming in the clouds": "India rose up from his golden bed: / As one awakened in the night" (E 130). These personified portrayals of

India "draws on the Oriental stereotypes of indolence and opulence" (Connolly, "The Authority" 158). The third reference in *Milton* is to "Hindu" (he uses it to signify place, not religion) in plate 35, where Blake refers to "Hindu"[8] as one of the places bound by Milcah:[9]

> Loud roll the Weights & Spindles over the whole Earth let down
> On all sides round to the Four Quarters of the World, eastward on
> Europe to Euphrates & Hindu, to Nile & back in Clouds
> Of Death across the Atlantic to America North & South. (E 135)

The first reference to India in *Jerusalem* is in the context of the description of the world of "Generation," "a depraved world of single unimaginative vision" (Stevenson 747) made by Urizen: "China & India & Siberia are his [Urizen's] temples for entertainment" (Jerusalem, plate 58, 39). In plate 67, India forms part of the geographical location that is being enclosed by polypus's fiber. Polypus in Blake is a colonial organism that symbolizes human society in this world and its religion (Damon 332–333). In plate 72, "Hindustan" is mentioned as one among "thirty-two nations," eight each from the four continents looking up "for the Bride" Jerusalem. In plate 80, India is one of those countries through which the "daughters of Albion" move: "Against Jerusalem they rage thro all the Nations of Europe / Thro Italy & Grecia, to Lebanon & Persia & India." Then in plate 82, "Hindustan" is once again shown as a part of the Generation: "the Furnaces of Los / Create Jerusalem, & Babylon & Egypt & Moab & Amalek, / And Helle & Hesperia & Hindostan & China & Japan" (E 239). These limited creations are part of Los's effort to save Albion from disintegration and death (Stevenson 805). In plate 84, "nations of India" are shown as flying away from Los. India, in Blake, is always a part of the Ulro or Generation and, therefore, becomes a symbol for an "ancient woven den" and Brahma is its weaver.

Like Hinduism, Blake was also deeply interested in Islam. Blake's first reference to Islam is in the *Song of Los: Africa*:

> The human race began to wither, for the healthy built
> Secluded places, fearing the joys of Love
> And the disease'd only propagated;
> So Antamon call'd up Leutha from her valleys of delight:
> And to Mahomet a loose Bible gave.
> But in the North, to Odin, Sotha gave a Code of War.
> Because of Diralada thinking to reclaim his joy. (plate 3, E 67)

Interpreting the poem, a large number of Blake's critics and editors have focused on Blake's use of the phrase "loose bible." Most of Blake's editors have pointed out that the Qur'an has been traditionally seen as "loose sheets" and Blake might be referring to this. In *Blake's Poetry and Designs,* John E. Grant and Mary Lynn Johnson observe that one etymology of the Qur'an is "a collection of loose sheets" (136). Similarly, W.H. Stevenson provides the following note to explain "loose bible": "The Koran; the name has been supposed to mean 'a collection of loose sheets'" (Stevenson 244). Harold Bloom, however, made a different interpretation of the epithet: the adjective 'loose' for him suggested that the Qur'an is "a poor reflection of the Bible" (qtd. in Whitehead 28).

However, these interpretations fail to give an insight into the text and the context of its occurrence. S. Foster Damon's interpretation of the adjective 'loose' seems more appropriate. According to Damon, Blake believed that Muhammad's attitude to sex was a reaction against the Christian ideal of celibacy, which threatened the continuation of the human race and for this: "Antamon (the male seed) call'd up Leutha (sex as sin) from her valleys of delight: / And to Mahomet a loose Bible gave" (*A Blake Dictionary* 259). Read in the context of how Islam had been associated with licentiousness and sexual profligacy in the Western imagination, it seems proper to interpret the term 'loose' as having something to do with the sexual behavior, and this interpretation also makes the context meaningful. As the human race began "to wither," there was a necessity of procreation and, therefore, of the "loose bible" (i.e. the Qur'an) valorizing the procreative act.

The interpretation of Blake's reference to the Qur'an, by linking it to the popular tradition that held Islam to be the religion that preaches sex and Bloom's interpretation of the "loose Bible" apparently mark Blake's prejudice against Islam. Nevertheless, from the beginning of the twentieth century, a considerable number of readers have indicated that the *Song of Los* is perhaps a tribute to Islam. Angus Whitehead, in "'A Wise Tale of the Mahometans': Blake and Islam 1819-26," quotes Percy H. Osmond, who in *The Mystical Poet of The English Church* (1919) judged the poem as "a eulogy of Mohammedanism at the expense of Christianity" (281). Saree Makdisi in *Blake and the Impossible History of the 1790s,* suggests that the text of plate 3 of *The Song of Los* in which "Los compares and demonstrates interactions of Eastern and Western cultures, reflects Blake's reversal of a pervasive Heliocentric model of Western European identity emerging in the 1790s, which involved the repudiation and denial (as 'other') of the Afro-Asiatic sources of the earliest European cultures" (qtd. in Whitehead 28). The corroborative evidence cited by Makdisi is from the song, "The Divine Image".

> And all must love the human form,
> In heathen, Turk or Jew
> Where Mercy, Love & Pity dwell,
> There God is dwelling too. (E 13)

Makdisi's perspective, however, came to be questioned in Edward Larrissy's article "Blake's Orient." Larrissy argues that Blake was familiar with the scholarly knowledge of the Orient and fell prey to the prejudices of the Orientalists. He interprets the word 'loose' as 'licentious.' Through the Orientalist notion of the "licentiousness of Islam," according to Larrissy, Blake conceives of "a particular aspect of fallen humanity." He quotes from Edward Gibbon and James Bruce to show that the idea that Islam is a religion of carnality and sacrilege was still prevailing during Blake's time (9–10). According to Larrissy, the concept of fallen sexuality is also there in "The

Laocoön." He cites the authority of Connolly who notes that the uncomfortable contortion of the body in the figures could represent diseased sexuality (10).[10] Larrissy concludes that "'loose' is not a word that one would associate with Blake's 'unironic utterances,' and this usage does contain an element of irony for the concept of looseness only comes into existence as a result of sex under law, or Leutha, with whose name it offers an approximate rhyme" (10). Angus Whitehead finds this interpretation "traditional and textually based approach to the poem." Whitehead compares Blake's representation of Islam with other eighteenth-century writings and the general attitude to the presence of the Muslim community in London and concludes that Blake's engagement with Islam was positive, during a "period in which the religious faith [Islam] was still regarded by many in Britain as the 'Devil's Methodism'" (30–32).

Notwithstanding Whitehead's observations, it is to be noted that Blake is certainly using one of the popular Orientalist tropes about Islam, but he is giving it a new twist. He is using it to criticize the Urizenic law that Christianity imposes on humanity. Islam, in this sense, becomes the religion that in some way frees humankind from the bondage of Christian monasticism. Twisting an image and giving it a new meaning is quite common in Blake. For example, the traditional symbol of the rose is endowed with a new significance in his poem "The Sick Rose." Blake always tried to create his own system and own meaning. He wrote: "I must Create a System, or be enslav'd by another Mans / I will not Reason & Compare: my business is to Create" (E 153). Larrissy rightly points to the fact that 'licentiousness' is the indicated meaning of 'loose', but he fails to appreciate the positive twist of the application of 'looseness' in the context of the poem.

Humberto Garcia, in his recent book *Islam and the English Enlightenment, 1670–1840*, argues that although the typical Enlightenment attitude to Islam is exemplified by such text as Voltaire's *Mahomet the Impostor,* certain subversive writings portrayed Islam in a different perspective. According to Garcia, this subversive tradition began with Henry Stubbe's *The Rise and Progress of Mahometanism* (1674). This work portrays Muhammad as a wise legislator who reinstated primitive Christianity's republican order. According to Garcia, the subversive thinking made a strong ground during the 1790s and he defines this phenomenon as "Islamic republicanism." The term is explained as descriptive of how radical Protestants in eighteenth-century England self-consciously recast Islam in a constitutionally nationalist term. Blake, according to Garcia, belongs to this subversive tradition. To make his point he refers to the essay, "The Prophetic Tradition" by Norman O. Brown. Brown's argument holds that Blake needs to be resituated within a larger prophetic tradition in which Islam is integral to Judeo–Christian history rather than a regressive, derivative religion: "We will not get 'Blake and Tradition' right until we see the tradition as the Prophetic Tradition, including Judaism, Christianity and Islam; and heresies in Judaism, Christianity and Islam" (367). Both Brown and Garcia make valid points, but there is a necessity to analyze the other references to Islam in Blake to understand the nature of his engagement with Islam.

The Song of Los presents an early engagement of Blake with Islam. Another allusion to Islam at the early stage of his career is found in his "Additions" to *The Descriptive Catalogue* of 1809. According to Erdman, Blake "contemplated holding another exhibition like the one of 1809, with another printed catalogue; he may have written these 'Additions' . . . before convinced of the failure of the first exhibition" (E 554). In his description of the painting, *A Vision of the Last Judgment,* Blake remarks on Muhammad's placement in it. To appreciate the kind of position assigned to Muhammad, it is necessary to understand Blake's design. Blake wrote about the design of the painting to Ozias Humphry Esquire on February 18, 1808: "Christ seated on the Throne of judgment [*The Heavens in Clouds rolling before him & around him*] before his feet & around him the heavens in clouds are rolling like a scroll ready to be consumed in the fires of the Angels who descend [*before his feet*] with the[*ir*] Four Trumpets sounding to the Four Winds" (E 553). The design is further illustrated: "The right hand of the Design is appropriated to the Resurrection of the Just the left hand of the Design is appropriated to the Resurrection & Fall of the Wicked" (E 553). Muhammad, in the painting, is placed just beneath Ishmael on the right side: "Beneath the Cloud on which Abel kneels is Abraham with Sarah & Isaac [&] also Hagar & Ishmael" and "[*Beneath*] <Ishmael is Mahomet>" (E 556).[11] As Whitehead observes, Blake is "alluding not only to the Judaeo-Christian-Islamic idea that the Arabs descended from the patriarch/prophet Abraham through his eldest son Ishmael but also to the Muslim belief that the Qur'an received by Ishmael's descendant Muhammad derives from the same divine source as the Torah of Moses, the Psalms of David and the Gospel of Jesus" (30).

This inclusion of Muhammad in the painting and placing him beneath Ishmael among the "Just" is very significant. In placing Muhammad among the "Just," Blake is making a statement breaking away from the popular misconceptions about Muhammad that go back at least to the days of the Crusades. He was also writing against the typical tendency of the period, exemplified by works like Voltaire's *Mahomet the Impostor,* which had been frequently staged and reprinted during the period (Garcia, *Islam and the English Enlightenment* 5). Appreciated in the light of the argument by Brown that Blake should be placed within the larger prophetic tradition that includes Islam, Blake's placement of Muhammad is not surprising. It is also in harmony with Garcia's configuration that "Islamic republicanism" made a strong ground during the 1790s. However, even this cannot be straightforwardly hailed as Blake's revolutionary statement since the question is: if Muhammad is a Prophet like Jesus, why does he need to be judged by Jesus. Moreover, placing of Muhammad among the "Just," in *A Vision of the Last Judgment*, stands in stark contrast to the illustration "The Schismatics and

Sowers of Discord: Mohammed."[12] In the painting, Blake closely follows Dante in placing Muhammad among the infernal spirits: his body cleft in two, the entrails coming out.

A history of the inception of the painting is provided in the Blake Archive. Blake began to compose 102 water-color illustrations to Dante's *Divine Comedy* in the fall of 1824 for his patron, John Linnell. From these Blake selected seven designs to engrave. "The choice of subjects, all from the "Inferno," may have been recommended, or at least approved, by Linnell. There may have been plans to engrave more designs, but even these 7 plates were left incomplete at Blake's death in 1827."[13] Dante represented Muhammad and his son-in-law, Ali as propagators of religious divisiveness and they are put in the ninth gulf of hell as a punishment for their schism. Muhammad's body is split from groin to chin: "His guts hung between his legs and displayed / His vital organs, including that wretched sack / Down the gullet" and Ali's face is "cleft from chin to crown grief stricken" (*Inf.* 28. 22–33). Blake seems to have stuck to the original description of Dante while depicting Muhammad in this illustration and it has puzzled critics for generations (Fuller, "Blake and Dante" 358). Angus Whitehead points to certain deviations that Blake has made from Dante. The deviations, according to him, are: Firstly, in the positioning of Dante and Virgil: Whereas in *Inferno*, Virgil and Dante are placed on a rock "having a privileged panoramic view as they look down on Mohammad and Ali," in Blake, Dante and Virgil are placed alongside Muhammad on the ground. Whitehead asserts that this positioning "suggests an intimacy and sympathy between the pagan and Christian poets and the Muslim prophet and first Shia Imam" (40). Secondly, Dante's description, according to Whitehead, is vague and indistinct. Blake gives Muhammad a distinct appearance and the bearded man in the middle of the portrait suggest "dignity" compared to the rudimentarily drawn fellow sufferers surrounding him. The design here resembles "Blake's representations of a suffering Job or the figure of the old man led by a child in 'London' of *Songs of Experience*, and *Jerusalem*, plate 84" (40). Thirdly, Whitehead notes that Blake departs from Dante in the depiction of Ali. Unlike Dante's weeping figure, Ali is depicted here as if making a gesture: "Ali's folded left arm and partially raised right hand may indicate a teaching posture." Whitehead suggests Blake may have known Ali's piety and his revered position in Islam from reading Sale's translation of the Qur'an (40). Fourthly, Blake also deviates from his source in the portrayal of the punishing fiend: In Dante, when Muhammad is questioned about his punishment, he is made to say that "a fiend / hacks us thus cruelly" (*Inferno* 191). In Blake's illustration here, there is no sign of cruelty and the fiend in question seems to be unwilling in his act. Whitehead compares Blake's illustration to that of his friend John Flaxman's illustration of the same to point out the difference. He concludes by referring to Robinson to whom Blake supposedly said, "Dante saw devils where I see none—I see only good" (Robinson 6), that "[T]he angel-demon, punisher and punished, are represented by Blake as nobly suffering figures enslaved by Dante's system of cruel vengeance" (41–42). Whitehead, however, seems to miss a point: the melancholy tragic air that hangs around the painting. It becomes apparent when we put it by the next painting of Blake in this series, "The Schismatics and Sowers of Discord: Mosca De' Lamberti and Bertrand De Born." The "demon" here is projected with his back to the sinners. One of the sinners stands with his chopped off head; the other has his hands chopped off. The bold and muscular nature of the figures suggests no sense of melancholy. The chopped head has a very confused look. The fiend though with his back before us seems to be an avenging figure with one hand on his hips and a raised sword in another hand.[14]

However, the question is, why Blake did not make any major change to Dante's portrayal, as twisting traditional images to tell a different tale is quite common in his poetry. Was he following Dante because he was commissioned by Linnell to do so? There seems to be no obvious answer to the question. However, an interesting analysis is provided by Humberto Garcia in his lecture entitled "Holy Entrails and Schismatic Bodies: Esoteric Embodiments of Islam in William Blake's Art." Garcia suggests that "William Blake's image of the split and porous body offers a productive site for investigating radical Protestant and mystical depictions of the Orient and Islam in particular." For him, Blake's "anatomical portrayal of the Prophet presents the intestinally exposed body as a microcosm of the universe." However, the portrait cannot be straightforwardly applauded because it is double-edged—"the Prophet's dangling entrails and Ali's cleft head literally confirm their heretical crimes only to figuratively exalt their prophetic-messianic mission."[15] What emerges, therefore, is that the painting becomes a space for the conflict of the residual negative portrayal of Muhammad and an emergent positive content.

Garcia's focus in this lecture is another painting of Muhammad by Blake, "The Visionary Head of 'Mahomet.'"[16] The painting belongs to a series that Blake executed between 1819 and 1825, "in the presence, and probably at the behest of astrologer John Varley" (Whitehead 35). Blake depicts Muhammad at a younger age as a clean-shaven youthful man. Martin Butlin finds the portrait of a "strong forthright character but with no specific sign of approval or disapproval" (720). David Fuller defines it as "open face which implies no criticism" (358). Whitehead refers to Morton Paley's suggestion that the painting resembles the traditional Muslim description of Muhammad only to reject it (Paley, *Traveller* 303). In creating this youthful image of Muhammad, Blake might have been influenced by the following account in Sale's "Preliminary Discourse": "[the] inhabitants of Paradise will enjoy a perpetual youth; that in whatever age they happen to die, they will be raised in their prime and vigour, that is, of about thirty years of age, which age they will never exceed" (qtd. in Whitehead 36). By referring to Blake's interest in phrenology, Whitehead concludes, "Blake, possibly informed by Sale and probably by early nineteenth-century British phrenological theory, appears, in his visionary portrait of 'Mahomet,' to have created an atypical, positive representation of the Prophet of Islam" (38).

Garcia construes this image via Brown's interpretation of the "prophetic tradition" and his idea of eighteenth-century Islamic republicanism. He argues that Blake represented himself through the portrait of Muhammad to assert his poet-prophet identity. He points to the similarity of Blake's 1807 oil portrait by Thomas Phillips to the "Visionary Head of Mahomet" by citing the authority of George Bentley (xx–xxvii). For Garcia, Blake's 'Mahomet' is not only an "incarnation of the 'Poetic Genius' dormant in all religions but his reincarnation in the 'White' English poet." And this 'whitewashing' is explained as an example of what Srinivas Aravamudan describes as "tropological" revision of the imperial and the racial ideologies.[17] It is an "anti-imperial gesture" where the reader is compelled to imagine "Islamicizing of a 'White' English individual, a disruption of the English national imaginary." Blake, he concludes, "refuses to orientalize Islam": Mahomet does not resemble the dark-skinned, turban-wearing despot traditionally depicted in Western writings, on the contrary, he is "Blakean poet against empire" (*Islam and the English Enlightenment* 18).

The most well-known and widely discussed comment on Islam by Blake is his supposed reference to a "wise tale of Mahometans" in table talk with Crabbe Robinson: "Perhaps the best thing he said was his comparison of moral with natural evil. 'Who shall say what God thinks evil? That is a wise tale of the Mahometans—of the Angel of the Lord that murdered the infant' [alluding to the Hermit of Parnell, I suppose]. 'Is not every infant that dies of disease in effect murdered by an angel'?" (7). Blake's "wise tale" is identified by Robinson to be the tale of *The Hermit* by Thomas Parnell. In Parnell's tale, a hermit sets forth to visit the world; he meets with a young companion and in the course of their journey, they encounter various types of people and the young man commits certain acts incomprehensible to the hermit. The hermit is most horrified when the young man mercilessly murders a child. To the stupefied hermit, the young man explains each of his actions revealing himself an angel. Basically, it is a moral tale where there is no reference to Islam. It was Goldsmith who remarked on the Arabian source of the tale, "I have been informed by some, that it is originally of Arabian invention" (143–144). Another possible Islamic source available to Blake was Sale's translation of the Qur'an, where, in *Surah Al-Khaf*, there is indeed a tale similar to Parnell's *The Hermit.* Here, Moses is amazed at the apparently inexplicable behavior of al-Khedr, who like the angel of Parnell's poem kills a youth: "[they] [. . .] proceeded: until they met with a youth; and [al Khedr] slew him. MOSES said, Hast thou Slain an innocent person, without *his having killed* another? Now hast thou committed an unjust action?" We get the following argument justifying the act of killing: "As to the youth, his parents were true believers; and we feared lest he, *being an unbeliever*, would oblige them to suffer *his* perverseness and ingratitude: wherefore we desired that their LORD might give them a more righteous *child* in exchange for him, and one more affectionate *towards* them" (Sale 246). The explanation provided by the angel in *The Hermit* for killing the child does not exactly follow this logic:

> Long had our pious Friend in Virtue trod,
> But now the Child half-wean'd his Heart from God;
> (Child of his Age) for him he liv'd in Pain,
> And measur'd back his Steps to Earth again.
> To what Excesses had his Dotage run?
> But God, to save the Father, took the Son. (*Select Poets* 256)

In the Qur'anic tale, the youth is killed because of his "perverseness." In Pernell's poem, there is no such issue involved, but the father is punished for being too eager in his love for the child, the indication being that the father would compromise his piety for his son. However, in both the tales, the death of the child/son is central. The important and relevant idea for Blake is that an angel or God's representative kills the child: "Is not every infant that dies of disease in effect murdered by an angel?" It can be concluded that Blake's reference to Islamic beliefs to explain "natural evil" conforms to the syncretism of the English-speaking Orientalists of the eighteenth century, though he was making this statement deep into the nineteenth century, on December 10, 1825.

Another important aspect of Blake's representation of the East can be seen in his portrayal of the fallen state of Africa and Egypt and his use of Gothic tools in representing the fallen world. Africa / Egypt in Blake is a claustrophobic space where the Urizenic forces unleash their reign of terror. In Blake, as pointed out by Punter, "the traditionalist features of the Gothic are pressed into the service of an all embracing vision of the horror of the fallen world" (*Literature of Terror* 104). The fallen world is like the Gothic dungeons defined by darkness as opposed to the enlightened world defined by light and open air. In *America: A Prophecy,* Blake uses such contrasting images: he refers to the "inchaind (sic) soul shut up in darkness" of the "dungeon" and exhorts "the slave grinding at the mill" to "[R] ise & look out" as the "dungeon doors are open": "The Sun has left his blackness, & has found a fresher morning" (plate 6, E 53).[18] The contrasting images of darkness and light, of bondage and freedom, of confinement and open air, are descriptive of the two contrary worlds—the fallen and the regenerated.

The darkness described by Blake is not merely physical but spiritual; the open air and light are symbolical of the spiritual light. The images describing the fall or the fallen man in *The Song of Los: Africa* are noteworthy in this regard. As noted earlier in this chapter, the "abstract philosophy" of Brahma is shown to initiate the fall of man and this fall is complete with the "philosophy of the five senses." As the result of this all-pervading Urizenic law, there looms the shadow of darkness over the "mountains of Lebanon round the deceased Gods / of Asia; and the deserts of Africa." In *The Song of Los: Asia*, the Asian kings are shown to have created a web of network for oppression, and hearing the revolutionary cry each of them "ran out from his Web . . . / For the darkness of Asia was startled" by the "thought creating fires of Orc." The tyrannical laws have turned Asia and Africa into a Gothic castle where forces of darkness rule. In examining the contrast between brightness and darkness, it should be noted that Blake associates the light of the sun with spiritual regeneration; however, the sun is also associated with blackness as the expression, "black grew the sunny African," shows. Blake might have two conceptions of the sun like the Swedenborgians, who believed that the true sun gives both light and heat but the fallen sun is a sun of heat alone (Beer, *Blake's Visionary Universe* 28–29).[19] The blackness of the African, therefore, is the result of fall and the fall is of the sun itself. The fallen sun is regenerated and it overcomes its blackness.

The repression of humans in Blake's poetry is also linked to the ravages of industrialization: "The terrible ball: the wedge: the loud sounding hammer of destruction" (*Jerusalem,* plate 73, E 228). According to Punter, "Blake builds, with the help of Gothic tools, a universe of man/machine chimeras, of dehumanized men and women and of machines with a curious and malevolent mode of life. In this universe all is threat and violence . . ." (*Literature of Terror* 104). The enactment of the violence and repression produces distortion as the following passage from the *Book of Ahania* (Chapter IV) reveals:

> The shapes screaming flutter'd vain
> Some combin'd into muscles & glands
> Some organs for craving and lust
> Most remain'd on the tormented void:
> Urizen's army of horrors. (E 88)

Oppression in Blake is thus related to deformity; repression by the Urizenic forces produces the tormented body. Blake's Urizen is almost like the Gothic figure of oppression. Jennifer Randonis has analyzed the *Book of Urizen* as incorporating many Gothic elements albeit some alterations. Blake, according to Randonis, incorporates the Gothic motifs of narcissism or self-isolation, the doppelgänger, and the quest in the *Book of Urizen.* The Gothic motif of wandering, according to Randonis, is transformed in the poem: Instead of depicting a hero embarking on the journey through the "chaos" in an "insane pursuit" of the Absolute, Blake transmutes the Gothic tradition by having Urizen formulate "chaos," the "eternal Abyss" itself.

Another hovering figure of Gothic terror in Blake is Polypus: "a mighty Polypus growing / From Albion over the whole Earth: such is my awful vision" (*Jerusalem*, plate 15, E 159). "The polyp is perhaps Blake's most terrifying symbolic creation, and it becomes in his mythology a proliferating monster of fearful asymmetry. . ." (Miner 198). Polypus is associated with Urizen. In *The Book of Ahania,* Urizen metamorphoses into a Giant Polypus of the heaven: its origin is in England and from there it extends to the whole world. Like the "science-fiction films, which enlarge a lizard to a dinosaur, Blake's polypus is a creature whose body extends along the circumference of the planet, entwining itself from west to east" (Paley, *The Continuing City* 214):

> In Verulam the Polypus's Head, winding around his bulk
> Thro Rochester, and Chichester, & Exeter & Salisbury.
> To Bristol: & his Heart beat strong on Salisbury Plain
> Shooting out Fibres round the Earth. thro Gaul & Italy
> And Greece, & along the Sea of Rephaim into Judea
> To Sodom & Gomorrha: thence to India, China & Japan.
>
> (*Jerusalem,* plate 67, E 220)

Talisa J. Ford observes, the mighty polypus, "a serpentine embodiment of imperial desire originates from Albion and assimilates to Albion, as Albion roots itself in every nation" (544).

For Ford, Blake uses the image of the Polypus to mock the imperial ambitions of England. The vision of the mighty polypus may indeed be interpreted as evidence of Blake's criticism of the empire, but the vision is double-edged since it enacts the colonial vision of British imperialism. Blake was writing the poem when Britain practically occupied and dominated a large part of the globe. Moreover, if Blake was concerned with the evil of empire, it was empire as a sickness—the polypus spreading out from England also comes back to its origin. In this respect, Blake's concern was similar to Burke's. Even though Blake is critical of empire building, his thoughts are Anglo-centric.

The Anglo-centric and Christo-centric outlook of Blake is evident in *Jerusalem the Emanation of the Giant Albion*. Blake wrote *Jerusalem* between 1804 and 1820. Its prolonged period of composition makes Blake's statements and views expressed in the poem trustworthy. The poem has the theme of the fall and resurrection of Albion, Blake's embodiment of "man-Britain." Blake projects London as the center of the origin of civilization and man:

> All these Center in London & in Golgonooza, from whence
> They are Created continually East & West & North & South
> And from them are Created all the Nations of the Earth
> Europe & Asia & Africa & America, in fury Fourfold. (plate72, E 227)

The centering "in London & in Golgonooza" not only locates Golgonooza—Blake's term for the earthly city of Jerusalem—in London but situates both London and Jerusalem as the center and origin of all the other "Nations of the Earth" (Ford, 531–532). Though this call to return to Jerusalem is to "dwell together as of old," Blake wants to return to a time when Albion encompassed all: "O Albion let Jerusalem overspread all Nations / As in the times of Old." The particular nations in question are then named in an impressive catalog:

> France Spain Italy Germany Poland Russia Sweden Turkey
> Arabia Palestine Persia Hindostan China Tartary Siberia
> Egypt Lybia Ethiopia Guinea Caffraria Negroland Morocco
> Congo Zaara Canada Greenland Carolina Mexico
> Peru Patagonia Amazonia Brazil. Thirty-two Nations
> And under these Thirty-two Classes of Islands in the Ocean
> All the Nations Peoples & Tongues throughout all the Earth.
> (plate 72, E 227)

During the Enlightenment period, there developed an imperialist "history" in England that located the origins of culture and Christianity squarely in England; an extreme version of this belief was that England was Jerusalem or the British were "true" Israelites. This is known as the Anglo–Israel movement. Barbara Tuchman has shown that how by "tortured interpretation of stray passages from the Bible," the enthusiasts of the movement "convinced themselves that the English are the true descendants of the ten lost tribes of Israel" (82). Blake's engagement with the Anglo–Israelites is evident in the subtitle of the poem, "The Emanation of the Giant Albion" and his treatment of the subtitle in Jerusalem's address "To the Jews":

> Jerusalem the Emanation of the Giant Albion! Can it be? Is it a Truth that the Learned have explored? Was Britain the Primitive Seat of the Patriarchal Religion? If it is true: my title-page is also True, that Jerusalem was & is the Emanation of the Giant Albion. It is True. And cannot be controverted. Ye are united O ye Inhabitants of Earth in One Religion. The Religion of Jesus: the most Ancient, the Eternal: & the Everlasting Gospel. (E 171)

Julia Wright's *Blake, Nationalism, and the Politics of Alienation* rightly observes that *Jerusalem*, "perhaps precisely because it is Blake's most 'consolidated' work, is also his most tyrannical, plotting the assimilation of the globe into his own political and religious vision." She concludes: "Despite Blake's early opposition to imperialism, Jerusalem envisions a kind of imaginative colonization, and religious proselytization, in which Albion's and Jerusalem's prior universality is reinstated over the national and cultural divisions of the present" (155). Blake imagines a regenerated world freed from the clutches of the Urizenic forces. This new world order will encompass all the people of the world as the long catalog of countries reflect. The problem with his vision, however, is it being one-dimensional; it is premised on the central role to be played by England and Christ. Blake is imagining a world without the imperial polypus, but the polypus is created anew with England / Albion/ Christ at the origin of it. In Blake, therefore, the radical subversions get contained by his Christo-centrism and Anglo-centrism.

Notes

1 Keri made an earlier attempt to establish that Blake had a connection with Mrs Bliss in his article "Mrs Bliss: A Blake Collector of 1794" in Steve Clark and David Worrall edited *Blake in the Nineties* (212–230).

2 Unless otherwise stated, all citations of Blake's poetry and prose are from *The Complete Poetry & Prose of William Blake*, edited by David V. Erdman, Electronic edition, Virginia: Institute for Advanced Technology in the Humanities, 2001. The copy of this edition available in the Blake Archive is used here: <http//www.blakearchive.org/blake/erdman.html>. In the parentheses, reference is given to page numbers (e.g. E 12) and when possible to the plate numbers as well.

3 There are two prefaces to Wilkins's translation of *The Bhagvat-Geeta*: one is written by Hastings in the form of a letter to Nathaniel Smith (5–16); the second is the translator's preface written by Wilkins (23–26). The 1785 edition of *The Bhagvat-Geeta* is used here for the references.

4 Burke, on the one hand, projected an image of the Indian society with its pre-lapsarian innocence and beauty; on the other hand, he depicted the despotic cruelty of the Indians supported by their company masters. He quoted from Holwell's "Interesting Historical Events" to show the Edenic beauty of the Indian society: "'In truth says this author, 'it would almost be cruelty to molest this happy people; for in this district are only vestiges of the beauty, purity, piety, regularity, equity and strictness of the ancient Hindostan Government. Here the property as well as the liberty of the people inviolate. Here no robberies are heard of either public or private'" (*Writings and Speeches of Burke* 6: 306). On the contrary, description of Devi Sing's seraglio sketches the cruelty meted out: crushed fingers and virgins raped in front of their fathers (*Writings and Speeches of Burke* 6: 420–421). Such descriptions, Franklin suggests,

sounded new depths of Oriental Gothic. "[This] rehearsal of atrocities only serves to reinforce stereotypes of the Oriental capacity for the capricious and diabolically inventive cruelty" ("Accessing India" 54).

5 According to Butler, apart from Volney, Thomas Paine's *The Age of Reason* and *The Rights of Man* and Alexander Geddes's *Prospects of a New Translation of the Holy Bible* (1786) were important influences on Blake. Geddes regarded Hebraism of the Old Testament as the religion of "stupid and carnal" people (407).

6 The third chapter of the book entitled "The oriental idyll" is particularly relevant in this connection (96–144).

7 Blake might not be always using the word 'nation' in the sense of 'political state' as is dominantly used now. In the eighteenth and nineteenth centuries, it could well mean 'people' in general or people of a particular (aristocratic) class. Blake might also be using the word in the Biblical sense of "the heathen nations, the Gentiles.' See Guido Zernatto, and Alfonso G. Mistretta. 'Nation: The History of a Word'. *The Review of Politics*, vol. 6, no. 3, 1944, pp. 351–366. See also "nation, n.1." OED Online.

8 'Hindu' might refer to Hindukush mountains here.

9 In the *Vala or The Four Zoas* Milcah is "the fourth daughter of Zelophehad. When man is being subjugated, Milcah is allotted the task of fastening his ear into the rock" (*A Blake Dictionary* 273).

10 See Connolly's *William Blake and Body* (60).

11 The punctuation marks or capitalizations in this quotation or other quotations from Blake are reproduced here as it is in Erdman.

12 See William Blake, "The Schismatics and Sowers of Discord: Mohammed." *Illustrations to Dante's "Divine Comedy" (1824–27),* rpt. in Butlin, Martin, *The Paintings and Drawings of William Blake* (New Haven: Paul Mellon Centre BA, 1981. Print; 812.56). For a quick look at Blake's paintings one may also visit The William Blake Archive, http://www.blakearchive.org/search/. For "The Schismatics and Sowers of Discord" series one may follow this link: http://www.blakearchive.org/search/?search=The%20Schismatics%20and%20Sowers%20of%20Discord.

13 See *Blake's Illustrations of Dante. The William Blake Archive*. Ed. Morris Eaves, Robert N. Essick, and Joseph Viscomi, 2005. http://www.blakearchive.org/exist/blake/archive/work.xq?workid=bb448&java=no

14 See William Blake, "The Schismatics and Sowers of Discord: Mosca De' Lamberti and Bertrand De Born," *Illustrations to Dante's Divine Comedy* (1824–1827), rpt. in Martin Butlin, *The Paintings and Drawings of William Blake*, New Haven: Paul Mellon Centre BA, 1981. Print; 812.57.

15 For an abstract of the paper one may visit the following website: http://williamblakeandenlightenmentmedia.wordpress.com/category/the-flames-of-orc-316/

16 See William Blake, *Visionary Head of Mahomet* (c. 1819), rpt. in Butlin, *The Paintings and Drawings of William Blake*, 720.

17 Srinivas Aravamudan in *Tropicopolitans: Colonialism and Agency, 1688–1804* speaks of "tropological revision of discourses of colonial domination." Such a revision is contestation of European rule by "tropicopolitans," inhabitants of torrid zones that were the objects of Europe's colonial ambition.

18 The images are repeated subsequently in *The Four Zoas* (E 402, 18–24).

19 Beer shows that Blake had a dual conception of the sun. He contends that in this respect, Blake was influenced by Swedenborg's presumption that the true sun is divided into heat and light and was also influenced by the Egyptian mythology of Osiris, the lost sun and Typhon, the fallen sun.

IV

"Orientaliana": Landor and Southey

William Blake's association with the East was rather oblique in keeping with his own mythography. However, Southey's output on the Orient and his engagement with the Eastern themes and issues are exceeded by no other Romantic poet, and only Byron comes close to him. That Southey had an encyclopedic range of reading on the East and he kept a track of his readings is evidenced by the large section in his *Commonplace Book* dedicated to the East. The extensive notes that Southey appended to his poems on the East also bear testimony to his wide range of reading. Southey's oeuvre on the Orient is very large and it includes massive volumes like *Thalaba, the Destroyer* (1801), *The Curse of Kehama* (1810), *Chronicle of the Cid* (1808), *Roderick, the Last of the Goths* (1814), and comparatively shorter compositions in the form of *Imitation from the Persian* (composed in 1828), *Ode on the Battle of Algiers* (composed in 1818), the fragment "Muhammed" (composed in 1799), and "The Kalendar" (composed in 1798–1799). Except for his "Hindu epic", *The Curse of Kehama,* all the other poems mentioned above have connections with the Middle East and Islam. For our convenience, the discussion on Southey will be divided into two sections—the first section will be on Southey's engagement with the Middle East and Islam, which will primarily center on *Thalaba, the Destroyer,* and the second will exclusively focus on *The Curse of Kehama* and the nature of Southey's engagement with India and Hinduism. However, an analysis of Walter Savage Landor's *Gebir* will be appropriate before turning to Southey, because *Gebir* was the first long narrative poem that set the tone for the Oriental verse romances—a genre that became very popular during the Romantic period.[1]

Landor's poem was unsuccessful in terms of its popularity and Robert Southey was one of the few admirers of the romance.[2] When *Thalaba, the Destroyer* was in the process of composition, Southey was reading Landor's tale. Southey wrote to William Taylor (October 22, 1799):

> I am finishing the fourth book of my Dom-Daniel-romance – the plan of the remainder is matured, my head full of eastern scenery & I look to speedily conclude it. have you seen a poem called Gebir? It appears to me the miraculous work of a madman – its intelligible passages are flashes of lightning at midnight – like a picture in whose obscure colouring no plan is discoverable, but in every distinct touch you see the Masters hand.[3]
>
> (*CL 1798–1803*, No. 449)

Gebir exercised considerable influence on Southey when he composed *Thalaba.* However, a point to remember is that Southey might have exercised a counter influence on Landor when Landor added notes to *Gebir* in the manner of *Thalaba* in its 1803 edition. Accordingly, Southey's *Thalaba* is considered the pioneering example of the annotated verse tales of the Romantic period having its precedence in Beckford's Oriental prose romance, *Vathek* and its poetic counterpart, *Gebir*. *Vathek* exercised a potent influence both on Landor and Southey, so did many other Oriental Tales. What is most common among these three tales is their attempt to tap in the new sources of creativity made available by the Oriental Renaissance. *Gebir*, however, was not Landor's only poem to dabble in Eastern themes. He published a hoax pamphlet of nine short poems entitled *Poems from the Arabic and Persian* in 1800, purporting to be based on the French translation of an Arabic manuscript, but originals by Landor himself; a few years later, he wrote *Count Julian: A Tragedy* (1812) on the conflict between Islam and Christianity. However, *Gebir* remains the earliest work by Landor to focus on the East, first published in 1798 and revised and republished with annotations and notes in 1803. The narrative centers on the story of the Spanish King Gebir's invasion of Egypt and his destruction in the hands of Dalica, the nurse of the Egyptian queen, Charoba.

The immediate source of Landor's *Gebir* was the prose tale *Gebirus* appended at the end of Clara Reeve's *Progress of Romance* (1785). Miss Reeve states in her preface that her story came from an Arabian manuscript by Murtada ibn al-Khafif found in the Mazarin Library and translated into French by M. Pierre Vattier. The Arabian manuscript has the title "The History of Ancient Egypt, according to the Traditions of the Arabians. Written in Arabic, by the Reverend Doctor Miurtadi, the Son of Gapiphus, the Son of Chatemn, the Son of Molseim the Macdesian." An English translation of it was done by John Davies in 1672, and Reeve might have seen this, but her story bears more similarity to the French version (Williams). Landor, though he was indebted to Reeve, boasted in the *Monthly Review* that the poem is "nothing more than the version of an Arabic tale" and "every line of appropriate description, and every shade of peculiar manners, were originally and entirely his own" (qtd. in Forster 78). Whatever Landor's claim might have been, reading the two stories makes it apparent that the tales have many similarities despite some differences. Reeve used the French version freely to create a feminist narrative making Charoba a patriot queen trying to save her country from the invader, Gebir. Landor builds a narrative where the invader, as well as the invaded queen, becomes the victim of the magic and witchery of Dalica. Moreover, there is no denying the fact that though Landor's immediate source was Reeve's tale, he drank deep into the tradition of romances, pastorals, epics, Oriental Tales, travelogues, the Gothic novels, and many other forms of writings. *Gebir* appears to be a kind of pastiche combining formal elements from diverse literary genres.

Commenting on the genre of the poem, Mohammad Sharafuddin refers to a note that Landor attached to the Latin version of the poem. Landor wrote: "Our first book is almost wholly in the pastoral genre:

nor could it be at all otherwise, having regard for propriety and the manner of the times in which it describes the events taking place; but from that step by step rise greater things up to the end of the poem" (qtd. in Sharafuddin 5). Following this note, Sharafuddin discerns the impact of various genres in each of the books: Book I is pastoral; Book II is romance; Book III is epic romance; Book IV has the excitement of epic narrative; Book V emphasizes the demonic aspect of epic narrative; Book VI contains epic prophecy; and Book VII relates Gebir's tragic destruction. He concludes that the poem shows a movement "irregular in detail but plain in its general curb: develops from pastoral to romance, from romance to epic, from epic to tragedy" (Sharafuddin 5). The problem with Sharafuddin's interpretation of the genre of the poem lies in overlooking the impact of the Gothic novels and the Oriental Tale. Influence of the Gothic finds no mention in Sharafuddin and his analysis of the influence of the Oriental Tale seems inadequate. The impact of Beckford's *Vathek* is obvious in many places, but nowhere is it more evident than in Book III, where Gebir descends into the underworld and meets his ancestors suffering the torments of hell. The spectacle of suffering of the race of Sidad resembles the description of suffering souls provided by Beckford at the end of his novel. The cause of suffering in hell, in both the tales, is the earthly ambitions of the sufferers and both tales seem to echo the Qur'an. In chapter 89 of Sale's translation of the Qur'an, there is a reference to a group of people called the Ad, the people of Irem who suffer in the hand of God due to their insolence on earth (488–490). The tale is used in the Qur'an to illustrate the idea that earthly insolence and covetousness leads to suffering in hell. While in the Qur'an, the people of ad are called Adites, in Landor's tale, Gebir and his people are referred to as Gadites. Humberto Garcia, however, points out that the Gadites (from Gad) and the Adites (from Ad) are the same people ("The Hermetic Tradition" 451–452).[4] Other Gothic elements are seen in Book V where Dalica makes her journey to the ruined city of Masar and meets with her sorceress sister, Myrther. Dalica and her sister seem to have their forerunners in the demonic women of the Gothic novels like Carathis in *Vathek* or Matilda in *The Monk*, who in turn look back to the figures of Eastern women like Cleopatra or the Eastern heroines of the Middle English romances. The element of lust is, of course, missing in the character of Dalica. Although Dalica is portrayed as a vicious woman by Landor, the queen, Charoba is characterized as innocent and meek. No such difference between Charoba and Dalica exists in the earlier versions of the tale. This distancing of the two women has made Landor's narrative problematic and added to the thematic complexities of the poem.

The story of the Iberian king, Gebir's invasion of Egypt and his subsequent amorous desire for Charoba (which becomes mutual in Landor's version of the tale) and his failure to unify Iberia and Egypt through love-diplomacy, because of Dalica's intervention, has been upheld as an anti-imperial epic. Marilyn Butler, for example, calls it "an anti-colonialist fable" where the would-be colonialist Gebir is killed on his wedding day ("Orientalism" 411–412). Butler reads Iberia as an allegorical representation of England. Mohammad Sharafuddin considers *Gebir* as an example of direct Orientalism having many conventional Eastern themes and motifs like necromancy, ruins, exotic eroticism, Oriental luxury, etc. However, he concludes that it is an anti-imperial tale, an expression of Landor's early "republican internationalism" (38–39). Such interpretations are possibly fueled by a remark the author made in the preface to the 1803 edition: "In the moral are exhibited the folly, the injustice and the punishment of Invasion, with the calamities which must ever attend the superfluous colonization of a peopled country" (qtd. in Sharafuddin15). However, the tale cannot simply be dismissed as an "anti-colonialist fable." The equation to be considered is: if Iberia is England, Egypt may be any of the British colonies. Butler herself concedes that "Landor's Egypt populated by shadowy cultists and murderous women, provides a model for Eastern court cultures in romances to follow" ("Orientalism" 412–413). If it is so, then Landor's would-be colony is not only a Volneyean ruin, but it is also what the pro-missionary lobby, led by men like Charles Grant, would make of the native religions and society, "priest-ridden, cruel and despotic, and thus asking for Western conquest" ("Orientalism" 411). Such a representation of the religion and society of the Eastern Other had colonial implications. In the example of India, we see how Charles Grant and his associates built a discourse around the supposed primitivism and degeneration of Hindus to justify the introduction of Christianity and opening up ways to convert the natives into their 'enlightened' faith. As Alan Richardson puts it, Landor's reliance "on colonialist figures of savagery, primitivism and the primacy of the West" "short-circuits" his own anti-colonial rhetoric ("Epic Ambivalence" 279). Moreover, Landor's "anti-colonial" statement in the preface is questionable. He condemns the folly of colonizing a "peopled country". Does this mean he would support the colonization of a country which is uninhabited? If yes, it is a very problematic idea since imagining a wild virginal space awaiting domestication was an element of the colonial imaginary.[5] Moreover, there had been occasions in the history of colonization when certain people had not been considered human at all. Therefore, Landor's statement is not as innocent as it looks.

The interpretation that the poem embodies an anti-colonial message has also to do with an overemphasis on certain sections of the poem, especially the description of the journeys in Books III and VI while neglecting a third journey in Book V. The element of wandering or journey is a recurring feature of the Romantic verse narratives. In *Gebir*, three journeys are undertaken: firstly, the subterranean journey made by the eponymous hero in Book III; secondly, the aerial journey made by the hero's pastoral brother and his nymph wife in Book VI; and the third journey in the poem undertaken by Dalica in Book V. The interpreters of the poem have chiefly concentrated on the first two journeys. Dalica's journey has received little critical attention. Gebir's descent into the abyss is a reflection of the past and Tamar's aerial survey with his beloved is a vision of the future, but Dalica's journey on the surface of the earth is concerned with the present—her immediate concern for the sovereignty of her native land. Book III begins with the description of Gebir's descent into the underworld. He meets Aaron who relates the story of Sedad's race to which Gebir belongs. The race of Sedad was once powerful on earth, but now in the abysmal hell they regret their earthly exploits: "How gladly would they poverty embrace / How labour even for their deadliest foe!" (Book III, 43–44).[6] The suffering of the conquerors depicted in this book indeed sends out an anti-imperial message. The meeting of Gebir with the "Tom-Painish" Aroar in the underworld has several references to European monarchs like George III, Louis XVI, William III, and Charles II and this makes the anti-imperial anti-colonial argument stronger.[7]

In Book VI, Tamar's nymph-beloved takes him on an aerial journey. It covers much of the world in its survey and a prophecy is made that all the proud tyrants, including Gebir, will be destroyed. There are moralizing lines commenting on the vainglories of the world:

> With horrid chorus, Pain, Diseases, Death,
> Stamp on the slippery pavement of the proud,
> And ring their sounding emptiness through earth. (Book VI, 113)

In the third book of the poem, the suffering of Gebir's ancestors and their regret that they ran after the glories of war and victory on earth drives home the moral lesson that earthly pomp and glory leads to suffering in hell. Similarly, in the sixth book, there is a kind of direct preaching against the earthly conquerors of the world and the nymph makes a prophecy for coming of a "mortal man above all mortal praise" (Book VIII, 111), who is projected as the harbinger of hope for a golden age. The reference to Corsica (Napoleon's birthplace) and the French Republic makes the identity of the redeemer clear.

Garcia argues that the placing of the prophecy in the mouth of an Egyptian nymph, who in this poem is a symbolic figure of hermetic magic and enthusiastic prophecy, gives Napoleon a "messianic status as the redeemer of world history" ("The Hermetic Tradition" 434). He explores the possibility of reading the poem as belonging to the subversive tradition of anticlerical historiographies written by radical Protestants and hermetic philosophers in the late seventeenth and eighteenth centuries. He argues, "because *Gebir* is based on a thirteenth-century Arabian romance that celebrates a hermetic-Islamic account of Mosaic history, Landor's oriental tale embodies a radical hermetic critique of Anglican-British imperialism" ("The Hermetic Tradition" 436). For Garcia, the sixth book is the most subversive because of its "provocative vision about the coming of an egalitarian social Utopia" ("The Hermetic Tradition" 433).

Such a reading is contested once we take a close look at the third journey of the poem made by Dalica in the fifth book. It begins with one of the standard scenes of Eastern ruins as Dalica travels to the ruined city of Masar. Once it was a glorious place—"a fair city, courted then by king, / Mistress of nations, thronged by palaces,"—but now is in utter ruin: "Bereft of beauty, bare of ornaments, / Stood in the wilderness of woe, Masar" (82). The place is characterized as "Treacherous and fearful" (82), populated by fierce animals like hyenas. "Masarian Dalica" (82) dares to visit this dangerous place and she meets her sister, Myrthyr who addresses Dalica as "Woman of outer darkness, fiend of death," and accuses her of overhearing the secret words of magic: "From what inhuman cave, what dire abyss, / Hast thou invisible that spell o'erheard?" Myrthyr does not mean to address her sister like this, but she fails to recognize Dalica and mistakes her for a common Egyptian woman. She accuses Dalica of profanity. Dalica passionately argues with her sister: "Dalica cried, 'To heaven, not earth, addressed, / Prayers for protection cannot be profane'" (84). The sisters recognize each other and from the conversation that follows, we get to know that they belong to a race of magicians preserving their tradition for generations. Dalica in a long speech explains to Myrthyr the cause of her visit, and she defines Charoba as an infant-like queen who neither knows the value of the crown ("She thought the crown a plaything to amuse"), nor is she capable of protecting the country: "Herself, and not the people, for she thought / Who mimic infant words might infant toys" (88). One notable aspect of her speech is her misreading of Charoba's behavior. She suspected that Charoba had fallen in love with Gebir, but the queen protests that she was in love: "Then saw I, plainly saw I, 'twas not love," because it is her "natural temper" that "what she likes / She speaks it out, or rather she commands." The silence of the queen is misinterpreted by Dalica and "the death of Gebir is resolved" (92–93). As the queen cannot protect herself and her country from the invader, Gebir, Dalica assumes responsibility and plans Gebir's death to protect the queen and her country. Accordingly, she is not the person to blame, yet she ends up as the villain and Gebir becomes the victim of her villainy attaining the status of a tragic hero.

If the poem is interpreted as a radical critique of British imperialism as indicated by Butler, Sharafuddin, and Garcia, Dalica should be considered the hero of the poem, since she is the instrument of justice; Gebir's colonial desire is thwarted by her. However, the problem is, her actions are not approved and the readers' sympathy is drawn toward Gebir, the dying hero and Charoba, the suffering queen. In Reeve's narrative, the queen and her nurse (Dalica) combine to kill the invader, but in Landor's scheme, Dalica alone commits the murder. She is presented as a sorceress who is a hindrance to the union of the invader and the invaded—the colonized and the colonizer. Her counterpart is primarily Tamar's beloved nymph who has magical power, but she does not use it against the invaders. The nymph is the docile sister of Dalica. Dalica also stands in contrast to Charoba, the innocent queen who is acquiescent to the desire of the king as she herself has fallen in love with the conqueror. She gives Gebir the upper hand: "He was a conqueror, still am I a queen" (Book IV, 71).

Therefore, reading Dalica's character in the context of Western polemics and the politics of colonialism, makes it difficult to interpret the poem as an anti-colonial tale.

Nigel Leask reads Landor's tale as depicting the fall of the old mercantilism (Gebir's colonizing mission) and the rise of the new free trade empire (Napoleon's redemptive freedom). Leask's study once again concentrates on the first two journeys; particularly, on the sixth book of *Gebir* (*British Romantic Writers* 25–26). Leask's reading has in focus the colonizers, not the colonized. If we concentrate on Charoba and Dalica instead of Gebir/Napoleon, we may better understand the politics in the poem. If we accept Butler's interpretation that Iberia is not Spain but England, then Gebir is the English invader/colonizer and Egypt may be any colonized/to-be colonized country. Following the same formulation, Dalica and Charoba are the natives. In Landor's poem, Charoba is conquerable and awaiting assimilation, whereas Dalica is resistant and unassailable. The tale, therefore, becomes a narrative of the "good native" and the "bad native." Gayatri Spivak's interesting formulations regarding the distinction between the "self-consolidating other" and the "absolute other" helps one to understand the politics in Landor's poem. Spivak analyzes the Western myth-making of the Other in terms of psychoanalysis and her psychoanalytical triangle consists of a self and two kind of Others "a self- consolidating other" and an "absolute other" (Spivak, "The Rani of Simur" 128).[8] In the allegorical framework of the poem, Dalica, who resists the imperial force is the "absolute other" and, therefore, the villain, and Charoba is the "self-consolidating other," who suffers with the helpless victim (imperialist), Gebir. *Gebir,* therefore, can be interpreted as an allegorical tale of colonization involving imperial anxiety. Shifting the scene of the poem away from the present into some ancient time lent it an allegoric orientation and helped Landor negotiate the British imperial anxiety.

One important characteristic of Landor's *Gebir* is the absence of any explicit reference to any religion. Southey's epic, *Thalaba* completely differs from Landor's poem in this respect. *Thalaba* is an Islamic Arabian tale, a kind of religious narrative.[9] In 1798, Southey wrote to Joseph Cottle about his aim in *Thalaba*: "My intention is, to show off all the splendor of the Mohammedan belief. I intend to do the same to the Runic, and Oriental systems; to preserve the costume of place as well as of religion" (*CL 1798–1803*, No. 344). It formed part of Southey's project to compose a poem on each of the religious systems. Since his younger age, he was attracted to different systems of faith. In retrospection, he wrote to John Martyn Longmire (November 4, 1812): "I got at Picart when I was about fifteen, & soon became as well acquainted with the Gods of Asia & America as {with those} of Greece & Rome. This led me to conceive a design of rendering every mythology which had ever extended itself widely & powerfully influenced the human mind, the basis of a narrative poem." Southey "began with the religion of the Koran, & consequently founded the interest of the story upon that resignation which is the only virtue it [Islam] has produced" (*CL 1810–1815,* No. 2172). While writing *Thalaba,* Southey also planned to write an epic on Muhammad in collaboration with Coleridge, and the poet extensively read on Islam and Prophet Muhammad. "Of the few books with me I am most engaged by the Koran," he wrote to John May, on July 29, 1799 (*CL 1798–1803,* No. 424). Entries in his *Commonplace Book* and the notes to *Thalaba* also prove his engagement with Islam during the period.

As Southey's plan to write the epic on Muhammad remained unfulfilled, much of his reading on Islam was worked into *Thalaba*. Naturally, Southey's initial plans for the epic on Muhammad and the little fragment that he wrote in 1799 are relevant to a reading of *Thalaba.* The epic was supposed to have the title, "The Flight and Return of Mohammed." In a letter to William Taylor (c. February 3, 1800), Southey elaborately discussed his plan for the epic:

> Mohammed will be, what I believe the Arabian was in the beginning of his career, sincere in enthusiasm – & it would puzzle a casuist to distinguish between the belief of inspiration & the actual impulse. from

> Coleridge I am promised the half, & we divided the books according as their subjects suited us – but I expect to have nearly the whole work. his ardour is not lasting, & the only inconvenience that his dereliction can occasion will be that I shall write the poem in fragments & have to seam them together at last. the action ends with the capture of Mecca. the mob of his wives are kept out of sight – & only [MS torn] the Egyptian introduced. (*CL 1798–1803*, No. 486)

The letter is also remarkable for its observation that Coleridge might not continue as collaborator and Southey's willingness to produce the epic all by him. Ultimately, neither Coleridge nor Southey completed the epic. Southey wrote an epic fragment and Coleridge a short poem "Mahomet."

One reason for Southey abandoning the epic, as it is expressed in the letter quoted above, was his doubts regarding its success: "Whether Mohammed be a hero likely to blast a poem in a Christian country is doubtful." The success of a poem was important to him, and the failure of *Thalaba* can be considered an important factor for abandoning the epic on Muhammad as well as his plan for other religious epics. Another reason for Southey forsaking the project might lie in his lack of clarity in the appreciation of Muhammad. His confusion is seen in his letter to John May (July 29, 1799): "What was Mohammed? self-deceived, or knowingly a deceiver? if an enthusiast, the question again occurs wherein does real inspiration differ from mistaken? this is a question that puzzles me" (*CL 1798–1803*, No. 424). Ernest Bernhardt-Kabisch points out that the poem was abandoned because of Southey's inability to suspend his "disbelief sufficiently to create Muhammed as the hero of a serious work" (*Robert Southey* 84). This confusion whether to adore Muhammad as a hero or to condemn him as an idolater becomes relevant to his representation of Islam in *Thalaba*. In the narrative of the poem, he celebrates Thalaba's belief in Islamic monotheism, but in the notes he seems to condemn everything that is Islamic and Oriental. A simultaneous feeling of attraction and repulsion is enacted in the text and the notes. Marilyn Butler has explained this as a characteristic of Romantic Orientalism. Butler considers the epic as laying down "the narrative paradigms of Romantic poetic orientalising, above all the cunning juxtaposition of desire and terror, the exotic and the grotesque, a formula which in the next generation sold plenty of other people's poems, if never enough his own" ("Orientalism" 415). Naturally, the issue of Southey's representation of Islam and the Islamic Orient in *Thalaba* has remained a matter of debate among the critics of Southey.

For a better appreciation of Southey's engagement with Islam and the Middle East, a very brief overview of his 109-line fragment "Mahomet," the supposed beginning of "The Flight and Return of Mohammed," would be relevant before turning to *Thalaba*. It begins with a description of Muhammad's flight to the cave. The enemies of Muhammad, who are waiting outside Ali's house to kill the prophet, find Ali coming out instead: "But when the youth went forth, they saw, and behold! it was Ali!" (*CPW* 839). Muhammad has escaped to the cave in fear of the Koreish people, who in their pursuit reach the cave, but the prophet is helped by providential power: at the mouth, the cave is covered with cobweb and "a pigeon fled from her nest" at the sound of the Koreish people coming (*CPW* 840). They conclude from these events that there is nobody in the cave and go back promising to return the next day. The fragment ends with Ali's arrival at the cave with the sad news that Muhammad's wife "Cadijah in sickness / Lies on her bed of pain" (*CPW* 841).

Anyone reading the passages from the fragment may find it similar to *Thalaba* differing only in the use of meter. The tone, the atmosphere, the setting, the sentiment and Southey's descriptive phrases seem to be echoes of *Thalaba* and vice versa. The Koreish people are like the idolaters of the Domdaniel and they search for Muhammad as the disciples of Eblis hunt for Thalaba. Southey seems to have realized his unfulfilled dream of composing an epic on the prophet of Islam by writing *Thalaba*. This seems to be more so when one considers the fact that Southey did not intend to make Muhammad the hero of his epic; his preference was Ali, the disciple of the prophet. He wrote in his February 1800 letter to William Taylor, "Ali is, of course, my hero." Thalaba, as Ali was, is a staunch adherent to the faith that remains unaltered in all circumstances. In *Thalaba*, Southey syncretizes Islamic theology "with what he valued from the Protestant religion" (Bolton, "Southey's Nationalist Romance," pa. 12). This would perhaps be difficult to do with Muhammad as the hero of his proposed epic.

However, it is not merely the religious syncretism that makes up the poem. The poet defines his creation as an "Arabian Romance" and Southey's interests and his sources, as revealed in the notes to the poem, were not confined to Islam, or any particular Eastern source material. He collected the materials from disparate sources and stitched them together in the epic. Like Landor's *Gebir, Thalaba* is also a kind of pastiche, patching together materials and inspiration from the East, the West, the North wherever possible, the Eastern sources being the dominant ones. Marilyn Butler identifies it as "an eclectic historical pastiche, most obviously of medieval romance and Spenserian epic" ("Orientalism" 413). However, Butler could not be oblivious to other sources as in a footnote she writes that Southey built up his "leading villains . . . from great variety of sources, including the rich Jewish-Christian-Muslim sources" (414).

The immediate source of *Thalaba*'s central plot was "the continuation of the Arabian Tales" where "Domdaniel is mentioned—a seminary of evil magicians under the roots of the sea" (*CPW* 225). The poem's meter—regular blank verse—Southey wrote, is used as an "Arabesque ornamentation to an Arabian Tale" (*CPW* 225). Southey's source story, "The History of Maugraby the Magician" narrates the tale of an Arabian hero, Habed who fights against the Domdaniel and the evil disciples of Zatani/Satan. Habed-il-Kalib, king of Tadmur, engages in spiritual combat with Maugraby. Maugraby specializes in kidnapping children, whom he takes to the caverns of the Domdaniel under the roots of the sea where they may be brainwashed and trained in the evil art of sorcery. Hadeb receives guidance in dreams, studies magic and undergoes an ordeal of initiation in preparation for his battle with the shape-shifting Maugraby.[10] Irwin observes that "this weird grim tale was unmistakably intended by Cazzotte to serve as a parable about the Martinist programme for spiritual reintegration and salvation." Southey, Irwin remarks, turned the story into "an allegory of Christian duty and endeavour" (*The Arabian Nights* 163). Seen from Irwin's perspective, Thalaba is rather a Christian hero than a Muslim one. Discussing Southey's debt to the "Tale of Maugraby," Sharafuddin observes: "Southey's elaboration of this story is extensive but his obligations to it are unmistakable" (51). He also relates various episodes in the poem to the Qur'an, particularly the episode of the destruction of the Adites and their false paradise Irem.

None of these critics, however, go into the specific features of the Oriental Tales and the Gothic writings to show how they are blended in Southey's annotated verse tale in the manner of *Vathek*. Similarly, the influence of pseudo-Oriental verse tales like Collins's *Persian Eclogues* in the description of the desert journeys goes unrecognized. It is important to note that in *Thalaba*, Southey exploited the taste for the Gothic together with cashing in on the Oriental Renaissance: The poem has scenes of Gothic ruins (ruined city of Bagdad); dark claustrophobic spaces (the cave of the Haruth Maruth, Maimuna's cave, Domdaniel under the sea); supernatural elements (the Simoom, a gust of wind intervenes and saves *Thalaba*); the element of magic (the breed of female magicians Maimuna, Khawla, Ocba who belong to the race of the demonic women in the Gothic novels), and a wandering hero (many journeys are undertaken). The Gothic features of *Thalaba* are, therefore, similar to *Vathek* or *The Monk* and it combines the Gothic and the Oriental Tale, although it should be noted that it does not have a villain-hero unlike most of the Gothic novels; the villains and the hero are demarcated in the poem. In this respect, it is closer to *The Castle of Otranto* where the villain is clearly marked off from the hero. Oneiza, the heroine is also closer to Isabella than to Nouronihar in *Vathek* or Matilda in *The Monk*.

In fact, the characters in the poem can be classed into two categories—the good, poor, and simple (Thalaba, Oneiza, and Moath) and the bad, rich, and villainous (all the members of the Domdaniel and Aloudin). This clear-cut division of characters in *Thalaba* can be interpreted with reference to Gary Kelly's theorization of the use of the Gothic and the Oriental elements in the eighteenth- and the nineteenth-century European literature. Gary Kelly argues that the images from the Gothic novel and the Oriental Tale have been used as the figure of the Other and the alien in European literature and culture. In the last half of the eighteenth century and the first two decades of the nineteenth, Kelly argues, these images of Otherness were used to criticize the feudal aristocracy as decadent and evil and bourgeois values were celebrated. There was a transposition of the Gothic Other upon the Oriental Other and the Romantic poets played a key role in this. The images of ruin, barbarity, cruelty, lust are Gothic motifs transferred to the Orient making the Oriental interchangeable with the Gothic Other (3–18). If *Thalaba* is "an allegory of Christian duty and endeavour," as Irwin puts it (A *Companion* 263), the hero illustrates bourgeois virtue as opposed to the "feudal vices" of the Oriental rulers represented by the Domdaniel. The images of Gothic horror in the poem, it can be further argued, suggest imperial anxiety—the fear that the dark forces from the imperial periphery might invade the metropolitan center. Edmund Burke, in his Hastings trial speeches, betrayed similar concerns. In his speeches, Burke employed the language of Gothic Otherness in distancing and defining the colonial subjects. In *The Rhetoric of English India,* Suleri notes that the portrait of Hastings in Burke's trial speeches is similar to the Gothic villains. The Gothic, Suleri argues, incorporates the fear and anxiety of empire as the vocabulary of these speeches reveals (32).

The Otherness in the poem has different facades and these are constructed by employing diverse techniques and tools, not merely through the conflation of the Gothic and the Oriental Other. There are debates, arguments and counter-arguments regarding the politics of representation in the poem: How one can summarize Southey's view of Islam in particular and the East in general. Whereas critics like Sharafuddin and Garcia have interpreted Southey's Orientalism in positive terms, others have found the poem as participating in the representational politics of the day.[11] According to Sharafuddin, Southey's aim in the poem "was to discover the common ethical denominator between Islam and Christianity so as to liberate the West from a self-regarding, therefore, tyrannical, perspective" (49). Praising Southey's Orientalism (together with Byron's) as "realistic" (49), he comments that Southey saw Muhammad as the "original biblical prophet" (90). Sharafuddin competently traces the Islamic sources of the poem, but at times, he turns a blind eye to the politics of Othering. Referring to one of the manifest examples of Southey's Orientalist construction of the East, Sharafuddin remarks, "it is the redemption of East *as the East*, and not in the imposition of western ideology, that is Southey's fundamental concern" (66). The concerned lines in Book V (stanza 6) of the poem run thus:

> So one day may the Crescent from the Mosques
> Be pluck'd by Wisdom, when the enlighten'd arm
> Of Europe conquers to redeem the East. (*CPW* 266)

It is very difficult to accept Sharafuddin's comment that the author did not wish to impose Western ideology because it goes against the text itself. Conceiving the West as redeemer of the East, Southey overtly expresses his Eurocentrism and foregrounds the idea of the East as inferior requiring the enlightening ideals of the West. Another problem for Sharafuddin and equally for Garcia when they talk about the positive or authentic representation of the East in Southey is that they do not pay adequate attention to the "paratexts" of the poem.[12]

In the preface to the 1837 edition of the poem, Southey claimed that *Thalaba* is an authentic document on Arabian life and Islam. He pointed out that *Thalaba* was not hastily written, and he was collecting materials for a "Mahommedan" poem for four (1795 to 1799) years: "I had fixed upon the ground four years before, for a Mahommedan tale; and in the course of that time the plan had been formed and materials collected" (*CPW* 224). However, Southey's authenticity was obviously textual. To give an example of the textual nature of Southey's East, a single line can be quoted from the preface to *The Curse of Kehama*. Explaining his depiction of the Middle East in *Thalaba*, he comments: "Everyone who had read *Arabian Nights' Entertainment* possessed all knowledge necessary for readily understanding and entering into the intent and spirit of the poem" (*CPW* 565). On the one hand, he claims his text to be an authentic depiction of the Eastern reality, and on the other hand, he sets a fantastic collection of tales as the touchstone for judgment. This reveals his lack of understanding of the East. Interestingly, Southey does not consider the *Nights* to have a great worth and describes it as full of "metaphorical rubbish" some of which have been filtered when it was translated into French (*CPW* 232).

Southey often repeats the traditional stereotypes of the East. Like the romance narratives of the medieval age, Southey presents Muhammad not only as lustful but the Arabs, in general, are presented with strong carnal passions. In a note to the poem, Southey observes that the Arab man "according to the custom of the nations has many wives, and when he gets fed up with one sends for another" (*CPW* 301). There are several harem images in the poem. In the sixth book of *Thalaba,* Southey describes a "voluptuous vale" where the very atmosphere is described in erotic terms. Beautiful women are shown gesticulating wantonly before greedy eyes of men: "a troop of female" dancers whose "ankles [are] bound with bracelet-bells" and who "Exposed their harlot limbs, / Which moved in every wanton gesture skill'd" "to the greedy eye" (*CPW* 277–278). Resignation is presented as an Eastern vice—the Easterners completely resign themselves to fate: "Ye can shake the foundations of earth, / But not the Word of God: But not one letter can ye change" of what "his Will hath written" (*CPW* 238). In a note to Book V, Southey quotes from the *Bahar-Danush* to prove the point: "The Mahummedans believe that the decreed events of every man's life are impressed in divine characters on his forehead, tho' not to be seen by mortal eye. Hence, they use the word Nusseeb, anglicé stamped, for destiny" (*CPW* 273). Southey observes: "No nation in the world is so much given to superstition as the Arabs, or even as the Mahometans in general" (*CPW* 274). Commenting on how the Europeans exploited the myths of the lazy Orientals, Syed Hussain Alatas in his book *The Myth of the Lazy Native* argues that "in its historical empirical manifestation the colonial ideology utilized the idea of the lazy native to justify compulsion and unjust practices in the mobilization of labour in the colonies. It portrayed a negative image of the natives and their society to justify and rationalize European conquest and domination of the area" (2). Elsewhere in the book, evaluating the European social thinkers' attitude to the Orientals in general, Alatas comments that the great majority of the socialists gave the impression that "there was an Oriental variety of ignorance, stupidity, intolerance and despotism"(235). He was speaking of the twentieth-century phenomenon, but his formulations to a great extent apply to Southey's representation of the East.

Not only are the men presented as cruel, but the women and children are also presented as equally barbaric in observing coolly the gory spectacles of crime. In the ninth book, a Christian boy is cruelly murdered in front of a regaling crowd: as the execution begins, men and women ("women that would shrink / And shudder if they saw a worm") watches it nonchalantly and "clap their hands for joy / And lift their children up /To see the Christian die."[13] The cruel woman behind the act is, of course, Khawla, Maimuna's sorceress sister. The passage is marked by a sense of religious hostility common in the medieval romances as the author highlights the enjoyment of the religious Other at the death of a Christian boy.

Equally notable in the text are the images of Eastern pomp and luxury, opulence and excesses: the over-opulent city of Irem which is destroyed by God's wrath; the false paradise of Alaodine; the once-opulent now-ruined city of Bagdad contain scattered images of Oriental opulence and wealth. Lobaba, for example, uses terms and phrases like "magnificent palaces," "lofty obelisks," "high-domed Mosques," "rich Bazars" to describe the city of Bagdad where "merchants meet, and market . . . / The World's collected wealth" (*CPW* 256). However, there are equally contrasting images of Eastern ruins described by Southey in the manner of Volney. The past glory of the city of Bagdad is compared to the present decay and degeneration. The description reminds us of the ruined city of Masar described by Landor in *Gebir*: "A labyrinth of ruins, / Babylon Spreads o'er the blasted plain." Thalaba is shown making his way "Thro' the broken portal, / Over weedy fragments" (*CPW* 266). One of the imperialist excuses to conquer the Orient was by recourse to the logic that the degenerated Eastern society needed the enlightened hand of Europe; Southey's evocation of the images of ruin and degeneration, therefore, could be useful to the empire builders. In *The Curse of Kehama,* Southey employs similar images of ruin to condemn Indian despotism and valorize the Western/ Christian civilizing mission.

There are several passages in the text as well as in the notes that deal with the tendency of the Easterners to ornamentation, and images of gilding are abundantly used in the poem. In the sixth book (which describes Alaodine's false paradise) itself, the word 'gold' or 'golden' is used forty-one times, and every time the word is used to show the excess in ornamentation. In the first book of *Thalaba*, for example, in the midst of the Arabian desert, Zeinab suddenly notices the palace of Irem and the narrator jumps on to the opportunity to show its ornamental excesses:

Here studding azure tablatures
And rayed with feeble light,
Star-like the ruby and the diamond shone:
Here on the golden towers
The yellow moon-beam lay;
Here with white splendour floods the silver wall. (*CPW* 226)

The note appended to explain this passage is more interesting. Southey quotes passages from Hakluyt and Tavernier to prove the excesses of Oriental artifice and then adds his own comment:

> A waste of ornament and labour characterises all the works of the Orientalists. I have seen illuminated Persian manuscripts that must each have been the toil of many years, every page painted, not with representations of life and manners, but usually like the curves and lines of a Turkey carpet, conveying no idea whatever, as absurd to the eye as nonsense-verses to the ear. The little of their literature that has reached us is equally worthless. Our *barbarian* scholars have called Ferdusi the Oriental Homer. We have a specimen of his poem; the translation is said to be bad, and certainly must be unfaithful, for it is in rhyme; but the vilest copy of a picture at least represents the subject and the composition. To make this Iliad of the East, as they have sacrilegiously stiled it, a good poem, would be realizing the dreams of Alchemy, and transmuting lead into gold. (*CPW* 318)

For Southey, the East is a place of excess and so it is with Eastern literature. The passage is remarkable for its oscillation between commodity and culture. The material and the textual coalesce together. Referring to the images of opulence, lasciviousness, lust, and exoticism in *Thalaba*, Diego Saglia observes that "Southey perceived the East as the reservoir of stories and objects and a material discursive-continuum" ("Words and Things" 172). He argues that the material and cultural benefits accruing to Britain from the East coalesce in the web of the empire, production, consumption, and knowledge. The Orient is the playground of the scholar and the administrator as well as of the artificer. He rightly contends that "the presence of a material and often overtly sensuous East in Southey's writings" is "one of the crucial expressions of Romantic period orientalism" ("Words and Things" 168).

Although Southey upholds several misconceptions about Islam and presents a stereotypical, homogenized, eroticized and exoticized image of the East and its people in *Thalaba*, his treatment of Islam cannot straightforwardly be dismissed as completely prejudicial, chiefly because of his characterization of Thalaba. *Thalaba* is a celebration of the unfaltering faith of its eponymous hero in the teaching of Muhammad. Even if Southey represents his own version of Christianity through Thalaba's unwavering faith in God, one cannot ignore Thalaba's story of success and sacrifice for the cause of destroying evil. The central conflict between Thalaba and magicians of the Domdaniel has been, and can be, explained with reference to the use of the Gothic language of Otherness where the Oriental Other and the medieval/feudal Other are conflated. Southey's valorization of working-class Thalaba and his scathing criticism of the rich magician members of the Domdaniel or other rich people of the East seems to have connections with his early republicanism. Southey's involvement in the anti-slavery campaign in the early days of his career had close connections with the unprecedented growth of republicanism and radicalism in England in the late eighteenth century. In the last two decades of the eighteenth century, British republicanism was at a peak and so was Southey's. With Grosvenor Charles Bedford, he wrote an article in *The Flagellant* in 1788. The article was critical of the British education system for adopting an authoritarian approach and favoring corporal punishment. He described flogging as the invention of the devil. This irked the authority and resulted in his ouster from the Westminster School. The mood of the paper reflects his radical sensibilities not uncommon among the Romantics in the 1790s (Bernhardt-Kabisch, *Robert Southey* 19). Southey's radicalism had also something to do with his dissenting sensibility. Southey was an admirer of Joseph Priestly and his Bristol upbringing helped him imbibe the dissenting influence. He attended a school run by William Foot, a dissenting minister. As Chene Sonoi points out, by the 1790s he had started mixing with dissenters like George Burnet and other Unitarians educated by Anna Barbauld. His dissenting sensibility shaped his political outlook in the early phase of his career (22). Southey also had connections with Henry Thornton as is evidenced by many of his letters written during 1795–1796. In one of his letters to his friend Grosvenor Charles Bedford in 1796, Southey wrote: "I mean to pass Saturday with Hannah More. you heard from me of my former visit to Cowslip Green. an elder brother of Cottles goes there Friday. with whom I shall return. he is a young man of some talents & patronised by Thornton the Friend of the Negroes" (*CL 1791–1797*, No. 159). Henry Thornton was a banker and a political economist and more importantly, was a cousin of William Wilberforce and a leading member of the Clapham Sect. In 1791, Thornton became chairperson of the Court of Directors of the newly constituted Sierra Leone Company, dedicated to establishing a colony of freed slaves in Africa.

Another factor that might have contributed to his republican attitude—his sympathy for the oppressed and antipathy for the wealthy oppressor—was the financial disparity that he noticed as a boy between his aunt Elizabeth Tyler's house, where he spent much of his childhood, and his own. The wealth and prosperity of his aunt stood in stark contrast to the poverty of their own. This was the common phenomenon at Bristol, where "Pride and Luxury" cohabited with "meanness" as the abolitionist poet Chatterton put it ("A Burlesque," 1–2). Even before he wrote on slavery, Southey diagnosed the sociopolitical situation in terms of mastery/slavery in *Wat Tyler* (Bolton, *Writing the Empire* 20). Southey was not alone in serving the domestic agenda by recourse to the discourse of slavery or colonialism but as a tactic it was used by Evangelicals like William Wilberforce for whom antislavery trade agitation was part of a larger attempt to effect a moral reform for the governing classes. In

Thalaba, by setting up a working class hero, who rebels against the immorality and the degeneration of the rich feudal members of the Domdaniel, Southey is also directing criticism toward the immoral, the degenerate and the wealthy of his own country. While Southey's radicalism mellowed down at the beginning of the nineteenth century, it was not completely lost and a displacement mechanism was at work in poems like *Thalaba* and *The Curse of Kehama*. His support for the oppressed working class and hatred for the life of luxury and opulence demonstrated in *Wat Tyler* (composed when Southey was just nineteen) now gets re-enacted in his poems set in the Middle East and India. Thalaba is a working-class hero like Wat. He stands for simplicity and hard work as opposed to the luxury and opulence of his enemies. Similarly, in *The Curse of Kehama*, poor and oppressed Ladurlad and Kailyal's fight against rich, powerful Kehama gives expression to Southey's republican sentiments.

Southey had started thinking of writing a Hindu epic when he was amending the final copy of *Thalaba*. In a letter to his friend Wynn (on July 23, 1800), Southey expressed his wish to compose a poem based on Hindu mythology: "I have some distant view of manufacturing a Hindoo romance, wild as Thalaba: & a nearer one of a Persian story of which see the germ of vitality. I take the system of the Zendavesta for my mythology, & introduce the powers of Darkness persecuting a Persian, one of the hundred & fifty sons of the Great King. . ." (*CL 1798–1803*, No. 538). On March 28, 1801, he wrote to Coleridge about it and by then, he had already decided upon a title for the poem: "I have planned a Hindoo romance of original extravagance, and have christened it 'The Curse of Keradon'" (*CL 1798–1803*, No. 572). Later, Keradon was changed to Kehama. Southey, therefore, began thinking of the romance by 1800, and he started composing it in 1802, but it was not completed until 1809.[14] During this time, Southey also considered writing an epic on the Zoroastrians as the letter to Wynn (on July 23, 1800) reveals. When *The Curse of Kehama* was still a "distant dream," he already had a plan for his epic on Zoroastrianism. Southey read

Anquetil-Duperron's (1731–1805) translation of the *Zend-Avesta* and he had a better opinion of the French translator compared to the English-speaking William Jones, for he wrote in the same letter: "[I]t is rather disgraceful that the most important acquisition of Oriental learning should have been given us by a Frenchman. but Anquetil du Perron was certainly a far more usefull & meritorious Orientalist than Sir Wm Jones, who disgraced himself by enviously abusing him" (*CL 1798–1803,* No. 538). The religious system of the *Zend-Avesta* might have been closer to Southey's heart, but the plan to write an epic based on his reading of Duperron's translation remained unfulfilled while *The Curse of Kehama* was completed after about a decade's delay. The failure to write an epic on a religious system that he preferred over Islam and Hinduism is explained by Lynda Pratt with reference to Southey's plan of the poem as a bridge between two "generically and geographically disparate part of his output: the epic and the romance, South America and the Orient" ("Where . . . success [is] certain" 135). According to Pratt, Southey wanted to fulfill his long-cherished dream of writing an epic on Manco Capac, the legendary progenitor of Inca Peru. Southey conceived of an idea of working him into a romance on Zoroaster and to bring Inca from Persia to Peru, but its geographical implausibility, according to Pratt, was responsible for the poem being abandoned (133–138).[15]

Southey's failure to write the "Persian epic" and delaying *The Curse of Kehama* for almost ten years might have had extra-literary reasons, especially monetary considerations. At a time when *The Curse of Kehama* was nearly finished, Southey pointed out the slow sale and lack of success that greeted *Thalaba*. In a letter to Landor (on February 21, 1809), he wrote: "I sold the first edition of Thalaba to Longmans for 115 £. they printed 1000, – that edition is just now exhausted, & a second about to come forth – But this has been a slow sale, – & when seven years ago I offered them another poem on the same terms (meaning to have finished Kehama for the purpose) they demurred & offered only the 100" (*CL 1804–1809*, No. 1585).

It is worth noting also that *The Curse of Kehama* was resumed and completed after Southey's meeting with W.S. Landor, who assured Southey of printing the poem.[16] Ultimately Southey declined the offer, but Landor's assurance gave him a push to complete the poem.

Another inspiring factor for Southey to embark on writing on Hinduism arguably was the topicality of the subject. India was the subject of much interest and discussion after the Hastings trial, and the debate between the Anglicists and the Orientalists that gained ground after 1787 (Lynda Pratt 138–140). Charles Grant published his "A Proposal Establishing Protestant Mission in Bengal and Behar" in 1787 and it was followed by "Observations on the State of Society Among the Asiatic subjects of Great Britain" in 1792 rousing the pitch for proselytization. A number of missionary societies were established during this time: The Baptist Missionary Society in 1792, the London Missionary Society in 1795, and the Church Missionary Society in 1799. *The Evangelical Magazine* was established in 1793 and it took up the task of creating public opinion in favor of evangelizing. The pitch for permitting the missionaries to proselytize in India was rising, and ultimately it led to the limited permission given to missionaries in the Charter Act of 1813. This success was largely due to Southey's friend William Wilberforce.

A related reason for not forsaking the Indian epic might also lie in Southey's personal interest in an Indian career. In his writings, Southey exploited the large resources of the East in an attempt to make money, and also thought of an Eastern career to become rich like many of his fellow citizens. In a number of letters written during 1799–1800, Southey talks about his interest in an Indian career. In a letter to Charles Danvers (November 6, 1800) he wrote: "[T]he East-Indian bar: where the climate is warm enough, & success certain. . ." (*CL 1798–1803*, No. 557). This attraction for the riches, however, was balanced by the fear of leaving England and living among the people he disliked: "[C]uriosity inclines me to go–but every other motive will certainly knock curiosity on the head. assuredly I would rather get two hundred a year in England, than two thousand in India & no after affluence could compensate for the misery of passing my best years among strangers" (*CL 1798–1803*, No. 557). A month before this, he wrote to his friend Wynn, "India is too hot for comfort – & I have an abhorrence of East-Indianised Englishmen" (*CL 1798–1803*, No. 556, October 30, 1800). Five years before, he was ready to leave the British isle with his pantisocratic dream, but now he spoke of missing the isle he had wanted to leave so eagerly. It indicates Southey's growing nationalism and conservatism and weakening of republican ideals he had earlier nurtured. Another letter written to Wynn (October 1800) expresses similar sentiments: "But of India I can talk and think in England – England – the land of intelect [sic] and morality – my own dear country, where I grew up and where I would be cut down" (*CL 1798–1803*, No. 549). During this time, he was in Portugal and that might have increased his love for his country, but it is the fear and anxiety of living in an unfamiliar territory among alien people, combined with his hatred for the "East-Indianised English men" that made Southey reject an Indian career.[17]

Although Southey declined Wynn's proposal to join the rank of the East India Company, he remained interested in Indian matters and was not averse to take textual journeys. He wrote to Humphrey Davy about his imaginative travels to the East: "So I travelled into Egypt & the Levant & Persia & the East Indies with every traveler whom I could find going that way" (*CL 1798–1803*, No. 447, October 18, 1799). He would not physically travel to the countries he names, but it would not be a problem for him to take a textual leap into the East. Therefore, he could plan writing a Hindu romance, even though he was averse to take up an Indian career. Lynda Pratt observes that Southey might have refused to go to India, "but that did not prevent him from making use of it – a use which was arguably as commercial as that made by those he condemned" ("'Where . . . success [is] certain'" 143). One of the important aspects of the late eighteenth- and nineteenth-century literature on the East was the author's aim to earn some quick money by exploiting the popular taste. Even a writer like Dr Johnson exploited the public taste for Eastern stories by writing *Rasselas* (Schmidt 104).

Eventually, *The Curse of Kehama* was completed, but in the ten years or so that Southey took in conceiving and completing the poem, his world had undergone a sea change particularly in relation to his radicalism and the British perception of India and Hinduism. This has larger implications for any reading of the poem. The poem might have its roots in the Jones era, but it was finished in post-Jones ideological formations toward the growing British empire in India. Southey conceived the poem when he was still a critic of British polity, but when he completed it, he became more of a nationalist, and his perspectives on continental and colonial politics underwent major changes. Southey's opinion on Hinduism, however, was not very favorable either when he first conceived the poem. Southey explained his plan for the "Hindoo tale" in the letter (October 30, 1800) to Wynn:

> For a Hindoo tale I have set another seed. there is a singular absurdity in that system – prayers and penance have a sterling – not a relative, value. they are actual coin for which the Gods are obliged to sell their gifts even to the wicked: & thus have they often given such power to the Penitents as they are called, as to endanger themselves. now one of these Penitents would I take, & set him on an enterprize to get at the Amortam. (*CL 1798–1803*, No. 556)

From the very beginning, the scheme of the poem was to depict the absurdity of the Hindu system and when Southey resumed writing *The Curse of Kehama* after meeting Landor, he had become a staunch supporter of the evangelical lobby. Between 1800 and 1809, Southey wrote a number of review articles on *Periodical Accounts relating to the Baptist Missionary Society.* In these articles, he argued in favor of the missionary efforts in Christianizing the natives. Reading in the light of Southey's reviews, Daniel White interprets *The Curse of Kehama* as Southey's "conversion poem." According to White, the question of how "to Christianize the natives became the question that motivated Southey first in his reviews and then in *The Curse of Kehama*" ("Idolatry" 5).

If Southey's desire for material success and serving the nationalistic and evangelical cause was the objective behind writing the poem, it must be noted that the poem was neither successful in terms of sales, nor in terms of its celebration of the national or the Christian. Contemporary reviewers criticized Southey for spreading the corrupting influence of a demonic religion upon the British public. He was accused of idolatry and was supposed to have been infected with the monstrosities of Hinduism. An unsigned review in the *Monthly Mirror*, for example, slyly remarked: "In his former works, he has prepared the reader for an indulgence in '*the wild and wonderous*,' but here he has out-run himself, and put *The Tales of the Genii* and the *Thousand-and-one Nights* utterly to blush" (Madden 132). After condemning Southey's implausible presentation of the Hindu deities, the review suggested that "Mr. Southey will never acquire all the fame, that his poem is capable of conferring until he obtains readers who reverence and adore his deities; and that time can never be until *The Curse of Kehama* be translated into *Hindoostanee*" (Madden 134). Another anonymous article in the *Critical Review* condemned Southey's poem as attractive at first glance but very tiring and "we seldom or never, perhaps, be tempted to renew our visit." The poem according to this reviewer "has scorned the limits of ordinary poetry" (Madden 134–135). Among the reviewers, John Forster was most scathing on Southey. Forster condemned almost every aspect of Southey's "monstrous" display in the poem, but he was chiefly critical of Southey's valorization of Hinduism, the "strenuous attempt to confer English popularity on the Hindoo Gods" (Madden 144). He famously compared the ludicrous nature of the mythological imports to "the shit of Lama." The poem is like a fine British fleet sent out to India,

> just for the purpose of bringing back, each ship, a basket of the Gods of crockery, or some portions of that materials with which the lama of Tibet is reported to enrich the craving hands of his devotees, and at length coming into the channel with flags flying, and their canons thundering, in celebration of the Cargo. (Madden 144)

These adverse reviews are proof that Southey's "conversion poem" failed to achieve its desired effect on the reading public. His depiction of Indian mythology no doubt aroused aversion which was his desired aim, but it also roused the fear of what Gouri Viswanathan defines as "reverse acculturation" (28). Southey shared the common anxiety about this "reverse acculturation" and he hated the "East-Indianized" English men. Ironically, Southey's critics feared for the "reverse acculturation" of the poet and his readers.

There had been different explanations as to why Southey failed to achieve his aim. The most common explanation has been the schism between the text of the poem and the notes. It is argued that the notes condemn what is upheld in the text within its imaginative boundary. Southey's text requires suspension of disbelief to appreciate the fictional world of Hindu mythology, but the notes act to the contrary as they condemn the mythological system. As a result of the conflict between the text and the notes, the readers and reviewers were confused. Javed Majid observes that the conflict between the scholarly and the administrative aspect of the poem is the reason behind the confusion (51–52). Lynda Pratt argues that Southey's poem was intended to demonstrate

> the superiority of all things national and Christian over all things "Hindoo," simultaneously feeding an appetite for the orient whilst demonstrating that "home" was best. What he saw as a poetic blend of the commercial with the national interest, others saw as deeply worrying and threatening. ("Where . . . success [is] certain" 148)

Some recent criticisms, however, deny the schism between the text and the paratext. Carol Bolton finds a link forged between the text and the notes in condemning Hinduism. She regards Kailyal and Ladurlad as "Christianly virtuous." Bolton writes: "Kailyal and Ladurlad are no less than Thalaba, on a Christian mission through a world of superstition – dominated by gods and demons – on the path to heaven." For Bolton, the text and the notes are in collusion in condemning Hinduism (*Writing the Empire* 243).

Readers' confusion has also been explained with reference to Southey's imposition of the English form upon an Oriental subject. In the preface to his 1837 edition of the poem, Southey defended its style and versification and illustrated how he had followed the British poetic standard. Southey wrote: "The spirit of the poem was Indian, but there was nothing Oriental in the style. I had learnt the language of poetry from our own great masters and the great poets of antiquity" (*CPW* 566). These comments by Southey lead to the discussion on the disjunction between form and content. However, the most obvious reason for the disjunctions within the text and the rupture between the text and the paratext is the long time that elapsed between its first conception and its completion. In the 1838 preface, Southey claims that the poem was "deliberately planned," but the preface also marks the halts in the process of its composition: "It is the only one of my long poems of which detached parts were written to be afterwards inserted in their proper places" (*CPW* 566). The patching together of different sources and information makes Southey's Oriental romances a pastiche, but another form of pastiche that works in *The Curse of Kehama* is the insertion of "detached parts" that were composed at different periods of time. Naturally, not only are there gaps between the text and the paratext, but there are also fissures within the text itself.

At the center of *The Curse of Kehama*, are two pairs of characters—a Brahmin king and his son, and a lower-caste pariah woman, Kailyal and her father, Ladurlad. Ladurlad has killed Kehama's son Arvalan to save his child from the sexual assault of the oppressor. It was an instinctive act on the part of Ladurlad: "Only instinctively . . . / Only to save my child I smote the Prince" (*Complete Poetical Works* 571). Arvalan's spirit seeks revenge upon the two through his mighty father, Kehama. As a part of Kehama's revenge, Kailayal is to be burned alive along with the wives (satis) of Arvalan. But, Kailyal escapes the wrath of the king helped by the goddess Mariatally. Ladurlad is punished by the king; he is cursed with unending suffering. The rest of the poem is Kailyal and Ladurlad's escape-adventure from the avenging spirit of Arvalan and the "man-Almighty" Kehama. The tale concludes with Kehama's failure to achieve supreme authority and his imprisonment in hell. Ladurlad and Kailyal are rewarded with residence in heaven.

When we consider this story in relation to growing Anglicism and Evangelism in Southey, the scheme of the poem is laid bare. Post-1800, Southey was siding with the growing demand of the missionaries to allow them to convert the natives of the colonized nations. He wrote in 1802 in *Annual Review* on the *Periodical Accounts relative to the Baptist Missionary Society* (1802) that

> Christianity would produce the greatest possible good, individual and general; because it would root out polygamy with its whole train of evils; because it would abolish human sacrifices, infanticide, and practices of self-torture; because it is a system best adapted for our happiness here as well as hereafter. (*Cuttings from the Annual Review* 207)

In another review of the Missionary Tracts, Southey argued:

> The better and the teachable natives would connect themselves with their civilized neighbours, and their children be exalted into the higher race; the more obstinate would cut off by spirituous liquors, their own vices and their own ferocity. This is the order of nature: *beasts give place to man; and savages to civilized man.* (*Cuttings from the Annual Review* 603, emphasis added)

This missionary zeal in Southey was ever growing. On July 14, 1813, he wrote in a letter to W. Wilberforce that the "Hindoos were easy proselytes to the Moors" and he wished "that Government should promote such plans [for proselytizing], furnish the means, & leave the Missionary to Societies to find men, & direct the execution. At present, there is no hope of this, but we are told to cast our bread upon the waters" (*CL 1791–1797,* No. 280). Southey's arguments in these reviews are similar to those of Charles Grant who wrote in his *Observations,* about the "general depravity of Hindus" and suggested a cure: "The true cure of darkness is the introduction of light. The Hindoos err, because they are ignorant; and their errors have never fairly been laid before them. The communication of our light and knowledge to them, would prove the best remedy for their disorders . . ." (148).

Just like Grant, Southey paints a picture of the Hindu society as degenerate, corrupt, priest-ridden and barbarous. In a note, Southey wrote that "of all false religions [Hinduism] is the most monstrous in its fables, and the most fatal in its effects," and it was responsible for the general degradation of the Indians (*CPW* 567). The backwardness and barbarity of the Hindus warranted a change, and Christianity would be the agent of this transformation. However, the representation of the natives simply as regressive and hostile could discourage the missionaries in their attempts to convert them and it would be equally discouraging to the imperial agency to find the hostile and powerful natives (like Kehama) unwilling to bow before them. Therefore, there was a necessity to portray a docile image of the natives. Thus, in Southey's scheme of things, Kehama and his idolaters, as well as Ladurlad and Kailyal, serve the evangelical purpose. Kehama is the image of the "Indian Bonaparte" whom the British dispensation in India was anxious to control, and Ladurlad and Kailyal are good natives who the missionaries could convert. They are the "better teachable natives" ready to be "exalted into the higher race."

In a letter to his brother Henry in December 1804, Southey went on to map the procedure of converting Hindus in India. He identified the caste system and the practice of sati as loopholes in Hindu society that could be exploited for conversion. The missionaries should aim at converting the lower-caste Hindus: "[I]t is the interest of all the oppressed cast[e]s to become Xtians, & the oppressors are everywhere the few. As for the Bramins let them alone – convert those who pay the Bramins & who support them – & the business is done. Xtianity would increase the temporal comforts of all. prove this by detailing the inconveniences of the Brahminical ritual" (*CL 1804–1809* No. 995). In Southey's scheme of things, the upper-caste Brahmins are the oppressors and not convertible, but the oppressed lower castes are open to conversion. Caste division becomes central to this vision of conversion. Southey referred to the evil of caste system in several other letters. Writing to John Rickman on October 14, 1802, Southey observed,

> the Trinity is better than the Trimourtree – I prefer the Devil to Seeva the Destroyer – a thousand arms are unpicturesque – & a sad plague to the taylor if he ... has to make a breeches pocket for each – give me horns – cloven feet – & a tail. – But man is a religious animal – & national faiths moulds the national character. the Hindoo system of caste is the worst ever devised for cramping human intellect – & anything to destroy it were desirable. there are diseases wherein arsenic becomes medicine.[18]
>
> (*CL 1798–1803*, No. 727)

It is this possibility of caste-based conversion that is suggested through his narrative in *The Curse of Kehama*. Southey foregrounds the caste identity of Kailayal and Ladurlad by identifying them as pariahs. At the very outset of the poem, he introduces the Hindu gods and goddesses that feature in the poem. Marriataly is introduced as "the Goddess who is chiefly worshipped by the lower castes." Kailyal and Ladurlad are worshippers of Mariatally and it is Mariatally who acts as the savior of Kailayal when she is to be burned alive:

> It chanced that near her, on the river-brink.
> The sculptured form of Marriataly stood;
> It was an Idol roughly hewn of wood.

Artless, and mean, and rude;
The Goddess of the poor was she;
None else regarded her with piety. (*CPW* 570)

In a note to this section, Southey refers to Pierre Sonnerat's *Voyage aux Indes Orientales* (*Journey to East Indies*, 1782) to explain the origin of the goddess as the deity of the pariahs (*CPW* 619).[19]

By the time Southey was writing his epic, the issue of caste and the case of the pariahs became well known in Europe and England.[20] Southey himself recounts the experience of William Carey who thought that caste was an obstacle in the process of conversion in the account of the Baptist Missionary Society. Wilkins, in presenting his translation of *The Bhagwat-Geeta*, set a contrast between the "learned Brahmins" and "the vulgar," the lower castes. Edmund Burke during the Hastings trial observed: "In that Country the laws of religion, the laws of the land, and the laws of honour, are all united and consolidated in one, and bind a man eternally to the rules of what is called his caste" (qtd. in Dirks 3). Among the Romantics, Thomas De Quincey talks about "the mystic sublimity of *castes* that have flowed apart, and refused to mix, through such immemorial tracts of time" in *Confessions of an English Opium Eater* (1821); S.T. Coleridge refers to the "Paras [pariahs] in Hindostan, who, however, maltreated, must not dare to deem themselves wronged" in the second chapter of the *Biographia Literaria* (1823). Both, the missionaries and Southey, configured caste system as an impediment to the improvement of the Indian (Hindu) society, an impediment to the civilizational mission of European modernity. However, there is one interesting difference between Southey and the missionaries in their conception of the caste: The missionaries conceived the caste system as an obstacle in the way of converting the Hindus while Southey represents caste division as an advantage to conversion; it was something usable to him and he thought it could be utilized in favor of Christianization and this, in turn, would help consolidate the empire.

In the letter to Henry (*CL 1804–1809* No. 995), Southey mentions two categories of victims among the Hindus—the women and the lower-caste people. Just like the persecution of the lower caste, cruelty against women is foregrounded in the very opening section of the poem. The poem begins with scenes of widow burning. Arvalan, Kehama's son is dead and his wives are now to be immolated. Although most British readers were familiar with the practice of sati, the details provided by Southey would have shocked many of them. Arvalan had two wives, Azla and Nealliny. Whereas Azla seems to have accepted her fate and sits on the pyre calmly, Nealliny is afraid and unwilling and is forced upon the pyre. Kailyal is also to be burned alive in an act of revenge. The other victims are several slaves, who dance around the funeral pyre and, one by one, plunge into the fire until "the devouring flames have swallow'd all" (*CPW* 569). In his notes, Southey quotes from a number of sources to show different facades of the sati. He gives accounts where the widows willingly sacrifice themselves on the pyre of their husbands, but also cites examples to show how widows were forcibly burned.[21] Southey quotes from the evangelical historian, Buchanan who hoped that the practice would end with the introduction of Christianity: "The civilized world may expect soon to hear of the abolition of this opprobrium of a Christian administration, the female sacrifice; which has subsisted, to our certain knowledge, since the time of Alexander the Great" (*CPW* 618). According to Bolton, Southey hated this barbaric tradition as he did loath the barbaric bullfighting in Portugal as it caused him pain, but this pain was necessary because in "recoiling from gruesome scenes, readers are expected to make a distinction between alien cultures and their own" (*Writing the Empire* 220–221). Southey's depiction of the ritual is aimed at producing this recoiling effect.

However, some of the passages that Southey quotes to historicize his description are marked by a sense of admiration for the calm and quiet way the women put themselves on the pyre (*CPW* 617), and this leads us to consider the question whether Southey had an ambivalent outlook to the practice of sati. Dissecting the Romantic artists' view of the practice of sati, Hermione De Almeida and George H. Gilpin point toward a kind of ambivalence in their analysis of Johan Zofanny's painting, *Sacrifice of an Hindoo Widow upon the Funeral Pyre of her Husband.* According to them, it "is perhaps the most comprehensive representation of what early English Romantic artists of India understood of the Ritual and its mythological imports." The painting depicts a complex scene:

> the sati, a woman portrayed slightly larger than life, occupies the centre stage of the painting. Beautiful and fine-featured and draped in volumes of white linen, she sits on a high platform, with the body of her husband resting at her feet and his head cradled in her lap. (229)

The Romantic poets seem to have nurtured similar ambivalence. P.B. Shelley in *The Revolt of Islam*, for example, glorifies the self-immolation of Cythna. In the opening scene of *The Curse of Kehama*, Southey is very critical of this evil practice, but he seems to endorse the self-sacrifice of Kailyal later in the poem when in section XIV, assisted by the enchantress Lorrinite, Arvalan's spirit attempts to rape Kailayal, and Kailayal decides to burn herself to save her honor. This is, however, another instance of victimization of women by the Brahminical society.

Southey in the poem valorizes Kailyal and Ladurlad but this valorization is problematic since it is done to justify the Christianization of lower-caste Hindus. As Southey's intention was to build public opinion in favor of conversion and Christianization of the natives, he draws the sympathy of the readers toward the lower-caste sufferers and they are portrayed in a positive light in contrast to the king and priest, Kehama. His method is to show the inconvenience of the Brahminical religion and their oppression on the one hand, and the docile and domesticable image of the lower-class and caste people on the other. This method juxtaposing the 'good' and the 'evil' is seen in the two opening sections of the poem. Along with the victims, Southey presents the perpetrators of the act and its spectators—Kehama, his idolaters, and the mob. Kehama is a combination of the Oriental despot and corrupt, tyrannous Hindu Brahmin. The source of Kehama's despotic power is not entirely earthly. His power comes from "prayers, penances, and sacrifices," from the very "absurdity" of Hinduism where even an evil person may acquire power through these means: "They are drafts upon Heaven, for which the Gods cannot refuse payment" (*CPW* 567). Kehama is not the only Brahmin in the poem who is projected as corrupt and despotic, but there are other Brahmins portrayed in section XIV ("JAGA-NAUT"). These Brahmins are equally corrupt, lustful, and fraudulent; in the name of their gods, they sexually abuse young women.

Kehama's despotism is revealed all through the poem. In the first two books, for example, we find his worldly power in commanding his people none of whom dares to face his anger. His power, however, extends beyond, and he can command the elements. He checks the elements from torturing Arvalan's spirit; he charms Ladurlad's life so that weapons, fire, flood or serpent, or a "beast of blood," or sickness or time "shall not harm" him (*CPW* 570); the earth will deny him food; water will "know thee and fly [from] thee"; the wind "shall not touch thee"; "And the Dews shall not wet thee" (*CPW* 570). Aided by the "unwilling" gods, Kehama attains superhuman power and he deploys it to exercise most barbarous cruelty upon his subjects. His brutality is seen on several occasions. In the opening section, he sacrifices many slaves at the funeral of his son. In section VIII ("The Sacrifice"), when he fails to sacrifice the animal because it was made impure by Ladurlad's touch, the "Rajah" slaughters thousands of those who did not prevent Ladurlad from his "impious" act. Kehama "gave command / To hem the off'nders in, and hew them down" and "At noon the massacre begun, /And night closed in before the work of death was done" (*CPW* 582).

Such a scene of sadistic massacre helped the poet to construct an image of the Indian despot because such an image of the Indian ruler was necessary to justify British imperialism. If the figure of Kehama is based on the mythical Ravana, his portrayal was also inspired by the British fear of Indian rulers like Tipu Sultan. The Mysore rulers, Haidar Ali and Tipu Sultan posed a major threat to British dominance in India. The third and the fourth Anglo-Mysore wars were given large attention by the British media. Tipu's defeat was celebrated. In a number of letters written after the third battle of Mysore (1789–1792), Southey referred to the publicity given to Tipu and the Mysore wars. For example, he wrote to his friend Grosvenor Bedford (c. July 9, 1792): "Let the newspapers now no more talk of Tippoo / Of the fine fighting Christian or pugilist Jew" (*CL 1791–1797*, No. 17). Again on October 23, 1795, writing to Bedford, he refers to "Tipooing": "[T]hat man deserves ten years more Tippooing for not writing his life" (*CL 1791–1797*, No. 137). As pointed out by Rajani Sudan, after the third battle of Mysore and in thirty years after his death in 1799, Tipu became a figure "the British loved to hate" (71–72). It is not unusual, therefore, for Southey to model Kehama on Tipu, who posed a major challenge to the British in the 1790s. Kehama as the despotic tyrant, it is also argued, reflects the British fear of the Napoleonic power. Bolton argues that Southey gradually turned into a patriot and a reformist from a republican, and from his altered ideological location he saw Napoleon as a threat to Britain with his expansionist policy. Southey, however, regarded Kehama as a greater threat than Napoleon; an "Eastern Bonaparte" like Tipu Sultan could upset the British regime in India (Bolton, *Writing the Empire* 221–224).[22] Kehama became a name for despotism even to Coleridge, who wrote that Jacobinism "still *walks* in Great Britain and Ireland . . . like the Kehama of our laurel-honouring laureate, one and the same, yet many and multiform and dividuous, assaulting with combined attack all the gates and portals of law and usage"(*Essays on his Times* 387, 405).

Ireland, we should not forget, was another colony of Britain. Irish people are demonized by Coleridge with the analogy of Kehama.

It is not only the Brahmins who are presented as corrupt and degenerate but under their debasing influence, the common lot has also relapsed into darkness. The state of the common people is represented through the mob in the poem. The crowd is chiefly present on three occasions in the poem: In sections I and II, they are spectators of the sati; in section VII and XII ("The Sacrifice" and "The Sacrifice Completed"), the crowd watches the king making the sacrifice, and in section XIV ("JAGA-NAUT"), the crowd participates in the Jagannath festival. The crowd is presented as an unmanageable herd of people having a slavish nature; they are savage and barbarous. Similar to the Turkish women enjoying the sight of a "red-headed boy" being killed in *Thalaba*, the mob enjoys the inhuman ritual of sati:

> Master and slave, old age and infancy,
> All, all abroad to gaze;
> House-top and balcony
> Clustered with women, who throw back their veils
> With unimpeded and insatiate sight
> To view the funeral pomp which passes by,
> As if the mournful rite.
> Were but to them a scene of joyance and delight. (*CPW* 568)

The crowd represents the general degeneration of the Indians as they are just a mob with no individual identity. Carol Bolton suggests that Southey often used the mob imagery in his letters displaying his fears of civil insurrection in Britain. Bolton quotes Southey's comment on the later Bristol riots (1833), where he speaks of the reformist crowd as an unstoppable force, a "brutalized populace [that] is ready to break in upon us." A similar concern with the crowd, according to her, is there in Wordsworth, but quoting from

Makdisi, she shows that Wordsworth's representation of the crowd/mob imagery in *The Prelude* is different:

> Wordsworth's ongoing effort to distinguish individual faces in the crowd is an attempt to keep the crowd from working any sudden (and not quite understood) transformation into a mob – as though to reassure himself, as he wanders through the streets of London, that what he sees is still 'only' a crowd, and not yet the mob of his nightmares.

In contrast to this, Southey "does not try to control his 'mob' in *Kehama*, but deliberately releases this huge, overflowing, intimidating element of his Indian world, so employing Wordsworth's 'nightmares' to exacerbate the horror of the scene" (*Writing the Empire* 219). In fact, during 1810–1811, Southey became increasingly worried about mob violence in the domestic context because he thought, "it would be instigated by the challenges of radicals to the government, as well as by pressure from the economic crisis of 1810–11" (*Writing the Empire* 66). In *Kehama*, there is no mob violence or mob frenzy, but the mob becomes a swarming mass of people with no will of their own, and who could be easily put in thraldom the way Kehama has done with them. In Southey's imaginative scheme, this mob requires moral lessoning—the teaching of Christianity to uplift them from their present state.

There is the recurring use of Gothic images in the poem, and Gothic scenes and images are associated with the forces of evil—Arvalan, Kehama, and Lorrinite. The images symbolically represent the fallen state of the East in general, and of Hinduism in particular. Gothic horror permeates the scene of burning the young women on Arvalan's pyre and equally horrible is Kehama's curse upon Ladurlad (Section II, "The Curse"). The section entitled "The Sacrifice" (VIII), once again presents before us the images of horror and cruelty with its description of the ritual killing of the horse, which will enable the king to achieve power over the gods and the ruthless killing of innocents that follows. The element of magic is introduced in the character of the malicious enchantress, Lorrinite, who promises assistance to Arvalan in fulfilling his lust and revenge. The motif of lust is introduced in the poem at the very beginning as Arvalan's death is due to his insatiable fleshly desire. He had a number of wives and slaves to satisfy his desires but he could not control his libidinal drives. Even after his death, the unappeasable libido leads to his pursuit of Kailyal. The incident at Jagannath showing the lustful Brahmins befooling the devotees and exploiting young women in the name of religion adds to the theme of lust in the poem. The Brahmins maintain a kind of harem in the temple with the help of a group of women. These women sing bridal songs and conduct Kailyal to the jaws of the lecherous Brahmins. The spectacle of the ruins becomes Southey's subject in sections XV, XVI, XVII, and XVII, "The City of Baly," "The Ancient Sepulchres," "Baly," and "Kehama's Descent," respectively. The images of ruin and a dark claustrophobic atmosphere prevail in these parts of the poem. To this are added the images of suffering, guilt, and punishment in the final sections ("The Padalon" (XII) and "The Amreeta" (XIV) of the poem. Commenting on the use of the Gothic in the poem, Leask observes: "Southey exposed the cruelty of sati (widow burning), temple prostitution, child exposure and Brahmin instigated sacrifices at Jagannath. In this respect, the poem anticipated the popular Victorian and Edwardian genre of 'Imperial Gothic' discussed in Brantlinger's *Rule of Darkness*" (*British Romantic Writers* 95–96). The poem is a case of demonization or Gothicizing of culture "through the Gothic languages of both fictional symbolism and critical Othering" (Smith and Hughes "Intro."). The Clapham sect, as Marilyn Butler observes, often used the sati and other indigenous images of horror to Gothicize India ("Orientalism").

Apart from the Gothic images of darkness, horror, dungeons, and ruins, images of sunny brightness, gardens, rivers, and fountains are also employed by Southey in the poem. The images of brightness and beauty that stand in strong contrast to the Gothic images of darkness and ruin are closely connected in Southey's binary model depicting his characters in the poem: On the one side of the binary are Kehama, his son Arvalan, and Lorrinite, and on the other side, stand Kailayal and Ladurlad. The despotic king, Kehama and his group could be the source of anxiety to the colonizers and missionaries, but the docile Kailyal and Laduralad could play an alluring and assuring role to the missionaries. Southey balanced the horrible with the alluring. Similarly, the images of danger, ruin, and darkness are balanced by the images of brightness and beauty. This balancing was necessary as a completely horrible, unattractive, and unmanageable picture of India could prove very unsuitable to the colonizers and the missionaries. The dangerous and the fearful are, therefore, balanced by the fascinating and the beautiful. The description of Indra's "Bower of Bliss" in the section "Swerga" as characterized by a combination of contrasting elements as is the palace in "Kubla Khan." The palace is built on a lake, "the waters were its floor"; and "its walls were water arch'd with fire";

> And domes of rainbow rest on fiery towers,
> And roofs of flame are turreted around
> With cloud, and shafts of cloud with flame are bound. (*CPW* 579)

The description of Indra's "bower of bliss," it is argued, was inspired by the popular narratives about Kashmir. In his *History of Hindustan*, Thomas Maurice describes Kashmir as the "present Paradise" (365). Maurice inspired both Coleridge and Southey.[23] In section VIII ("Mount-Meru"), Southey describes the source of the Ganges in the following terms: "A Stream descends on Meru Mountain; / None hath seen its secret fountain" (*CPW* 584). In the third stanza of this section, there is another description of the river that reminds us of Coleridge's "Kubla Khan":

> It springs at once, with sudden leap,
> Down from the immeasurable steep.
> From rock to rock, with shivering force rebounding.

> The mighty cataract rushes; Heaven around.
> Like thunder, with the incessant roar resounding.
> And Meru's summit shaking with the sound. (*CPW* 584)

According to Javed Majid, images of fountains and rivers in *Thalaba* and *The Curse of Kehama* are suggestive of the poet's effort to appropriate the new sources of creativity made available by the Oriental Renaissance. The description of the source of the Ganges as secret and pure, untainted by any human hand is, therefore, also symbolic of Southey's exploration of the pure and untainted territories of the East for English poetry. Majid identifies in Southey's *Thalaba* and *The Curse of Kehama* "a preoccupation with plumbing and probing depths" (49) as indicating "a tentative exploration and probing of new sources of creativity and material" made available by the Oriental Renaissance (50–51). He quotes a passage from the eleventh book of *Thalaba* to prove his point:

> The spring was clear, the water deep,
> A venturous man were he and rash
> That should have probed its depths,
> For all its loosened bed below
> Heaved strangely up and down,
> And to and fro, from side to side
> It heaved, and waved, and tossed,
> And yet the depths were clear,
> And yet no ripple wrinkled o'er
> The face of that fair Well. (*CPW* 317)

Such passages are quite common in the poem and the images of well, river and springs are recurrent. In the fifth book, for example, there is a passage similar to the above one in its use of the images of fluidity:

> Blue flames that hovered o'er the springs
> Flung thro' the Cavern their uncertain light
> Now waving on the waves they lay,

And now their fiery curls Flowed in long tresses up,
And now contracting glowed with whiter heat.
Then up they poured again
Darting pale flashes thro' the tremulous air;
The flames, the red and yellow sulphur-smoke,
And the black darkness of the vault
Commingling indivisibly. (*CPW* 209)

There is, however, an obvious difference between this passage and the earlier one: whereas in the first, images of light prevail and the well is deep but visible, in the second, the smoke and flames of different color give it a demonic quality. If the images in the first passage are attractive, the images in the second are terrible. Such contrasting qualities in the images of liquidity lead Majid to conclude that the attempts to tap in new sources of creativity posed a threat to the cultural superiority of the Greco–Roman heritage (84). It may be contended that Southey was also concerned with the primacy of the British and Christian cultural heritage as opposed to the Eastern religious and cultural tradition. It also helps in decoding the possible reason behind Southey's condemnation of Eastern art and literature as, "A waste of ornament and labour…." Elsewhere he condemns the Eastern style as "oriental bombast" (*CPW* 232). Jones's praise for the Eastern poets and literature is no longer acceptable to Southey: "Our barbarian scholars have called Ferdusi the Oriental Homer" (*CPW* 232), he wrote. Southey's condemnation of the Oriental art and literature seems to foreshadow Macaulay in his condemnation of the Indian culture, education, and knowledge in the infamous *Minutes*.

This change in perspective marks the shift in the dynamics of England's relationship with the colonies and it can be interpreted as signs of Southey's changing ideological position during the time. From a half-rebel, he gradually became a conformist. The bonhomie of the Hastings era underwent a sea change during the 1790s with the Hastings trial and the rise of the Anglicists led by Charles Grant and William Wilberforce. The events changed

Europe's attitude not only to India but also to Oriental art, literature, and culture in general. The "magisterial" approaches were gradually replacing the "curatorial" and exoticist approach of the Jones era; "Indianism" was being substituted by Anglo-centrism and Anglicanism. The "oriental Homer" now can be condemned together with the Western "barbarian" who equated Ferdowsī with Homer. The dichotomy of Southey is: He uses both Ferdowsī and Jones as creative inspiration only to condemn them in his critical verbiage. *The Curse of Kehama*, therefore, becomes a text documenting Southey's transformation from a republican thinker and a dissenting Christian, who favored syncretism in the 1790s, to a conservative Anglicist, who embraced the theory that Christianization of Hindus in India is a precondition for civilizing them. Coleridge perhaps had an inkling of this much in advance. As early as in November 1796 in a letter to John Thelwall, Coleridge noted the patriotic tendencies in Southey. Commenting on Southey's *Joan of Arc*, Coleridge remarked: "Homer is the poet for the warrior—Milton for the Religionist—Tasso for Women—Robert Southey for the Patriot" (*LSTC* 178). By the time he completed *The Curse of Kehama*, his patriotism was in full bloom and the patriot Southey was to become the poet laureate very soon.

Notes

1 An earlier version of the section on *Landor's* Gebir was published in the journal *Impressions* in July 2017.

2 Landor and Southey shared the same fate when it came to the lack of popularity of their poems. Writing to Thomas Moore on the subject of using the East as the source of poetic inspiration, Lord Byron condemned Southey's Oriental epics as "unsalables" (*BLJ* III 101). However, the most unsalable of the verse narratives based on the Orient was Landor's *Gebir*, which sold only a few copies.

3 A scholarly web edition of Southey's letters is published in the website *Romantic Circles* (<http://www.rc.umd.edu/>) in four parts. The general editors are Lynda Pratt, Tim Fulford, and Ian Packer. The letters are numbered in this edition and the volumes are chronologically arranged. This edition will be referred to as '*CL*' in the parenthesis. Instead of mentioning the volume number, the year covered in each volume (as it is in the title) will be mentioned together with the letter number, e.g. *CL 1791–1797*, No. 159. Unless otherwise stated, all references to Southey's letters are to this edition. Punctuations, capitalizations, or bracketing are reproduced as it is in this edition. Often in these quoted letters there is no capitalization at the beginning of a sentence, and it is reproduced here without any changes.

4 Elsewhere Garcia interprets the poem as an "anti-colonial allegory condemning William Pitt's reactionary policies and Bonaparte's false prophecies as the 'Grand Sultan' of Egypt" (*Islam and English Enlightenment* 182).

5 In their Pantisocracy project, for example, Coleridge and Southey wanted to establish a colony at Susquehanna which they imagined as a habitat of wild animals uninhabited by human beings. See James McKusick's "Wisely Forgetful: Coleridge and the Politics of Pantisocracy" in *Romanticism and Colonialism* (107–128).

6 All citations of Landor's *Gebir* are from *Gebir: A Poem Seven Books* (London: Printed by and for Slatter and Munday; R.S. Kirby, 1803). Numbers in the parenthetical citations are page numbers from this edition.

7 Sharafuddin quotes from De Quincey who commented that "Aroar is too Tom-Painish and seems up to a little treason" (39).

8 John Barrel talks about the geopolitical ramifications of the theories of psychic processes that Spivak draws on and develops in *The Infection of Thomas De Quincey: A Psychopathology of Imperialism*. New Haven, CT, and London: Yale University Press, 1991.

9 An earlier version of the section on *Thalaba* has been published in *Romantic Weltliteratur of the Western Hemisphere*. Ed. Dr Agnieszka Gutthy. New York: Peter Lang, 2019.

10 This short summary owes much to Robert Irwin's *The Arabian Knights: A Companion* (263).

11 See *Islam and Enlightenment 1670–1840*, Chapter V: "The Flight and Return of Mohammed: Plotting Samuel Taylor Coleridge's and Robert Southey's Unitarian epic" (157–188).

12 For Gérard Genette, the paratext equals to peritext plus epitext. The peritexts are those elements in a published work that accompany the text, things such as the author's name, the title, preface or introduction, or illustrations, etc. The epitext refers to materials outside the book but may help in interpreting the text. Genette observes: "More than a boundary or a sealed border, the paratext is, rather, a threshold." It is "a zone between text and off-text, a zone not only of transition but also of transaction: a privileged place of pragmatics and a strategy, of an influence on the public, an influence that . . . is at the service of a better reception for the text and a more pertinent reading of it" (1).

13 This passage that occurs in the penultimate stanza of the ninth book in the 1801 edition of *Thalaba, the Destroyer* was deleted from the later editions.

14 Southey wrote to Landor on November 26, 1809: "Yesterday I finished Kehama. There will be a few things in the course of corrections to explain the story more clearly, – a few trifles altered, – & many improvements to be made in metre" (*CL 1804–1809,* No. 1716).

15 Javed Majid believes that Southey could write the "Persian epic" later in his career, but publication of Thomas Moore's "The Fire Worshipper" in *Lalla Rookh* based on *Zend-Avesta* pre-empted any such possibility (47–48).

16 Southey's failure to write the "Persian epic" and delaying *The Curse of Kehama* for almost ten years has something to do with his lack of success with *Thalaba.* He was more interested in writing prose pieces and reviews that fetched him quick money than composing another unsuccessful poem like *Thalaba.* See Southey's letter to Walter Savage Landor, May 2, 1808, where he wrote: "I have sent you all that is written of the Curse of Kehama. You offered to print it for me, – if ever I finish the poem it will be because of that offer, tho[ough] without the slightest intention of accepting it" (*CL 1804–1809,* No. 1455).

17 The hatred for the "white nabobs" was not uncommon among the British. P.J. Marshall in his article "British–Indian connections c.1780 to

c.1830: the empire of the officials" has analyzed the attitude of the British gentlemen toward the English officials working in India. There were also caricatures of the "white nabobs" in England. Christina Smylitopoulos, in her interesting essay, "Portrait of a Nabob: Graphic Satire, Portraiture, and the Anglo-Indian in Late Eighteenth Century," has illustrated how the East India Company officials were mocked in British society by drawing attention to the contemporary representation of them.

18 It is interesting to note, however, that he calls Christianity "arsenic," a poisonous substance. Is it that he would prefer something else than conversion?

19 See Rupa Viswanath's *The Pariah Problem: Caste, Religion, and the Social in Modern India* for an idea of the caste identity of the pariahs.

20 Charles Gold, for example, drew his painting "Barbarous Ceremony: in honour of Mariatale, Goddess of the Smallpox," which was published in 1806 in *Colored Engraving. Oriental Drawings.*

21 Southey provides extensive notes on this. He uses Bernier's testimony for both the purposes: Two incidents as reported by Bernier are quoted by Southey; one that happens in Surat which shows the willing submission of the widow and the other that happens in Lahore, where a young girl is forced upon the pyre (*CPW* 617–618).

22 In a letter to Bedford, Southey defines Indian despots like Kehama as "Eastern Buonapartes" (*CL 1798–1803*, No. 784, Robert Southey to Grosvenor Charles Bedford, May 20, 1803).

23 According to Tim Fulford, "oriental bowers were movable fantasy zones, products of European desire for a free and fecund arcadia . . . they constantly retreated just ahead of the advance of knowledge. Imagined first in Palestine, they were relocated in Arabia, Persia, Kashmir, Tartary and Tibet when remaining essentially unchanged in their nature and function." During the Romantic period, Cashmere was regarded as the "Paradise of the East" having beautiful gardens, fountains, and rills ("Poetic Flowers" 113).

V

The "damsel with a dulcimer": Coleridge, Wordsworth, and the Eastern Muse

The Anglo-centrism and Evangelism evident in the works of Southey, to some extent, also colors the works of his friend and collaborator, Coleridge. Working in close tandem, Southey and Coleridge influenced each other and their collaborative readings on the East bore fruit as they used their knowledge gained from the readings in their poetic output. However, it is pertinent to remember that though they worked with almost similar materials, the results were not identical. Whereas Southey excelled in narrative epics, Coleridge's attempts at it were unsuccessful; it is rather Coleridge's short lyrics, ballads, and narrative fragments where one can find his deep engagement with the East. Unlike Southey, Coleridge did not write overtly Orientalist poems, excepting perhaps, "Kubla Khan" and a small narrative fragment "Mahomet." Of course, the play *Osorio* (later revised and rechristened *Remorse*), set with Spanish Inquisition and religious conflict in Spain in the background, is a significant text in terms of Coleridge's exploration of religious syncretism. A subtle incorporation of Eastern philosophies, theological beliefs, and literary conventions are also seen in a large number of his poems and foremost among them are *The Rime of the Ancient Mariner*, "Christabel," "The Pains of Sleep," and "The Lewti."

One of the earliest Romantic poems that experimented with poetic form and theme was Coleridge's *The Rime of the Ancient Mariner.*[1] Written in 1797–1798 and published in the first edition of the *Lyrical Ballads*, the poem has been conventionally interpreted as a spiritual autobiography—an inner drama of sin, punishment, and redemption.

It seems that the 1817 version of the poem published in *Sybilline Leaves* has dominated the critical discourses that read the poem as a spiritual autobiography. In 1817, Coleridge added the explanatory glosses to the poem, leading the readers' attention to the sin-punishment-redemption trajectory. On the other hand, the new historicist readings of the text have focused on the slave trade as its context and it has been interpreted as an "allegory of imperial expansion and the slave trade" (Attar 41). The poem has been regarded either as an example of Coleridge's critique of the trade or as evidence of his increasing distance from his early radicalism.[2] Few commentators, excepting some recent ones, have focused on Coleridge's enchantment with the Oriental Tale and the Gothic writings and how his reading of these genres had shaped the poem. However, if we explore the formal and thematic elements of the poem and the workings of imagination in it, Coleridge's experimentation with the contemporary taste for the Oriental Tales and Gothic narratives becomes perceptible.

The presence of elements from the Oriental Tale in *Ancient Mariner* was mapped out by J.L. Lowes in his 1927 book, *The Road to Xanadu: A Study in the Ways of the Imagination*. He wrote that "the attempts to trace the prints of the *Arabian Nights*, and the *Seven Champions*, and *The Hermit*, and 'Tom Hickathrift' in 'The Rime of the Ancient Mariner' and 'Christabel' and 'Kubla Khan' were like seeking the sun and the rain of vanished yesterdays in the limbs and foliage of the oak. But the sun and the rain are there" (460). Following the path laid down by Lowes, Tim Fulford in the essay, "Coleridge and the Oriental Tale" points to two tales in the *Nights* as a major influence on Coleridge. The concerned tales are, "Tale of the First Calendar Prince" and "The Merchant and the Genie." Fulford contends that from the first tale, Coleridge got the frame narrative and the story of the shooting of the albatross. Fulford quotes a passage from the tale where the hero-narrator attempts to shoot a bird and misses it and happens to hit the vizier's eye:

> When I was a stripling I loved to shoot in [sic] a cross-bow; and being one day upon the Terrass of the Palace with my Bow, a Bird happening

> to come by, I shot, but miss'd him, and the Ball, by Misfortune, hit the Visier, who was taking the Air on the Terrass of his own house, and Put out one of his Eyes. (218)

After this incident the vizier persecutes him. According to Fulford, the tale is characterized by an absence of logic or appropriate justice. A similar lack of causality marks the second tale. When the Merchant throws the shells of dates in the well, it hits the genie's son. The genie that springs up from the well must kill the merchant to avenge his deed. As Fulford points out, the dislocation of the conventional causality, the sudden appearance of the supernatural beings, the absence of narratorial moralizing, the enclosure of the voyage with a framing story, are all features of "The Merchant and the Genie" that give *Ancient Mariner* its nightmarish fascination (220). The whole collection of tales (the *Nights*) shares the above characteristic features and *Ancient Mariner* retains most of these features.

It is the lack of causality or moral coherence in *Ancient Mariner* that Mrs Barbauld objected to and Coleridge in his reply remarked that the *Nights* should be the touchstone for moral judgment on the Mariner's tale:

> MRS BARBAULD once told me that she admired the Ancient Mariner very much, but that there were two faults in it, —it was improbable, and had no moral. As for the probability, I owned that that might admit some question; but as to the want of a moral, I told her that in my own judgment the poem had too much; and the only, or chief fault, if I might say so, was the obtrusion of the moral sentiment so openly on the reader as a principle or cause of action in a work of such pure imagination. It ought to have had no more moral than the Arabian Night's tale of the merchant's sitting down to eat dates by the side of a well, and throwing the shells aside, and lo! A genie starts up, and says he must kill the aforesaid merchant, because one of the date shells had, it seems, put out the eye of the genie's son.
>
> (qtd. in Fulford, "Coleridge and the Oriental Tale" 217)

The passage indicates the deep influence of the *Nights* upon Coleridge's mind. The *Nights* imbibes a different aesthetic principle which was alien to the aesthetic judgment of Mrs Barbauld. Coleridge's incorporation of the 'spirit' of the *Nights* into the poem also resulted in Wordsworth's criticism of it. Wordsworth pointed to three faults in *Ancient Mariner*: Firstly, the Mariner "has no distinct character, either in his profession of Mariner, or as a human being who having been long under the control of supernatural impressions might be supposed himself to partake of something supernatural"; secondly, "he does not act but continually acted upon"; and thirdly, "the events having no necessary connection do not produce each other": and lastly, that "the imagery is too laboriously accumulated" (Mason 39). As Fulford remarks, "adapting the structure of the *Nights'* narrative to a traditionally English genre (the ballad) Coleridge was able to unsettle British expectations about moral order" ("Coleridge and the Oriental Tale" 220). In a notebook entry of April 1805, Coleridge comments on the unpredictable nature of the Oriental tales: "The favorite Object of all oriental Tales, & that which inspiring their Authors in the East inspires still their Readers everywhere is the impossibility of baffling Destiny, & that what we considered as the means of one thing becomes in a strange manner the direct means of the Reverse" (Perry 111). Wordsworth and Mrs Barbauld failed to judge the poem because they were baffled by the imaginative leap Coleridge took in the poem. However, there is another issue that must be taken up: Coleridge's view that the poem has "too much" of moral and it is an obtrusion upon the imaginative nature of the tale. Coleridge was making this observation in May 1830 and it would not be wild to surmise that Coleridge was thinking of the 1817 version of the poem where he superimposed the moral gloss upon the amoral spirit of the poem. Coleridge's conception of the poem was based upon the world of the *Nights* but inserted a Christian morality into the poem in 1817.

At various stages of his career, Coleridge referred to the *Nights* and his fascination with it. Coleridge wrote to Thomas Poole (October 9, 1797) on the impact of the *Nights* on him:

> I found the Arabian Nights' Entertainments, one tale of which . . . made so deep an impression on me . . . that I was haunted by spectres, whenever I was in the dark: and I distinctly remember the anxious and fearful eagerness with which I used to watch the window in which the books lay, and, I would seize it, carry it by the wall, and bask and read. My father found out the effect which these books had produced, and burnt them. (*LSTC* 1: 22)

It is no coincidence that Charles Lamb used the same language of enchantment while describing the effect of reading *Ancient Mariner* on him:

> For me, I was never so affected with any human Tale. After first reading it, I was totally possessed with it for many days. I dislike all the miraculous part of it, but the feelings of the man under the operation of such scenery dragged me along like Tom Piper's magic Whistle. (159)

On another occasion, in one of his lectures in 1811, Coleridge wrote: "Give me the Arabian Nights' Entertainments, which I used to watch, till the sun shining on the bookcase approached, and, glowing upon it, gave me the courage to take it from the shelf" (qtd. in Caracciolo 124).

By taking into consideration Coleridge's enchantment with the *Nights*, Samar Attar identifies three tales that, according to him, have exercised a considerable influence on *Ancient Mariner*: "Sindbad the Sailor," "Tale of the Merchant and the Genie," and "Tale of the Porter and the Three Ladies of Bagdad." The elements she traces back to the *Nights* are: the frame story and the power of narratives to change life; the Wedding Guest as a compulsive listener; the exclusion of women from a man's life; the theme of predestination and the lack of causality; the killing of the albatross (30–37). For Attar, Coleridge is particularly indebted to the tale of Sindbad the Sailor:

> Sindabad is a merchant; the Mariner is a lost soul. Both are condemned to a life of wandering. Both experience shipwreck and horrors. They deserve their misfortune, Sindbad because of his high greed for more wealth and excessively inquisitive nature about other people and their ways of life and the mariner for not only shooting the Albatros but also for harbouring some secret guilt. Providence plays some important role both in Sindabad's and the Mariner's life—almost every incident seems to be predestined. But although both men lose many years of sinful life, they seem to gain an eternity of bliss at the end of their adventure. (410)

Attar concludes that Coleridge undoubtedly borrowed from the *Nights* but "his Ancient Mariner emerged as something different from Sindabad the Sailor" because Coleridge has transformed his past and present experiences into literature "in his attempt to write the self." Though the poet is not identical with the mariner, "he certainly shares many of his qualities" and "the 'Rime' is an unconscious autobiography in disguise and an expression of Coleridge's fears and anxieties" (41).

However, the poem is more than an "unconscious autobiography," because it is rooted in the European enterprise of (slave) trade and commerce. Attar ignores the fact that *Ancient Mariner* like the tale of "Sindbad the Sailor" contains an element of greed; it is the greed for wealth that led European traders to the perilous seas and the inhuman practice of the slave trade. Another driving force for the mariners and European travelers, of course, was their inquisitiveness, and this is a central stimulus behind all the journeys undertaken by Sindbad. The eighteenth and the early-nineteenth-century Orientalists and colonizers were deeply concerned with gathering knowledge about the life of the Other. The story of Sindabad, therefore, provided Coleridge with the kind of model that was necessary for writing on the European enterprise of trade, commerce, and colonialism. The inter-textual reading of Attar fails to take note of this worldliness of the poem. Therefore, her conclusion, that it is an "unconscious autobiography," will remain an inadequate description of the poem, unless the contemporary colonial and imperial discourses are considered a part of the spiritual autobiography.

Another problem with Attar and Fulford is that they do not explore how Coleridge combined elements from the Oriental Tales with the Gothic in *Ancient Mariner*. Coleridge was an avid reader of the Gothic novels and wrote a Gothic drama, *Osorio*. He employed Gothic images in many of his poems (Punter, *Literature of Terror* 105).[3] In "Religious Musings" Coleridge describes the effects of commerce, war and sexual exploitation by deploying Gothic images:

> O thou poor wretch
> Who nursed in darkness and made wild by want,
> Roamest for prey, yea thy unnatural hand
> Dost lift to deeds of blood! O pale-eyed form,
> The victim of seduction, doomed to know
> Polluted nights and days of blasphemy; (*Complete Poems* 109, 301–06)

That Coleridge located the shared affinities of the Gothic and Oriental Tale can be guessed from these lines from the "Verses" (1796): "Mists in which Superstition's pigmy band/Seem'd Giant Forms, the Genii of the Land!" (*Complete Poems* 11, 15–16). In his analysis of "Christabel" Fulford shows how Coleridge was engaged with M.G. Lewis's works in 1797 and 1798. He observes: "'Christabel' is a corrective reply to popular 1790s taste, a reply in which Coleridge adapted aspects of the *Nights* to produce a more credible supernatural tale than that produced by contemporary Gothic writers—principally Matthew Lewis. . ." ("Coleridge and Oriental Tale" 224). If in "Christabel" elements from the *Nights* are incorporated into the Gothic, in *Ancient Mariner* he incorporated the Gothic elements into the structure of an Oriental Tale. The element of wandering, the theme of guilt and punishment (undeserved), the spectre-bark (instead of the castle), the vicious woman (life-in-death), the ghostly atmosphere, scenes of death and horrors are all manifestations of Gothic found in *Vathek*,

The Monk, *Melmoth, the Wanderer* or *Gebir*, *Thalaba, the Destroyer* and *The Curse of Kehama*. Punter observes that in poems like "Pains of Sleep" the Gothic is a vehicle for expressing his personal fears and anxieties (*Literature of Terror* 104), but the use of the Gothic in *Ancient Mariner* seems to be political, if not radical, as in "Religious Musings," since the Gothic images are used as a tool for exploring the horrors of slave trade.

Helen Thomas discovers in Coleridge's writing a tendency to move into the inner space, a move toward the form of spiritual autobiography beginning from the late 1790s. She claims that the spirit of Romantic poetry was shaped by combining the spiritual autobiography with the anti-slavery ideology: "Coleridge's poetical schema prescribes both a revival and revision of spiritual autobiography, established by radical dissenting Protestantism, and reveals the subtle relationship between the emergence of anti-slavery ideology and the development of the Romantic genre" (*Romanticism and the Slave Narratives* 103). Coleridge was as interested in *Robinson Crusoe* as he was in the *Nights*. Defoe's novel is a celebrated model of spiritual autobiography, but Crusoe's tale is not a simple spiritual autobiography. It is an expression of the enterprise of Protestant capitalism of the emerging bourgeoisie and is equally concerned with the issue of colonization if not with empire building. The inner space, therefore, is conflated with the outer space, both in *Robinson Crusoe* and in *Ancient Mariner*: Poetics and politics cannot be separated. Defoe provided Coleridge the model for combining the personal and the political. In *Robinson Crusoe,* Defoe seems to endorse Crusoe's project, but in Coleridge's poem, fear and anxiety dominate.

However, *Robinson Crusoe* and the spiritual autobiography was one element in the poem among many others—the Gothic, the Oriental Tale, the ballad, and the travelogue. Coleridge fused disparate forms in writing *Ancient Mariner*, and even though it was presented as a story of sin-punishment-redemption, its wayward Eastern spirit could not be contained. Therefore, the poem puzzled readers like Mrs Barbauld whose horizon of expectation was unsettled by the poem even after the glosses were added in 1817. It is also necessary to note that the technique of adding glosses comes from the annotated Oriental Tales. Coleridge appropriated the paratextual elements from the annotated tales to superimpose the Christian moral upon the poem. Therefore, the journey of the poem from the 1798 version to the 1817 one with its glosses can be read as symptomatic of Coleridge's growing insularity and a poetic and political compromise.

Tim Fulford traces the origin of the poems like *Ancient Mariner*, "Christabel" and "Kubla Khan" to a note by Coleridge in 1797. 'The Sister of Haroun—beloved by the Caliph—Giafar' and 'Her verses to Giafar—Giafar's answer," Coleridge wrote, constituted "good subjects" for poetry (*Coleridge's Notebook* 1:58). Coleridge was referring to the tale of Abbasa.[4] In the tale of Abbasa, the Khalif Haroun-al Raschid gets his half-sister Abbasa married to his vizier, Giafar on condition that they would not consummate the marriage because Haroun himself loved Abbasa. Abbasa, however, develops a passion for Giafar and by writing verses to him, she persuades him to consummate the marriage and a child is born in secret. At the discovery of this, the Khalif executes Giafar and all his followers. Fulford observes that Abbasa's narrative "is about the power of narrative to create change." So are the stories of Shahrazad. Fulford connects Bard Bracy, the Mariner, and the Abyssinian maid by identifying their common ability or desire to change the world through their narratives. According to him, the "Oriental tales provided, Coleridge, a model for poetry that is concerned with, and itself, exploits the power of its own fictional world to intervene in the real world of its audience." Coleridge derived from them "a non-realistic aesthetic in which the poet does not aim, as most eighteenth-century poets aimed, to offer accurate pictures of the ordinary world but seeks instead to create fantastical worlds which nevertheless affect our understanding of (and actions within) that ordinary world." His "fresh interpretation of the Eastern tale helped him form the new poetry and new poetic that we have come to call Romantic" ("Coleridge and the Oriental Tale" 223).

"Christabel" is an instance of Coleridge's "new poetry and new poetic" exemplifying his creative hybridity. In "Christabel," Bracy "vowed with music loud / To clear yon wood from thing unblest, / Warned by a vision in my rest!" (528–530). However, the poem has puzzled critics for generations, and until recently, little attention has been paid to the features incorporated to form the Oriental Tale in the poem which may give us a clue to understanding what Coleridge defined as "nothing more than a common Faery Tale" (*Biographia Litararia* 345). It is important to note that it is the element of the fairy tales that might have puzzled the critics. The lack of causality that characterizes the tales of the *Nights* and *Ancient Mariner* also found its way into "Christabel." Another characteristic feature that might have resulted in the puzzlement is its hybridity of the genre. The poem is apparently a ballad, but it incorporates elements from a Gothic novel, romance, Oriental Tale and travelogue.

The first part of the poem was composed in 1798 and the second in 1800. Prior to its publication, it was circulated in manuscripts among his friends. It was revised several times and was not published until 1816. The poem was published at the request of Byron, who worked magic with his Eastern Tales. Byron was apparently very impressed with the poem and defined it in a note to *Siege of Corinth* (one of his Eastern Tales) as a "wild and singularly beautiful poem" (qtd. in Jackson 224). Notwithstanding Byron's appreciation, "Christabel" was adversely received by critics at its publication. Hazlitt wrote that "the general story is dim, obscure, and visionary" (qtd. in Attar 54). The chief controversy was regarding the character of Geraldine. A number of questions were raised in *The Champion*: "What it is all about? What is the idea? is lady Geraldine a sorceress? or a vampire? or a man? what is she, or he or it?" (qtd. in *Coleridge's Poetry and Prose* 159).

To understand Coleridge's presentation of Geraldine, one needs to look into the Oriental Tales and the Gothic novels among other things. There are elements and episodes in "Christabel" that can be traced back to the Oriental Tales. Fulford traces two episodes in "Christabel" to Coleridge's favorite "Tales of the Genii": the story of Geraldine's abduction and the scene where Geraldine tricks Christabel to bed. In one of the tales, an enchantress attempts to deceive the sultan by telling him a story about how she was abducted in the forest by "four ruffians," who led her to a castle where they imprisoned her and she escaped. In the tale of Urad, the virtuous heroine is tricked into bed by a woman called Lahnar who undresses in Urad's chamber and she discovers that Lahnar is not a woman (Fulford, "Coleridge and the Oriental Tale" 225–226). Samar Attar refers to a few other stories from the *Nights* as having influenced Coleridge and she points out that the seductive vampire or witch, the lesbian, the spirit of the mother, the large castle with secret passages and the prophetic vision in a dream may be borrowings from the *Nights*. "The stock images that delineated the fantastic and the sinister, the realistic and the uncanny, seemed to have been engraved in Coleridge's soul since he discovered the book *The Arabian Nights* in his childhood" (50).

However, the elements from the Oriental Tale are transformed in "Christabel" and they enter the poem mediated by the Gothic. In his analysis of "Christabel," Fulford marks the influence of M.G. Lewis's *The Castle Spectre*. Coleridge, according to Fulford, adapted *The Castle Spectre* in "Christabel" "to make the action believably dependent on human feelings and relationships." Both "Christabel" and *The Castle Spectre* deal with the social and sexual power of the knightly patriarch over innocent women. The damsel, Angela in *The Castle Spectre*, is a prototype of both Christabel and Geraldine. In Lewis's story, Angela is the daughter, whose resemblance to her dead mother makes Lord Osmond desirous of her. The Orient in the play is represented by the "four blacks" and Osmond himself might be a West Indian plantation owner or an Indian nabob infected with the sexual profligacy of the Orientals ("Coleridge and the Oriental Tale" 224–225). Fulford, though he mentions it, ignores the influence of *The Monk* upon Coleridge. In 1797, Coleridge reviewed *The Monk* and its story was based on an Oriental Tale "The Santon Barsisa." Coleridge's Geraldine resembles Matilda, Lewis's heroine, in her beauty and behavior. Matilda seduces Ambrosio and Geraldine seems to be trying the same with Sir Leoline. She is a devil in disguise and leads Ambrosio to the path of evil. Though Coleridge denied that Geraldine is a witch, the poem suggests her supernatural power and her being an evil spirit. She does "witchery by daylight," to appropriate Coleridge's own language (*Coleridge's Poetry and Prose* 160).

As noted in the second chapter, the late-eighteenth-century Gothic novel had two types of female characters—the innocent heroine and the terrible (and sometimes also beautiful) woman. Christabel resembles the innocent type whereas Geraldine belongs to the second category of women with deadly devilish witchery at their disposal—the race of Maimuna, Khawla, Matilda or Carathis. Further, the issue of incest, which often forms a part of the Gothic, is an important element in *The Monk* and Coleridge's "Christabel." Geraldine is the daughter of Sir Leoline's friend and therefore, the relationship between the two verges on the incestuous. The feudal lord of the Gothic novels and the figure of the Oriental despot merge in the character of Sir Leoline. Fulford is right to point out that the despotic sadistic patriarchs of the Gothic novels are modeled on the Caliph of the *Nights* ("Coleridge and Oriental Tale" 225). If we accept Fulford's observation that Sir Leoline is modeled on Osmond, "who is either . . . a West Indian plantation owner (as Lewis himself was) or as a returned nabob"—someone who has a connection with the empire, we may also interpret Geraldine as the figure of the imperial Other infiltrating the domestic space. Empire comes home in *Ancient Mariner* in the figure of the Mariner and his haunting tale. The Wedding-Guest is held up from joining the domestic space and in "Christabel," Geraldine's entry into the domestic space destroys the filial relationship. Michelle Levy in "Discovery and Domestic Affection in Coleridge and Shelley" submits that both Coleridge and Mary Shelley were fascinated with

Oriental Tales and texts of discovery and exploration, but they were repulsed by the real discoveries and explorations as dangerous to the society and civilization. By making Bard Bracy promise to drive out the evil from the castle, Coleridge seems to take up the task of purging the domestic space of imperial infection. The paradox is Coleridge's belief in the power of his narrative itself comes from the East.

In 1824, Coleridge added some explanatory notes to "Christabel" in the manner of the *Ancient Mariner* to remove the obscurity in the poem. However, long before this, inspired by "Christabel," Southey (in December 1800) composed an episode for *Thalaba* of several hundred lines and wanted it to be the final book of *Thalaba.* Tim Fulford, in his article "Coleridge's Sequel to *Thalaba* and Robert Southey's Prequel to *Christabel*," defines Southey's composition as a prequel to "Christabel." Southey's narrative seems to develop the hidden implication of Coleridge's poem. A clear-cut distinction between good and evil is made by Southey and Geraldine is presented as an enchantress, a witch who turns Sir Leoline against his own daughter. In Southey's version, Thalaba brings Sir Leoline out of enchantment and father and daughter are reunited. Southey's effort to write this prequel was the result of the renewed friendship between Coleridge and Southey in 1799 and their new effort to collaborate. What these affinities make clear is that "Christabel" should be read as an Oriental Tale in the form of a ballad.

Coleridge and Southey separated in November 1795 due to their unresolved differences over the Pantisocracy scheme.[5] Their friendship was renewed in 1799 and Western Somerset "became a meeting point of Eastern fantasies" in 1799 (Fulford, "Coleridge's Sequel" 56). One of the fruits of their "Eastern fantasies" was Coleridge and Southey's plan to compose an epic on Muhammad. By the autumn of 1797, Coleridge acquired extensive knowledge of Islam and its followers. By this time, he read Sale's translation of the Qur'an, Gibbon's *The History of the Decline and Fall of the Roman Empire*, Thevenot, and Harris's *Collection* and the *Universal*

Histories (Shaffer 56). All this reading went into the conception of the epic on Muhammad. The proposed epic was to be named "The Flight and Return of Mohammed." In 1799, Coleridge composed a fourteen-line fragment which was supposed to be the beginning of the epic. It was published only in 1834 with the title "Mahomet." In the case of "Christabel," Coleridge, in the 1816 preface claimed that he had a plan for three more sections but the plan is found nowhere in his writings; however, a plan for the failed epic on Muhammad indeed existed and Coleridge wanted to finish the poem. He wrote to Southey on October 15, 1799: "Mohammed I will not forsake; but my money-book I must write first" (*LSTC* 1: 310). The plan of the epic was retrieved by Warren U. Ober from the Mitchell Library of Sydney and it is reproduced by Humberto Garcia in the appendix to his book, *Islam and the English Enlightenment, 1670–1840* (233–235).[6] The plan made by Coleridge and Southey shows that the epic would have ten books. It would begin with the death of Abu Taleb and Muhammad's flight to Medina; would cover major events in his life and end with his return to Mecca defeating his enemies. Ultimately, the epic was abandoned by both the poets, and the little fragments they composed were not published until very late, in Southey's case posthumously.

However, the question is why they attempted to write an epic on Muhammad. In the previous chapter, we saw that Southey had a plan to compose poems on each of the religious/mythological systems. E.S. Shaffer points to a letter by Coleridge to Southey to show that Coleridge was also interested in various religious systems. Coleridge wrote on December 25, 1799:

> [T]he oak of Abraham planted at Mamre, was still existing in the time of Constantine and destroyed by his orders; –a famous mart being held there every summer, persons of all religion both Jews & Christians & Asiatic Gentiles in general confluence doing honor thereto/–what a delightful subject this for an eclogue, or a pastoral, or a philosophical poem. (qtd. in Shaffer 35)

For Shaffer, Coleridge's fragment "Kubla Khan," the unfinished epic "Mahomet" and the unwritten epic "The Fall of Jerusalem" exemplify his syncretism. Shaffer traces Coleridge's development as a poet and thinker and argues that Coleridge turned into a defender of Christianity from being a sceptic, and this happened largely due to the influence of German high criticism of Harder, Eichhorn, and Klopstock. The high criticism interpreted the Bible (both Old and New Testament) as literature and Christianity as a myth. There was a parallel development that tried to disregard revealed religion as false; together with Muhammad, Christ and Moses came to be regarded as impostors. Shaffer argues that the lack of credibility of the Bible as history led to the construction of revealed religion as myth. Coleridge would write the "Fall of Jerusalem" in defense of Christianity with Christ as the prophet. To defend Christianity as a true religion, Coleridge had to defend Muhammad. Therefore, Coleridge and Southey thought of writing the epic on Muhammad (Shaffer 1–61). Humberto Garcia places the origin of the epic in the context of "Islamic Republicanism," Romantic Unitarianism and Napoleon's Egyptian expedition of 1798–1799—the "French campaign to bring Islamic liberty to Egypt" (*Islam and English Enlightenment* 158). The epic would be an expression of their Unitarian Jacobinism. Coleridge was greatly influenced by the Unitarians during the 1790s. As Daniel White argues, young Anglicans like Coleridge and Southey were drawn to Unitarianism "for its liberal appeals to free thought and for its anti-authoritarian association with political and religious liberty" (*Early Romanticism and Religious Dissent* 128). Coleridge looked forward to Islamic monotheism as a way of returning to primitive Christianity. As he argues in *Anima Poetae*, the epic would be a "disputation between Mahomet as representative of unipersonal theism with the Judeo-Christian machinery of angels, genii and prophets, an idolater with his gods . . . and a fetish-worshipper who adored the invisible alone" (290). Muhammad and Islamic monotheism for Coleridge, therefore, became the symbol of liberty, both religious and political.

Historically, Muhammad was largely responsible for ending the pagan idolatry in the Arabian countries. In the fragment, Coleridge presents Muhammad as iconoclastic: "Prophet and priest, who scatter'd abroad both evil and blessing / . . . but crush'd the blasphemous rites of the Pagan / And idolatrous Christians. – For veiling the Gospel of Jesus," (*Complete Poems* 221, 2–4). The reference to the "idolatrous Christians" strengthens the argument that the poem "embodies a Unitarian critique of the Anglican establishment" (Garcia, *Islam and English Enlightenment* 159). The prophet is represented as the man who ended priestcraft. Such an iconoclast could stand for the Napoleonic force and the next few lines with a rhetoric of war make it clear:

> Naked and prostrate the priesthood were laid, — the people with mad shouts
> Thundering now, and now with saddest ululation
> Flew, as over the channel of rock-stone the ruinous river
> Shatters its waters abreast, and in mazy uproar bewilder'd,
> Rushes dividuous all – all rushing impetuous onward.
>
> (*Complete Poems* 221, 11–14)

Muhammad is represented as a west-wind-like force sweeping away the rust. He becomes a Napoleonic figure heralding political reform. Garcia concludes that "Islamic teaching embodies an egalitarian form of Old Testament prophecy that can serve as a practical guidebook for practical dissenters battling against eighteenth century state priest craft" (Islam *and English Enlightenment* 168). "Mahomet," Garcia contends, dramatizes this politicized Unitarian fantasy. Islam in the poem, therefore, becomes a tool in the hands of Coleridge—a tool to attack European corruption and false practices of Christianity. In other words, Coleridge appropriates Islam to serve his Unitarian and radical purpose (Abbasi and Anushiravani).

However, one cannot ignore the element of ambiguity in the fragment. Nigel Leask observes that in "Mahomet," Coleridge tries to balance good and evil in the figure of the prophet ("Road to Xanadu Revisited"). To understand this balancing act, it would be good to consider this ambiguity first and then move on to the cause of abandonment of the project. If Muhammad is a Napoleonic figure, the ambiguity might be the result of Coleridge's confusion regarding the French Revolution and the resultant events. His confusion over the French Revolution and Napoleon is revealed in "France: An Ode" which was published as "The Recantation: An Ode" after the French attacked Switzerland in March 1798. The poem is at once a celebration and condemnation of the French Revolution. The French also invaded Egypt and Syria in 1798 and it is not that Coleridge could outright celebrate Napoleon's Egyptian invasion. The Egyptian expedition of France had an anti-England aspect since Napoleon's invasion was to thwart the growing power of the British in India. In 1798–1799, Coleridge might not have been a nationalist, but later Coleridge advocated that England should occupy Egypt (Keane 60–62).

There might have been another cause for the ambiguity. Though Coleridge and Southey might have a positive opinion of Muhammad, they could not ignore the residual traces, centuries of misrepresentation of Muhammad as an impostor. Muhammad, in the fragment, is conceived of as a warrior–hero not as a prophet–philosopher. Two years before Coleridge and Southey began working on the epic on Muhammad, Coleridge wrote his first play, *Osorio*. In *Osorio*, Coleridge again characterizes Islam as heroic. In the final act of the play, there is a dialogue between Alhadra, a Muslim Moorish woman and Maurice, a Christian. Francesco, an evil Catholic priest is brought by the Morescos to be killed, and Maurice pleads in the name of mercy. The theological debate is whether Islam preaches mercy. Maurice says that "Mahomet taught mercy and forgiveness. I am sure he did!" The Old Man (a Moresco) laughs at the words 'mercy' and 'forgiveness.' When Maurice replies that if Muhammad did not teach mercy "he needs it for himself," Alhadra accuses

Maurice of blasphemy and says that "the law of Mahomet / Was given by him, who framed the soul of man. / This the best proof — it fits the soul of man!" Vocabulary of war is used to characterize Islam: "Ambition, glory, thirst of enterprise, / The deep and stubborn purpose of revenge" (172). It teaches 'ambition', 'glory', 'enterprise,' and 'revenge' as understood by Alhadra, and perhaps by Coleridge. As the scene goes on, all the Morescos want Francesco to be killed, though finally, Alhadra commands that he should be taken to the ship. The similarity in the vocabulary of "Mahomet" and Alhadra's speech is striking.

In a notebook entry in 1805, Coleridge refers to the Unitarian years as a time of confusion: "Thinking during my perusal of Horsley's Letters in Rep[ly] to Dr P[riestley's] objections to the Trinity on the part of Jews, Mahometans, and Infidels, it burst upon me at once as an awful Truth what 7 or 8 years ago I thought of proving with a *hollow Faith* and for an *ambiguous purpose*, my mind then wavering in its necessary passage from Unitarianism. . . ." He continues that "Unitarianism in all its Forms is idolatry" and compares Horsley and Priestley's philosophy to the "the trick of Mahomet." He asserted his absolute faith in Trinitarian Christianity: "[M]y mind may be made up as to the character of Jesus, and of historical Christianity, as clearly as it is of the Logos and intellectual or spiritual Christianity – that I may be made to know either their especial and peculiar Union, or their absolute disunion in any peculiar Sense" (Perry 106). Coleridge compares Mohammed to Priestly and calls his religion idolatry. Therefore, it was not unlikely that he would have an ambiguous attitude to Muhammad and Islam in 1799–1800.

As Shaffer has documented it, Coleridge's attitude to Christianity began to change after the failure of the Pantisocracy scheme and his visit to Germany (17–60). Coleridge was completely transformed after his self-imposed exile in Malta (1804–1806). In Malta, Coleridge had the opportunity to see a mixed breed of people and had his experience in the colonial government. Malta has been the site of East–West conflict from the time of the Crusades and was under French invasion in 1798, but was ultimately retained by the British. In 1804, while residing in Malta, Coleridge collaborated with Admiral Alexander Ball on a series of papers that expounded an imperialist philosophy. In the "Observations on Egypt," Coleridge suggested that to prevent the French from occupying Egypt "we should take it ourselves" (qtd. in Keane 61). Erdman defines Coleridge's calculations in this paper as those of "a master race-economist" and Donald Sultana comments that Coleridge was now "committed to the cause of imperialism" (qtd. in Keane 61).

Coleridge was an advocate of the anti-slavery movement and opposed the racist logic of the slave-trade lobby at the beginning of his career, but with the passage of time, he moved away from his earlier position. Similarly, Coleridge's perspective on Islam and Muhammad was not static. Coleridge appropriated Muhammad and Islam when it was necessary and condemned him as he turned a Trinitarian leaving behind his Unitarian past. He wanted to use Muhammad for unveiling "the Gospel of Jesus." He discovered new methods of "unveiling" and naturally the epic was abandoned; his political position changed and he turned to Anglicism. He could have completed the project before the change of his political position but a few problems were there. He became busy with "Christabel" and the "money-book." Critics have also argued that the "narrative epic" was not Coleridge's genre (Fulford, "Coleridge's Sequel" 59); he could only compose it with Southey, but Southey left for Portugal and became busy composing *Thalaba*. Southey used his knowledge of Islam and the Islamic Orient in *Thalaba*. It can be argued that just like his friend Southey, Coleridge transferred his reading on Islam to "Kubla Khan." The prime cause of abandonment of the project, however, was transformed ideological position, from Unitarianism to Trinitarian Christianity. This ideological transformation of Coleridge is equally visible in his approach to India and Hinduism.

Coleridge was born fifteen years after the Battle of Plassey and eight years after the Battle of Buxar and seven years after the right of the East India Company as the official tax collector of Bengal was established. These are moments of history that would become grand originary moments of the British empire in India. By the time Coleridge was a young man, India was all around him and young British men went on fortune-hunting to India. Together with the rich material India, textual India was also a palpable presence as scholarly translations and research essays originating in Bengal were disseminated all over Europe. Coleridge was an avid reader and some of his readings on India included Wilkins's *The Bhagvat-Geeta* (1785), Jones's *Ordinances of Manu* (1796), Maurice's *History* of *Hindostan* (1795), Dubois's *Description of the Character, Manners and Customs, of the People of India* (1817). On the personal front, he had an Indian link with two of his brothers joining the rank of the East India Company. Unfortunately, both of his brothers died in India. Coleridge's elder brother John sailed to India in 1770 and died in 1787 in Kerala and his brother Frank died after being wounded in the siege of Seringapatam (1791–1792).[7] Wordsworth's brother John also died in the sea traveling to China via India. Coleridge himself could have ended up in India as his family wanted to enlist him in the military. In one of his letters to Thomas Poole on January 26, 1804, Coleridge wrote about his meeting with James who once offered him an Indian career: "My dearest Poole, —I have called on Sir James Mackintosh, who offered me his endeavours to procure me a place under him in India, of which endeavour he would not for a moment doubt the success; and assured me on his Honour, on his Soul!!" (*LSTC* 2: 454). All these events might have left some mark upon his mind.

Coleridge's relationship with Indian theology and philosophy is normally divided into two distinct phases: the early phase of enthusiastic reception of Indian thoughts (1783–1815) and a later phase of rejection of everything Indian (1816–1833). Natalie Tal Harries, however, traces three different stages of Coleridge's involvement with Indian thoughts:

a period consisting primarily of positive views (1793–1802); a second period where his opinion remains balanced (1802–1821); and a third phase predominantly critical (1821 onwards) (131). The primary focus of this section will be on the early phase of enthusiasm. As early as on October 16, 1797, in a letter to Thelwall, he compared himself to the Indian Vishnu: "I should much wish, like the Indian Vishnu, to float about along an infinite ocean cradled in the flower of the Lotus, and wake once in a million years for a few minutes just to know that I was going to sleep a million years more" (*LSTC* 1: 172). The letter is an indication of the deep influence Indian thoughts had on Coleridge. He refers to the image of the floating Vishnu on other occasions as well. In "The Night Scene: A Dramatic Fragment" (*The Collected Works* 16: 653–656) Coleridge used the same image:

> The God who floats upon the Lotos leaf
> Dreams for a thousand ages; then awakening,
> Creates a world, and smiling at the bubble
> Relapses into bliss. (51–54)

In this fragment, Sandoval mocks Earl Henry when he defines the pleasure he had with Oropreza in a bower of bliss as a "Deep self-possession, an intense repose." Coleridge here speaks of a state of contemplation, as he does in the letter to Thelwall. The fragment was written in 1800–1801 when Coleridge's attitude to India started undergoing some transformations.

Coleridge's sources for this image might have been more than one, though it is customary to refer to Wilkins's translation of *The Bhagvat-Geeta*. Thomas Maurice's *The History of Hindustan: Its Arts and Sciences* (1795), John Holwell's *Interesting Historical Events relative to the Provinces of Bengal and the Empire of Indostan* and William Jones's "Hymn to Narayana" are three other important works containing the description of Vishnu or Narayana floating on the water. Refracted forms of these images are reflected in Coleridge's image of the floating God, as Aparajita Majumdar claims in her article, "Coleridge, Vishnu and the Infinite." Edward Moor's *The Hindu Pantheon* is an unlikely source for Coleridge's early images because it came out only in 1810. In Maurice, there is a plate depicting Vishnu floating on the water on the hooded serpent (*Sesh Nag* symbolizing infinity), not on the lotus. The caption below the plate reads: "VEESHNU reposing during a CALPA, an Astronomical period of a thousand Ages . . . copied from a sculptured Rock in the Ganges" (401). Maurice's visual source was Holwell (Majumdar 36). In Jones's *Hymns* Brahma is depicted on the Lotus, not Vishnu.

The reference to Vishnu in the letter to Thelwall comes in the context of contemplation—Coleridge's inability to comprehend the whole: "I can contemplate nothing but *parts*, and parts are all *little*! My mind feels as if it ached to behold and know something *great*, something *one* and *indivisible*. And it is only in the faith of that that rocks or waterfalls, mountains or caverns, give me the sense of sublimity or majesty! But in this faith *all things* counterfeit infinity." He inserts some lines from "The Lime Tree Bower my Prison" to explain a heightened state of contemplation where he feels the presence of "the Almighty" in every living thing:

> Struck with deep joy may stand, as I have stood,
> Silent with swimming sense; yea, gazing round
> On the wide landscape, gaze till all doth seem
> Less gross than bodily; and of such hues
> As veil the Almighty Spirit, when yet he makes
> Spirits perceive his presence. (*Complete Poems* 129, 38–43)

Coleridge laments that such states of thought seldom visit him: "It is but seldom that I raise and spiritualize my intellect to this height." The letter shows the mark of the Gita in its idea of meditation as a means to understanding the unity of all: "God all in all." As Tal Harries puts it, Coleridge was "clearly attracted to the practice of meditative contemplation as a method of comprehending the 'vast' and achieving a sense of 'something one and indivisible'" (132). Poems like "The Eolian

Harp" (first published as "Effusion XXXV"), "Religious Musings," "Ode on the Departing Year," and "The Destiny of Nations" written in 1795 contain similar ideas. In "The Destiny of Nations," the pantheistic belief of Oneness runs through the following lines:

> Glory to Thee, Father of Earth and Heaven!
> All conscious presence of the Universe!
> Nature's vast ever-acting energy!
> In will, indeed, impulse of All to All. (*Complete Poems* 103, 459–462)

Similarly, in "Religious Musings," Coleridge writes that God is "Diffused through all, that doth make all one whole" and he defines it as the "Supreme Reality" (*Complete Poems* 106, II, 130–134). The same sentiment is expressed in the very famous stanza of *Ancient Mariner*:

> He prayeth best, who loveth best
> All things great and small
> For the dear god who loveth us,
> He made and loveth all. (*Complete Poems* 145, 645–650)

There are two aspects to these passages: a belief in the Oneness, and contemplation as a means to understand this Oneness. Tal Harries explains this with reference to the passages from the Gita:

> According to the *Gita* 'the tumultous senses hurry away, by force, the heart even of the wise man who striveth to restrain them' but the 'man of a governable mind enjoying the object of his senses, with all his faculties rendered obedient to his will', 'who hath all passions in subjection,' possesses 'true wisdom' and 'obtaineth happiness supreme' (*The Bhagvat-Geeta* 1785, 42). These attributes are continually reinforced throughout the *Gita* and Coleridge's poetic expression of visionary meditation contains the same elements. (134)

The pantheism of Coleridge has been explained with reference to the philosophy of Spinoza, but Spinoza's ideas were viewed as Eastern in origin (Libbrecht).

A sustained engagement with the principle of Oneness and the philosophy of the Gita is seen in *Osoria,* Coleridge's Gothic tragedy written in 1797, later revised and performed as *Remorse.*[8] Coleridge quoted a few lines from *Osorio* in the letter to Thelwall discussed above. The lines are spoken by a Moorish Muslim woman Alhadra. Her husband has been murdered by Osorio and she is burning in vengeance, but simultaneously, she thinks of an alternative way of life:

> It were a lot divine in some small skiff,
> Along some ocean's boundless solitude,
> To float for ever with a careless course,
> And think myself the only being alive! (169, 5. 1)

That a Muslim woman is made to speak this indicates that Coleridge might be thinking of contemplation as a common Eastern trait. However, in the play, there are similar lines placed in the mouths of the Western characters as well and both the villain and the hero speak in a similar vein.

The play is set in the years of the Spanish Inquisition (that started in 1418) when non-Catholic Christians, Jews, and Muslims were persecuted by the Catholic army. There are three different groups of characters in the play: Catholic oppression and cruelty are represented through Francesco, Osorio, and Valez; Islam is represented as the heroic religion through Alhadra, Ferdinand, and his Moorish companions (Morescos); the third group is represented by Albert, Maria, and Maurice. Though they are Christians, throughout the play, they speak the language closer to the precepts of the Gita. They speak of One Life and universal love. Osorio speaking to Ferdinand about Maria says that she does not think like a Christian: "Her lover school'd her in some newer nonsense" (35, 2.1). The "newer nonsense" is the language of universal love and philosophical understanding of One Life that Coleridge found in the Gita. However, the rhetoric of One Life is not confined to these characters alone; even Osorio, the villain speaks the language. Arguing with his father about the sin of committing a murder Osorio says:

> I kill a man and lay him in the sun,
> And in a month there swarm from his dead body
> A thousand — nay, ten thousand sentient beings
> In place of that one man whom I had kill'd.
> Now who shall tell me, that each one and all,
> Of these ten thousand lives, is not as happy
> As that one life, which being shoved aside
> Made room for these ten thousand? (85, Act 3)

The sentiments expressed here seem to echo Krishna's argument in the second chapter, "Lecture II: On the Nature of the Soul and Speculative Doctrine" of Wilkins's translation of *The Bhagvat-Geeta.* Krishna advises Arjun to understand the indestructible nature of life: "Learn that he by whom all things were formed incorruptible, and that no one able to effect the destruction of this thing which is inexhaustible" (36). Krishna argues that the body may perish, but the soul lives on taking new bodies. Osorio's speech can be compared to what Albert says when in the dark dungeon Osorio comes with a goblet of poisoned wine for him:

> Yon insect on the wall,
> Which moves this way and that its hundred legs,
> Were it a toy of mere mechanic craft,
> It were an infinitely curious thing!
> But it has life, Osorio! life and thought;
> And by the power of its miraculous will
> Wields all the complex movements of its frame
> Unerringly, to pleasurable ends! (147, Act 4)

The reference to the insect as having "life and thought" and its comparison to the toy seem redundant unless Coleridge intended to make it a philosophical statement emphasizing the concept of One Life. Maria expresses her abhorrence for the life in the convent and wishes to live in the midst of nature. Recalling how she enjoyed the company of nature with Albert, Maria says, she hears "The voice of that Almighty One, who loved us, / In every gale that breathed, and wave that murmur'd! (121, Act 4). Maria offers an alternative way of living. Away from the cloistered life of the convent, she would live in the midst of nature where the voice of the almighty can be heard in the 'gale' and the 'wave.'

The whole play is a theological and philosophical debate. The story of the play centers around Osorio's villainy. Osorio wanted to kill Albert, his brother, to marry Albert's beloved, Maria. Ferdinand, a Moresco who was appointed to kill Albert, was moved by Albert's goodness and did not kill him. After a long absence, Albert now returns and takes the disguise of a sorcerer. On Ferdinand's advice, Osorio hires disguised Albert to convince Maria of Albert's death through a magical fit. This is necessary to persuade Maria to marry Osorio, who has been repeatedly refused by her. Commissioned by Osorio, Albert in disguise performs the scene of his supposed death. Osorio, however, sniffs something wrong with the magician as the performance seems to reveal Osorio's guilt. Osorio has Albert imprisoned and murders Ferdinand to wipe out any evidence of his crime. Imprisoned in the dungeon of the castle, Albert reveals his identity to Osorio when they meet. Osorio prays for mercy and expiation of his sins. Meanwhile, Ferdinand's wife, Alhadra and the Morescos come to destroy the house of Valez. On their arrival, however, they pardon everyone except Osorio who they wish to take away. This could be a simple tale of revenge, but Coleridge seems to be more interested in exploring the philosophical and theological ideas. The Spanish setting gives him the opportunity to explore the evils of Catholicism. The Spanish setting also enables him to accommodate different faiths, for Spain was a country with a history of contact and conflict; it was a "contact zone." It was easier for Coleridge, therefore, to showcase his new learning of the philosophy of the "potentates of Ind" in the play, as he would later refer to it.

Coleridge's pantheistic ideas have often been explained with reference to Neo-Platonism and the philosophy of Spinoza. Coleridge became an admirer of Spinoza and wanted to write an epic on him in 1799 and 1803 (Vallins 113). Spinoza's philosophy was regarded by Coleridge as well as by his German mentors as Eastern in its origin. Later in his career, Coleridge would reject both the philosophy of the Gita as well as Spinoza. In explaining Coleridge's pantheism and his concept of One Life, one must also take account of *Hayy Ibn Yakzan*, which was available in English translation. The twelfth-century Arabic novel by Tufayl was first translated into Latin by Pico della Mirandola. Spinoza is said to have translated or ordered a translation of this philosophical novel into Dutch. Philosophers in western Europe including Spinoza were greatly influenced by this book (Attar 8). If Coleridge was borrowing from Spinoza, his debt *Hayy* is undeniable.

Coleridge, however, became more insular in his thoughts at the beginning of the new century as he embraced Trinitarian Christianity. Tal Harries identifies a kind of vacillation in Coleridge's work from 1802 to 1821 between sympathy and apathy to Indian philosophy. In poems like "The Pains of Sleep" and "Dejection: An Ode," according to Tal Harries, Coleridge fails to achieve a state of meditative contemplation. In this period, he was still attracted to the concept of divine unity, exemplified by his poem "God's Omnipresence: A Hymn" (1814), but by this time, Coleridge had also started criticizing pantheism. In *Opus Maximum*, he criticized "Pantheism" as "the natural result of an imbecile understanding <producing indistinction> by half-closed lids, when all the hues and outlines melt into garish mist, [they] deem it unity" (*The Collected Works* 15: 281). He was clearly criticizing the Vishnu-like state of contemplation. On the Gita, Coleridge observed: "If we consider the [Gita] as poetry; it has the mortal disease of all Indian poetry: the attempting to image the unimageable, not by symbols but by jumble of images. . ." (*The Collected Works* 15: 394). In "On the Divine Ideas," Coleridge condemns Hinduism as "Atheism in the form of Polytheism" (qtd. in Warren, "Coleridge, Orient and Philosophy" 118). Coleridge also criticized Jones who in his essay "On the Gods of Greece, Italy, and India" argued that India had a direct influence on ancient Greek thought (Vallins 120). Considering these late reactions, Shaffer observes that of "all forms of oriental thought Coleridge had least sympathy with Hinduism, at least in his later years" (133).

The reasons behind Coleridge's early reception and late rejection of Eastern traditions of thoughts have been variously explained. His growing Hellenism has been identified as one of the reasons behind this. He wrote that though many of the philosophical ideas can be traced back to the East, he would prefer the Grecian: "This is not Greek theology merely. It is a fair account of the Egyptian, of the Indian, and of every other, but I speak of the Greece because it was the only country that dared to ask why" (*The Collected Works* 5: 58–59). Andrew Warren explains Coleridge's rejection of the Eastern and Indian philosophical ideas regarding the changing philosophical position of the latter. The central text taken up by Warren in "Coleridge, Orient and Philosophy" is Coleridge's *Lectures on the History of Philosophy* (1818–1819). He discovers a triad in Coleridge's philosophical ideas, which come from three different sources: Hebrew, Greek, and the East. This triad is related to another parallel triad Will, Reason, and Nature. In his mature years, Coleridge rejected Nature / East in favor of Will and Reason. According to Warren, Coleridge rejected Spinoza's materialism in favor of Fichte's idealism. Similarly, David Vallins argues that in Coleridge's writing, there is a conflict between the ideal on the one hand and the material on the other. In his later writings, Coleridge condemns Hinduism and pantheism as problematically identifying the human with the divine. Coleridge also blames the same idolatrous tendency in Catholicism—in their saint worship—where the human and the divine are confused.

Shaffer traces Coleridge's evolution of ideas and concludes that Coleridge's Orientalism is neither "affection nor antiquarian fancy nor an escape into the exotic." Coleridge's concern was "for the primitive spring of faith in one God for all mankind, and his special concern for the seed-time of European civilization." Shaffer identifies Coleridge's Christian-centrism, but she ignores the overarching nature of the Christian-centric discourse—the gradual creation of a center that would push all into the margins. Changes in Coleridge's attitude toward India and Hinduism cannot be dissociated from the rise of the evangelical lobby and the Clapham in England. Coleridge's criticism of Hinduism, therefore, must be read in the context of the changing policy of imperial Britain toward India. Moreover, rejecting Hindu philosophy was an act of assertion of the Western cultural hegemony. Shaffer argues in her book that one of the causes of the rise of the concept of the Bible as myth was the dissemination of the knowledge about Hinduism, which threatened the primacy of the Bible. Shaffer observes, "in the context of Oriental history, the claim of the Bible to be the origin and pattern of religious civilizations was reduced to a moral and finally to a symbolic claim only" (56). The necessity to defend Christianity might have resulted in Coleridge's condemnation of Hinduism.

Some these conflicting ideas and ideals of Coleridge seem to have been encoded in "Kubla Khan" with its sources of inspiration traceable to all the continents of the world. In 1927, J. L. Lowes observed that in "Kubla Khan" "with the kaleidoscopic swiftness of a dream, the scene shifts from Abyssinia to Cashmere" (379). Three distinct strands of source hunting of the images in "Kubla Khan" can be seen in critical circles leading to China and the Far East, the Indian subcontinent, and the Middle East including North Africa. The source that Coleridge refers to in the 1816 preface to the poem has fueled the critical imagination because Purchas' book is very vast in its geographical and temporal scope. The title of the book reads:

> Purchas his Pilgrimage Or Relations of the World and the Religions Observed in All Ages and Places Discovered, from the Creation up

> to this Present. In Four Parts. This First Contains a Theological and Geographical History of Asia, Africa and America. Declaring the Ancient Religions before the Flood, the Heathnish, Jewish, and Saracenical in all Ages since . . . with brief Descriptions of the Countries, Nations, States, Discoveries, Private and Public Customs.

Purchas's book maps a geography that extends through all the continents of the world. Similarly, the geopolitical space in "Kubla Khan" runs through the Near East, Persia, and North Africa to India and the Far East.

The poem has been read from different critical perspectives. Lowes follows the images of the poem and traces them to multiple sources. Though critical of Lowes, Shaffer also moves through different texts and contexts to contextualize "Kubla Khan." She argues for the biblical root of Coleridge's Orientalism. Quoting from Goethe, Shaffer observes that in speaking of "Oriental poetry we must speak of the Bible as the oldest collection" (106). She traces various influences on Coleridge, including that of Jones's translations of Eastern poetry, and combination of various forms such as the ballad, the ode, the "oriental idyll," the epic and the biblical prophecy etc. According to Shaffer, "Kubla Khan" "the apocalyptic epic is the apotheosis of a new form, the lyrical ballad" (95). She also cites a number of Islamic and proto-Islamic sources as influences on Coleridge.

In recent years, new sources for the poem have been identified, analyzed and discussed in the critical arena. Humberto Garcia, for example, argues that "Kubla Khan" is a miniature version of the "Arab-Islamic epic in which the Garden of Iram / Irem myth is the master trope for plotting the French revolution's rise and fall" (*Islam and English Enlightenment* 184). Coleridge had multiple sources for the story of the garden of Irem and its destruction: Southey's *Thalaba*, Landor's *Gebir,* William Jones's "On the Poetry of the Eastern Nations," (1772) and Sale's translation of the Qur'an. Jones wrote:

> Mahommed, in his Alcoran, in the Chapter of the Morning [Al-Fajr], mentions a garden called Irem [or Iram], which is no less celebrated by the Asiatic poets than that of the Hesperides by the Greeks. It was planted, as the commentators say, by a king named Shaddad and was once seen by an Arabian, who wandered far into the desert in search of a lost camel. (Pachori 138)

In fact, throughout the Qur'an, there are many references to paradise and paradisal landscapes.[9] Coleridge read Sale's translation of the Qur'an in 1797 and also studied the works of Jones. The Garden of Irem built by the Adites is destroyed by God through the prophet Hud when Shedad and his people ignore God's warning. In Coleridge's poem, Kubla Khan hears the ancestral voices prophesying war/ destruction.

Apart from these purely Qur'anic descriptions of paradise, there had been numerous other contemporary accounts on the Near East which might have equally influenced Coleridge. A book of particular interest to Coleridge was James Bruce's *Travels to Discover the Source of the Nile* (1790). Lowes argues that Coleridge adopted many striking images from Bruce and that his Xanadu resembles the area around the fountain from which the Nile originates, the Nile itself being the equivalent of the river Alph. Lowes links Mount Amora to Abola and connects Coleridge's Abyssinian maid with Bruce's narrative (371–373). In Purchas's book, there are numerous descriptions of seemingly paradisal landscapes and one of such passages contain a reference to Mount Amara, of which the Abyssinian maid, Coleridge's muse, is singing. There is a detailed description of the hill anticipating what is there in the poem. The hill is a steep one, "dilating itself in a round form . . . with impassable tops thereof, many fruitful and pleasant vallies wherein the kindred of [Prester John] are surely kept . . . a mountain glittering in some places like the sun, saying all that was gold" (Purchas 672). A similar description of Amara Valley is provided by Johnson in his *Rasselas*. Like Purchas,

Johnson also describes Abyssinia as the land of a "mighty emperor," where the Nile, "the Father of Waters, begins his course, and whose bounty pours down the streams of plenty, and scatters over half the world the harvests of Egypt" (qtd. in Khan 101). European Christians believed in the legend of an earthly Paradise in the realm of a Christian monarch named Prester (or Presbyter) John, and it was thought to be somewhere in the East, possibly Ethiopia, also known as Abyssinia. The heavenly realm was believed to have been the land of four major rivers flowing out of it—the Nile, Senegal, the Niger, and the Congo, whose origins explorers sought to find (Khan 100).

The source for Coleridge's Abyssinian paradise has also been traced through Milton's *Paradise Lost.* Milton refers to "Abassin Kings," "Mount Amara," and the "True Paradise under Ethiop Line / By Nilus head, enclosed with shining rock, (*PL* IV, 280–283). The Abyssinian maid has been related to the Egyptian goddess Isis. Coleridge, in 1796, borrowed the *Metamorphoses* of Apuleius which refers to goddess Isis as a "radiant figure carrying a timbrel of brass in her right hand, that produces a shrill and clear sound" and a boat-shaped cup of gold in her left hand (Beer, "The Language of Kubla Khan" 236–238). During the Romantic period, Yemen was another Middle Eastern locus for the earthly paradise. William Jones described Yemen as "the most secure" and "the most beautiful region of the East," enclosed on the one side by vast rocks and deserts, and defended on the other by a tempestuous sea" "under a serene sky" (Pachori 136).

Critics like Fulford and Attar consider "Kubla Khan" as chiefly growing out of Coleridge's interest in Oriental Tale. Fulford regards "Kubla Khan" as a dreamscape shaped by several Eastern tales, particularly, "Tales of the Genii" and the Persian–Arabic collection *Bahar-Danush* or *Garden of Knowledge* translated into English by Jonathon Scott. The *Bahar-Danush* contains a description of a garden and the theme of poetic inspiration. A visit to the garden inspires the poet to creative ecstasy—"the Wujd of ecstasy."[10] Fulford observes that Coleridge "was introduced by Southey to Persian tales that identified the ruler/artist contrast as an Oriental topos. That topos, of course, is central to "Kubla Khan" where the poet-figure, inspired by his Abyssinian maid-muse, will build in air the dome that the Khan wants to build on the ground ("Coleridge and the Oriental Tale" 229). Attar points to a few sources little discussed by earlier critics. In *Purchas His Pilgrimage*, there is a detailed discussion of the Assassins' paradise. Attar refers to the story related by Marco Polo about the master of Alamut's fortress, who used to hypnotize his self-sacrificing followers with the use of *hashis* and would introduce them into his false paradise with ladies and damsels dallying with the entrants. Attar suggests that Alaodine, the leader of the assassins, changed role with Kubla Khan in Coleridge's opium-induced dream. He connects the warrior king Kubla Khan, the excited Assassins of Alaodine's paradise, and the half-crazed narrator of the poem (46–47). In Purchas, there is a passage describing Alaodine's paradise: "Hee had in a goodly Valley betwixt two Mountaynes very high, made a Goodly garden, furnished with best trees and fruits he could find, adorned with divers Palaces and houses of pleasure, beautified with gold Workers, pictures and Furnitures of silke" (qtd. in Lowes 329). Similar descriptions of gardens are there in the tale of Aladdin in the *Nights*. Attar quotes the relevant passage from the tale "Aladdin and the Wonderful Lamp":

> Build me a palace of finest marble, set with jasper, agate, and other precious stones. In the middle you shall build me a large hall with dome, its four walls of massy gold and silver, each side having six windows whose lattices, all except one, which is to be left unfinished, must be set with diamond and rubies. (46)

"The Sixth Voyage of Sindbad the Sailor" might have inspired the river image in the poem and the image of the measureless caverns; the woman wailing for her demon-lover might have drawn its inspiration from "The story of Young King of the Black Isles" where the wife of the king laments for lost Ethiopian lover in a wasteland. The Abyssinian maid might have come from the tale of "Noureddin and the Fair Persian" where there is an exquisitely beautiful lady, who dances and sings. She is a symbol of poetic inspiration and creative energy. Kabbani Rana has interpreted the figure of the "damsel with a dulcimer" with reference to the recurring image of the sensual East in Western literature. According to Rana, Coleridge drew his poetic muses from "imagination's Orient."

> His Abyssinian maid is the spouse of his poetic fancy; like Southey's 'snowy- Ethiop', she is exotic but familiar—being fair-skinned like Circassians of the Orientalist painting. She is a later version of the Circassian Lewti in the poem of that name, in which, Coleridge adopts the trappings of Persian poetry. [11]

Both Lewti and the Abyssinian maid, according to Rana, are figures of sensuality (35).

The second strand of the poem's source hunting leads us to India, and Kashmir becomes the focal point of this strand. It is argued that the image of Kubla's garden might have been influenced by the contemporary writings on Kashmir, or the gardens from Indian myths might have made their way into the poem. Fulford suggests that Coleridge's dream-vision of a paradise garden in "Kubla Khan" might reflect aspects of Jones's "The Palace of Fortune: An Indian Tale" (1772) "in which a paradise garden is also viewed only in a dream-vision" ("Poetic flowers" 118). In Jones's poem, there are images of "living rills of purest nectar flow / O'er meads that with unfading flowerets glow" (65–66); "A rising fountain play'd from every stream" (83); and "a rock of ice, by magic rais'd, / High in the midst a gorgeous palace blaz'd" (99–100). Both Coleridge and Southey read Maurice, Bernier, and Tavernier and their description of Kashmir as the earthly paradise. As John Drew notes, when the interest in Orient became centered in India in the 1790s, Kashmir rose in the English consciousness and Kashmir could be an "objective correlative for the highly-charged interior landscape of 'Kubla Khan'" (205). Drew also traces the origin of the Abyssinian maid to Kashmir and sees her as the poetic equivalent of the Indian goddess Sarasvati (186–226).

If Kashmir inspired the image of paradise, there were images of beautiful palaces and their ruination in William Hodges's *Travels in India* that might have inspired the "ancestral voices prophesying war." Deidre Coleman in her article "The 'dark Tide of time': Coleridge and William Hodges's India" shows that Coleridge had knowledge of Hodges's book and his paintings. Hodges's paintings were exhibited in London and forty-eight of his paintings were available between 1785 and 1788 entitled *Select Views of India*. Coleman argues that Hodges's paintings with its depiction of the fall of grand Mughals "provided a sort of warning to eighteenth century imperial Britain." Coleman identifies a number of issues common to Hodges's book and "Kubla Khan": the dreamy nostalgic evocation of the Miltonic garden of Eden, the false paradise, territorial conquest, war and the loss of empire. Coleman argues that Hodges depicts Mughal life as characterized by contrasting images of energy and delight, twined with stasis and annihilation and it resonates in Coleridge's poem in the contrasting images of "gardens bright" and "lifeless ocean" presided over by Kubla Khan's "pleasure dome" (48). In the final part of the essay, Coleman attempts to show how Hodges's notion of the cave as discussed in *Dissertation on the Prototypes of Architecture, Hindu Moorish and Gothic* influenced Coleridge's idea of "Romantic sublimity." The cave temples of Elephanta are linked to the "deep romantic chasm" of "Kubla Khan"—a place at once "holy and enchanted." Coleman gives instances from contemporary writings on India to argue how the cave or cavern was connected to the Sanskrit texts by the Orientalists. She cites from William Jones's "Hymn to Surya" and from *Quarterly Review* to prove her point. The "dark caves" becomes "the dark caverns of Sanskrit literature." Coleman points out how Jones's syncretism becomes a cause of concern for Coleridge—the 'holy' caverns of Sanskrit literature for Jones become the demonic chasm for Coleridge (52–53). However, the residual impact of the 'holiness' remains in "Kubla Khan."

When this interpretation of Coleman is linked to the issue of imperial anxiety in Coleridge's poem and the contemporary British fear of another Mughal descendant, Tipu Sultan and his depiction in popular British media, Kubla Khan becomes a very complex figure. He is not only the Chinese emperor but also the contemporary Tipu and simultaneously the British rulers, who are following in the footsteps of the Mughals. The poem incorporates both the fear of empire as well as the fear of losing it when read in the context of the growing British empire in India. The fear of losing the Indian empire becomes the immediate concern when we take into account Napoleon's Egyptian invasion, which was planned to curtail British power in India. However, the failure of the Napoleonic invasion was also a kind of warning to the British as were the pictures of the ruination of the Mughals in India in Hodges's narrative.

The third strand of tracing Coleridge's sources in "Kubla Khan" takes us to China. David Vallins identifies China as an alternative space in Coleridge's poetry. Vallins contends that in some of his earlier works, Coleridge explored the possibility of uniting the divine and the human, the conscious and the unconscious, the material and the spiritual, the real and the imagined, the mundane and the divine. Coleridge tried to do this by locating his poems neither in Christian Europe nor the known Orient (India/Middle East), but by displacing the settings into some lesser-known areas: China in "Kubla Khan," South Pole in *Ancient Mariner,* and Circassia in "The Lewti." The vague geography of these settings, Vallins argues, allowed Coleridge in integrating the earthly and the spiritual, the mundane and the imaginative, the sensuous and the intellectual, the spontaneous and the philosophical. Finding an alternative space beyond the Judeo–Christian and the Hindu framework helped the poet in uniting the opposite poles of his mind beyond duality (119–130).

However, interpreting the poem philosophically ignoring the contemporary geopolitics concerning China would be an incomplete reading of it. Just as the Hastings trial brought India to the attention of the British, the Macartney embassy of 1792–1794 to China brought China to the forefront. The mission was a diplomatic failure but the ambassador and his companions produced books and journals on their Chinese experience, and these accounts essentially changed the European perception of China. The cause of the failure of the embassy was reported to be the refusal of the British ambassador to kowtow before the Chinese emperor. The Chinese ritual kowtowing became widely known during the Romantic period and, as Kitson notes, it became a symbol of Oriental despotism: "The kowtow like the infanticide, the sati, the lingchhi, or cannibalism became a scandal in the nineteenth century British discourse, a marker of barbarism indicating lack of civilization" ("The 'Kowtow' Controversy" 20).

Although the declared source of the poem is Purchas's *Pilgrimage*, Sir William Chambers' "Dissertation on Oriental Gardening" contained many passages describing Chinese gardens, and the landscape of "Kubla Khan" seems to follow the discourse on the Chinese garden in Chambers. Two other sources for Coleridge might have been Macartney's journals and George Staunton's *An Authentic Account of an Embassy from the King of Great Britain to the Emperor of China* (1797) as both of the authors dwelt in detail on the Chinese garden. Chambers argued that the Chinese artfully employed the "pleasing, horrid and enchanted" features of nature in designing their garden. The pleasing aspect of the Chinese garden is seen in lines six to nine, the horrible in lines fourteen to sixteen and the enchanted in lines seventeen to twenty-nine in "Kubla Khan" (Katsyuama 197–199). An extensive description of King Qianlong's garden at Yuen-min-yuen and in Beijing, and also his summer palace at Zhe-hol is given by Staunton and Macartney. There are many passages with descriptions of Chinese landscape almost similar to "Kubla Khan." One of such passages may be quoted here:

> In many places immense woods, chiefly oaks, pines and chestnuts, grow upon almost perpendicular steeps and force their sturdy roots through every resistance of surface, and of soil, where vegetation would seem almost impossible. These woods often clamber over the loftiest pinnacles of the stony hills, or gathering on the skirts of them, descend with a rapid sweep, and bury themselves in the deepest valleys . . . a cataract tumbling from above, raging with foam and rebounding with a thousand echoes from below or silently engulphed in a gloomy pool or yawning chasm. (Macartney 132)

That Coleridge was following the development in China is evident from his writings. In his *Lectures 1795: On Politics and Religion,* Coleridge referred to the ritual of the kowtow: "I have . . . read in some Eastern courts the ambassadors from Europe have their arms pinioned while they speak to the despot"(*The Collected Works* 1: 294). Considering the possible Chinese influence on Coleridge, "Kubla Khan" is interpreted by Nigel Leask as a "Chinese poem." Leask argues that in "Kubla Khan," Coleridge is presenting a coded satire on George III's government for his attempt to terrify the people into submission in the manner of the Chinese emperor Kubla Khan and his contemporary descendant, Qianlong ("Road to Xanadu Revisited").

The interpretation of "Kubla Khan" changes with the change in its locus. In the context of India, it becomes a poem concerned with imperial anxiety. Read in the context of Egypt, it is a critique of Napoleonic imperialism—a critique of his "commanding genius" as opposed to the "absolute genius" of the poet.[12] China, as a geopolitical space, gets connected to Coleridge's critique of despotism, Eastern or Western. In whatever way we chose to interpret the poem, "The Orientalist exterior," as Fulford argues, "uncovers an occidental and psychological interior" (Fulford, "Poetic bowers" 118). We may reach an interesting conclusion by taking a lead from Javed Majid who interprets the imagery of plumbing and probing depth in Southey's Eastern epics as symbolic of the attempt to tap in new sources of creativity made available by the Oriental Renaissance. Coleridge's images of the river, fountain, and the "damsel with a dulcimer" have been interpreted with reference to poetic inspiration in the Greco-Roman tradition, but like the other Romantics, Coleridge was also trying to tap in the new source of creativity. Negotiating this new source of creativity, however, was fraught with problems. The Oriental Renaissance, as we have seen, challenged the superiority of the Greco-Roman cultural tradition and the primacy of Christianity. Jones knew this even when he compared "Oriental Firdous" with Grecian Homer or wrote on the ancientness of the Hindu scriptures. The demonic aspect of Kubla's pleasure garden reflects the anxiety and fear of the poet caused by the Oriental Renaissance. The 'sun' and the 'ice,' the 'holy' and the 'savage', could co-exist only because both fear and fascination with the East gripped the Western psyche. The figure of the Abyssinian maid seems to be Coleridge's solution to the anxiety. By locating the muse in Abyssinia, Coleridge tries to steer clear of this anxiety. During the Romantic period, Iran and Ethiopia were in contention for the seat of an ancient civilization. Abyssinia was associated both with the East and the West, as argued by Shaffer and Beer (*Coleridge the Visionary*). Shaffer has shown regarding the writings of Jones, Lowth, and Eichhorn that in the eighteenth century, Abyssinia was regarded as the geopolitical center of Oriental civilization with a Mosaic link. Further, Shaffer points out that India and Abyssinia might have been also linked in Coleridge's imagination through the figure of the Egyptian goddess Isis and the Indian Goddess Isani as known in Bengal (118–121). Abyssinia, therefore, provided the poet with a perfect setting for domesticating the oriental 'springs.'

Finally, a point must be made about the preface that Coleridge wrote to introduce the poem in 1816. In the preface, Coleridge presents the poem only as a "psychological curiosity." In 1816–1817 Coleridge published "Kubla Khan" and "Christabel" and republished *Ancient Mariner*. All these poems were written in the late 1790s, and in 1816–1817, he added the paratexts—prefaces and glosses—apparently to make the poems more intelligible to the readers. Tim Fulford in his essay "Coleridge and the Oriental Tale" draws our attention to the changes that Coleridge made while republishing *Ancient Mariner* in 1817. The 1797 version of the poem had a subtitle "A Poet's Reverie," "manifesting the structure of a waking dream" (221). In the 1817 version, the subtitle was omitted. Similarly, "Kubla Khan" was conceived as a dream poem, but Coleridge dismisses it as a psychological curiosity in the 1816 preface. The poems could no longer be projected as reveries. Fulford argues that it was the result of Coleridge's compromise with his growing conservatism and increasing distance from early radicalism. Coleridge tried to dismiss his earlier effort at syncretism and disown the Eastern influence. From a radical, a 'Jacobin' and a Unitarian in the 1790s, Coleridge became a supporter of the state and the Anglican Church after 1805; from an opium enthusiast and wayward genius, he was trying to project himself as a rational poet and thinker.[13] Coleridge's attitude toward the East, colonialism and slavery also underwent drastic changes after the Maltan phase of his career. His gradual turn to parasitism and Trinitarian Christianity led the poet to contradict his earlier positions. Therefore, Garcia is right to define the preface to "Kubla Khan" as a "conservative act of self-effacement" (*Islam and English Enlightenment* 181). In the 1790s, Coleridge could think of a poem based on syncretism, but in 1816, he rejected his earlier syncretism as a mere fancy.

Coleridge was involved in collaboration with two of his fellow poets. His collaboration with Southey led to the production of some famous specimens of literary Orientalism. The most celebrated collaboration of the Romantic period, however, was between Wordsworth and Coleridge and it gave birth to the defining moment for Romanticism with the publication of the *Lyrical Ballads* (1798). Wordsworth's reading on the Orient might not be equivalent to that of Coleridge or Southey and his poetry does not contain extensive references to the East, but there are poems by Wordsworth with a distinct Eastern strain. More significantly, Wordsworth's poetic theory in the Preface to *Lyrical Ballads* is indebted to the Eastern poetic customs. It bears distinct marks of Jones's formulations on poetry and poetic diction.

As early as in 1946 V. de Sola Pinto pointed out the similarities between Jones and Wordsworth in their poetic theories. He observed that the principle in which Jones finds the origin of poetry and the other arts is "a strong and animated expression of the human passions, of joy and grief, love and hate, admiration and anger, sometimes pure and unmixed, sometimes modified and combined." For Pinto, it "anticipates (and probably influenced) the views of Wordsworth, Coleridge, and Shelley, and it foreshadows the teaching of Benedetto Croce" (690). The 1772 publication of William Jones's *Poems Consisting Chiefly of Translations from the Asiatic Languages* and the two essays added to this, "On the Poetry of the Eastern Nations" and "Essay on the Arts, Commonly Called Imitative," according to M.H. Abrams, deliberately set out to revise the base of the neoclassical theory of poetry and poetic genres. Jones did this, Abrams suggests, by weaving together ideas drawn from Longinus, the old doctrine of poetic inspiration, and recent theories of the emotional and imaginative origin of poetry, and a major emphasis on the lyric form and the "primitive and spontaneous" poetry of the Eastern nations. What the "Asiatick" "primitive and spontaneous lyric" shows, according to Jones, is that Aristotle was wrong: poetry is not produced by imitation, but by a very different principle, "which must be sought for in the deepest recesses of the human mind." Abrams concludes that well before the *Lyrical Ballads* was published, "the association of the lyric with an expressive theory of culture complemented its abstraction in the new modern system of genre" (84–88). Similarly, Garland Cannon observes that both "philosophically and artistically, Jones early perceived the poor state of English poetry." Cannon comments that if the relevant questions asked by Jones in various books and answers suggested to these are synthesized into a single critical essay, it would have anticipated Wordsworth's "philosophical essay" in the 1800 edition of the *Lyrical Ballads* ("Oriental Jones: Scholarship" 42).

None of the above critics, however, has been bold enough to use the term 'influence'; they have spoken of a possibility. It was Javed Majid, who used the term 'influence' (171–173) for the first time. The reason behind this 'probability' theory, perhaps, is the lack of evidence that Wordsworth read Jones's essays. Duncan Wu, in *Wordsworth's Reading 1770–1799*, suggests that Wordsworth read the review of Jones's *Institutes of Hindu Law* by Coleridge published in March 1798 in *The Critical Review*. If Coleridge reviewed it, it is also possible that Wordsworth had read the works of Jones because Wordsworth worked in close tandem with Coleridge during 1797–1798. It is possible, therefore, that Wordsworth was also familiar with the 1772 edition of Jones's *Poems* or other works by Jones. That Wordsworth had sustained interest in the East and Eastern literature, is proved by the catalog of Wordsworth's book prepared by his daughter. The list of books includes several versions of the *Nights*, *Arabian Tales or continuation of the Arabian Nights Entertainments*, *The Thousand and One Days or Persian Tales*, and *The Tales of the Genii.* Apart from these Oriental (or pseudo-Oriental) Tales, Wordsworth had a grammar of Arabic language by Thomas Arpenius, translations of Sa'di's works, J.D. Carlyle's *Specimens of the Arabian Poetry*, and several other works on the Orient by European authors, Simon Ockley's *The History of the Saracens,* Jean Louis Marie's *Travels through Barbary,* Purchas's *Pilgrimage,* Jean Antoine Dubois's, *Descriptions of the Characters, Manners and Customs of the people of India,* Lady Wortley Montague's *Letters,* to mention a few of them.[14] Wordsworth's interest in Eastern poetry in the 1790s is also substantiated by the fact of his reading of Ahamad Ardabili's *A Series of Poems, Containing the Plaints of Consolations and Delights of Achmed Ardebeili, a Persian Exile* (1797). Wordsworth read the poems in 1797 (Wu, *Wordsworth's Readings* 6). Another relevant point to remember in this context is, once Wordsworth was advised by his uncle to do a course in Oriental literature. He wrote in a letter to his friend, William Matthews on November 23, 1791: "My uncle, the clergyman, proposed to me a short time ago to begin a course of Oriental literature, thinking that it was the best field for a person to distinguish himself, as a man of letters. To oblige him I consented to peruse the plan after my return from the continent" (*Letters of the Wordsworth Family* 38). Wordsworth's reading list also shows that he was familiar with Sa'di's works and other Perso-Arabic poets upon whom Jones founded his poetics. An examination of the themes and issues taken up by Jones in his essays and prefaces and Wordsworth in his Preface to *Lyrical Ballads* and the parallels in their argument make the case of Eastern influence on Wordsworth stronger.

Jones's theory that poetry is not imitative but expressive and Wordsworth's formulations in the Preface are almost identical. Prefiguring Wordsworth's claim that poetry has its origin in powerful feelings, Jones wrote in his "Essay on the Arts, Commonly Called Imitative": "poetry was originally no more than a strong and animated expression of the human passions of *joy* and *grief*, *love* and *hate*, *admiration* and *anger*, sometimes pure and unmixed, sometimes variously modified and combined. . ."[15] (Pachori 13). Jones goes on enumerating his expressive theory:

> Thus will each artist gain his end, not by *imitating* the works of nature, but by assuming her power, and causing the same effect upon the imagination, which her charms produce to the senses: this must be the chief object of a poet, a musician, and a painter, who know that *great effects are not produced by minute details, but by the general spirit of the whole piece, and that a gaudy composition may strike the mind for a short time, but that the beauties of simplicity are both more delightful, and more permanent.* (Pachori 135)

The passage is remarkable for several reasons: Firstly, Jones clearly states that imitation is not the end of poetry; secondly, imagination is identified as an important force to achieve the desired poetic effect;

and thirdly, for Jones's rejection of the gaudy in favor of the simple.' In a similar vein, Wordsworth would argue in favor of expressive poetry, eulogize imagination, and condemn poetic diction of the neoclassical writers for their "gaudiness and inane phraseology" (Preface 163).[16] One cannot miss the striking intertextual parallels.

The role of imagination in the creative process is deliberated on by Jones again in his "Essay on the Poetry of the Eastern Nations." He praises the "Asiaticks" for the "liveliness of their fancy and the richness of their invention" (Pachori 135) connecting his theory of imagination to Eastern poetics. Jones's view that the poet assumes "her (nature's) power" "causing the same effect upon the imagination" is also repeated by Wordsworth. The view that imaginative power helps poetry to act by a "kind of substitution," is reflected in Wordsworth when he remarks that the poet has the "ability to conjuring up in himself the passions which are indeed far from being the same as those produced by real events, yet . . . do more." The only difference between the two is, Wordsworth is more positive than Jones about what the later calls 'substitution': "The power of imagination to produce images in the absence of objects is crucial to Wordsworth's own poetry and to his theory of it" (Majid 172).

Jones's "Essay on the Arts Commonly Called Imitative" is also remarkable for linking poetic inspiration to nature. Jones writes that living amid beautiful forms of nature, the Arabians drew their stimulus from it: The Arabians took "all their notions of *felicity* . . . from the *freshness* and the *verdure.*" "[T]hey pass their lives in the highest pleasure, of which they have any conception, in the contemplation of the most delightful objects, and in the enjoyment of perpetual spring" (Pachori 138). One is reminded of Wordsworth's "Tintern Abbey," especially the poet's address to Dorothy where the poet advises her to contemplate the scene at the abbey as a perpetual source of pleasure. Jones observes that

> the Arabians being perpetually conversant with the most beautiful objects, spending a calm and agreeable life in a finer climate, being extremely addicted to the softer passions, and having the advantage

> of a language singularly adapted to poetry must be naturally excellent poets, provided that their manners and customs be favourable to the cultivation of their art. (Pachori 139)

This observation on the relationship between poetry and beautiful forms of nature is echoed by Wordsworth in the Preface. For Wordsworth, the elemental passions of men remain pure in individuals who live amidst nature and in that life of simplicity the durable passions are best assimilated. Wordsworth considers the life of the people living close to nature as the true subject matter of poetry.

Regarding the language of prose and poetry, Jones observed that "*fine sentiments delivered in prose were like gems scattered at random, but that, when they were confined in a poetical measure, they resembled bracelets and strings of pearls*" (Pachori 140). Wordsworth expresses a similar view. For Wordsworth, there is no essential difference between prose and poetry except that of meter: "And it would be a most easy task to prove to him, that not only the language of a large portion of every good poem, even of the most elevated character, must necessarily, except with reference to the metre, in no respect differs from that of good prose" (168). Jones concludes his essay with the observation on the lack of poetic inspiration for English poetry and suggests:

> That, if the principal writings of the Asiaticks, which are reposited in our publick libraries, were printed with the usual advantage of notes and illustrations, and if the languages of the Eastern nations were studied in our places of education, where every other branch of useful knowledge is taught to perfection, a new and ample field would be opened for speculation; we should have a more extensive insight into the history of the human mind, we should be furnished with a new set of images and similitudes, and a number of excellent compositions would be brought to light, which future scholars might explain, and future poets might imitate. (Pachori 144)

Wordsworth, in the Preface, seems to develop the full implication of Jones's observations. He took the responsibility to revive English poetry following the suggestion of Jones, though he did not shift his poetic scene to the Orient. His ideas of poetic diction, poetic language, the subject matter of poetry, view of Nature and man, view of poetry as expressive owe to the writings of Jones. Needless to say, Jones's views were inspired by his reading of Eastern poetry. Wordsworth in writing the manifesto of Romanticism, therefore, was indebted to the Oriental Renaissance of the eighteenth century and to a large extent to "oriental Jones."

When it comes to Wordsworth's poetic practice, the dream of the Arab episode in Book V of *The Prelude* resonates with Jones's idea that the home of impassioned poetry is the East. Referring to the writings of the Arabians, Jones, in his "Essay on the Arts," observes that among the Arabians "*dramatick poetry* of every sort is wholly unknown, yet, where the pleasing arts, *of expressing the passions in verse, and of enforcing that expression by melody*, are cultivated to a degree of enthusiasm" (Pachori 131). Wordsworth's dreamer in Book V hears a voice from the shell that can be defined as a passionate "expression by melody." The language of the voice is not known to the dreamer, yet it impresses meaning upon him because of the passion contained in it:

> And heard that instant in unknown tongue
> Which yet I understood, articulate sounds,
> Aloud prophetic blast of harmony. (Book V, ll. 94–99)

Wordsworth seems to follow Jones's (and his own) dictum that "greatest effect [of poetry] is not produced by imitation but by a very different principle which must be sought for in the deepest recesses of the human mind" (Pachori 131). The "powerful feelings" coming out of the "deepest recesses of the human mind" would cut through the linguistic borders. So, the "passions" uttered in an "unknown tongue" impress meaning upon the dreamer.

Book V of *The Prelude* with its enigmatic dream of the Arab is very significant in terms of evaluating Wordsworth's debt to the Oriental Renaissance. The dream sequence has received much critical attention and has been interpreted from multiple perspectives. The central concerns of these interpretations have been: firstly, whose dream it is; secondly, whether the dream is real or just an artificial strategy; and thirdly, what the dream does signify. In all versions of *The Prelude* before 1839, the dream was attributed to a friend. Later, Wordsworth removed the friend from the narrative and introduced himself as the dreamer. This has led to speculations about the possible identity of the dreamer. James Worthington Smyser interprets the dream of the Arab as derived from the three dreams of Descartes on November 10, 1619. In the last of these dreams, Descartes beheld two books—a dictionary containing all scientific knowledge and a book of poetry. Regarding this, he interprets the stone and the shell as representing science and poetry, respectively. Smyser acknowledges that the friend Wordsworth refers to might be Coleridge, but he argues in favor of Michel de Beaupuy.[17] David Chandler in "Robert Southey and 'The Prelude's Arab Dream" interprets the dream episode with reference to Southey's dream of the deluge, and his intention to write a poem on it and connects the Arab Bedouin hero in *Thalaba* to the presentation of the Bedouin in *The Prelude*. He concludes that the friend is none but Southey, whose dream is delineated by Wordsworth. However, there are others who interpret the dream as Wordsworth's own and consider it a more logical explanation. In 1926, Selincourt defended the dream as Wordsworth's own (526), but J. Hillis Miller in 1972 interpreted the dream as a deliberate invention (138).

Most of the recent interpretations have analyzed the dream sequence as an embodiment of Wordsworth's idea of poetry and poetic creation. Galperin, for example, observes that we must consider Wordsworth's account of the dream vision in Book V as self-reflexive: "Through the Arab dream, Wordsworth – the resisting writer – depicts himself, the 'Poet,' for what he is: a crazed, deluded wanderer implicated in a mythic or representational structure that is uncompletable" (621–622). Gordon K. Thomas provides an almost similar perspective and according to him, Wordsworth is concerned with the lasting quality of written language. For Thomas, the dream is real, though borrowed from Descartes. Robert Philmus subjects the dream to Freudian interpretation. For Philmus, "the real thought-content of the dream . . . dramatizes an anxiety about the destructibility, the mortality, of the dreamer, not about that of all humankind or of the embodiments of its spirit" (186). Whether the dream is real or imaginary or by Wordsworth or his friend, the critics agree that it is associated with poetry and poetics.

Although there had been much source hunting for the dream episode in *The Prelude*, little or no exploration has been made into the possibility of reading the dream as influenced by the *Nights*, a book Wordsworth repeatedly refers to in Book V. However, there is a contention regarding the editions Wordsworth possibly read. He refers to a "yellow canvas-covered" (461) abridged version of the *Nights* and a four-volume set (466). In *Wordsworth's Reading 1770–1799,* Duncun Wu suggests that Wordsworth was possibly referring to the four-volume edition of the *Arabian Nights Entertainments: Consisting of One Thousand and One Stories…* that was first published from Manchester in 1777 and many times thereafter (6). However, there were many other multi-volume editions available in England, and Susan Wolfson claims that in all likelihood, Wordsworth was referring to the four-volume edition published in 1778 and reprinted in 1789 by T. Longman.[18] Going by Wolfson's suggestion we may identify a tale in the 1789 T. Longman edition that bears a strong similarity to Wordsworth's dream sequence.

The concerned tale is "The History of the Third Calender, a King's Son," where Agib, the prince relates his experience of a shipwreck in a sea voyage and what happens thereafter. The shipwrecks near the Magnet Mountain as all its iron nails fly off. Every person on board dies except the prince, who is miraculously saved from drowning by holding on to a plank. When borne ashore, Agib finds a flight of steps leading to the summit of the mountain. As it was foretold by the pilot of the wrecked ship, he finds a dome of brass at the top of the mountain and the on top of the dome "stands a horse of the same metal, with a rider on his back, who has a plate of lead fixed to his breast, upon which some talismanical characters are engraven. . . ." Exhausted, Agib falls asleep under the dome and dreams:

> I pass'd the night under the dome, and in my sleep an old grave man appear'd to me, and said, Hearken, Agib, as soon as thou art awake, dig up the ground under thy feet; thou shalt find a bow of brass, and three arrows of lead, that are made under certain constellations, to deliver mankind from so many calamities that threaten them. Shoot the three arrows at the statue, and the rider shall fall into the sea, but the horse will fall down by thy side, which thou must bury in the same place from whence you took the bow and arrows: This being done, the sea will swell and rise up to the foot of the dome that stands upon the top of the mountain: When it is come up so high, thou shalt see a boat with one man and an oar in each hand: This man is also of metal, but different from that thou hast thrown down; step on board to him, without mentioning the name of God, and let him conduct thee. He will in ten days' time, bring thee into another sea, where thou shalt find an opportunity to get home to thy country safe and sound, provided, as I have told thee, thou dost not mention the name of God during the whole voyage.

After he wakes up he performs the bidding of the mysterious voice:

> When I awak'd I was very much comforted by the vision, and did not fail to observe everything that he had commanded me. I took the bow and arrows out of the ground, shot 'em at the horseman, and with the third arrow I overthrew him, and he fell into the sea, and the horse sell by my side, which I buried in the place whence I took the bow and arrows; and in the mean; time, the sea swell'd and rose up by degrees: When it came as high as the foot of the dome that stood upon the top of the mountain, I saw as far as, a boat rowing towards me, and I returned God thanks that everything succeeded according to my dream.
>
> At last the boat came ashore, and I saw the man was made of metal, according as I had dreamt. I stept aboard, and took great heed not to pronounce the name of God, neither spoke I one word at all; I sat

> down, and the man of metal began to row off from the mountain. He row'd without ceasing till the ninth day, that I saw some islands, which put me in hopes that I should be out of all the danger that I was afraid of. The excess of my joy made me forget what I was forbidden to do: God's name be blest, said I, the Lord be praised.
>
> I had no sooner spoke those words, but the boat sunk with the man of metal, and leaving me upon the surface, I swam the remaining part of the day towards that land which appeared nearest to me.[19]

The content of the dream, as well as what happens before and after it, are relevant to a reading of the dream sequence in Wordsworth. The Bedouin in Wordsworth seems to be a combination of the horseman sitting at the top of the dome who rides a horse of brass and the mysterious boatman, who brings the prince to safety, but casts him in the sea when he takes the name of Allah. Wordsworth's Bedouin rides a horse, and like the boatmen looks like a savior to the dreamer: "Much I rejoiced, not doubting but a guide/ Was present..." (81–82); yet the boatman/horseman leaves the dreamer hopeless: "...he hurried on/ Reckless of me..." (16–17). The two paddles in the hand of the boatman from the dream of the prince might have been fused with the two books of Descartes. Both the dreams have the seashore as their setting and a fear of the deluge is integral to both of them. Very significantly, the motif of the messiah or savior is central to the tale as well as to Wordsworth's dream. The similarities between the tale and Wordsworth's dream are so striking that one cannot but conclude that Wordsworth was inspired by the tale of the Third Calender prince. The argument becomes stronger when one considers the fact that Book V of *The Prelude* contains a long panegyric to the *Nights*. The passages describe Wordsworth's enchantment with the *Nights* and gives details of its effect upon his young mind. As Wordsworth describes it, the "precious treasure" (460), "the tales that charm away the wakeful night in Araby" (520) had a lasting impact on the poet.

Smyser interprets the dream as expressing Wordsworth's idea that poetry is more valuable than science. In the dream episode,

Wordsworth comments on the comparative value of the two books: "the Arab told me that the stone" was "Euclid's elements" and the shell "said he" was "something more worth" (85–90). For Wordsworth, "poetry is the impassioned expression which is in the face of all Science" (Preface 174). Theresa M. Kelley argues that Wordsworth does not mean to assert the dominance of poetry over science. For Kelley "the shell embodies a new kind of knowledge which is at once geometrical and poetic" (565). This interpretation is more acceptable since the Arabs were preservers not only of poetic tradition but also of the scientific tradition. As Ernest Bernhardt-Kabisch puts it, "As an Arab, he (the Bedouin) is one of a nation of preservers and transmitters who rescued Greek science and metaphysics from oblivion . . . and the Age of Wordsworth also regarded Arabia as a fountainhead of romance and eloquence specially of figurative expression if not the originators of modern Romantic poets as such" (qtd. in Caracciolo 66).

Bernhardt-Kabisch's observation leads to a recent analysis by Samar Attar, who traces the dream of the Arab episode to the Arabian novel, *Hayy Ibn Yakzan*. According to Attar, Wordsworth must have heard of *Hayy Ibn Yakzan* as it was translated into English by Simon Ockley, whose *History of the Saracens* was in his library. Attar argues that Wordsworth might not have read Ibn Tufyal's novel, but a number of philosophers who Wordsworth read were influenced by the novel. Rousseau was one of the admirers of the novel and his *Emile* was inspired by it; Godwin admired Tufyal; Descartes was inspired by Hayy in whose figure reason is combined with imagination: "*Hayy Ibn Yaqzan* who introduced rationalism in Europe . . . also spoke about the significance of that mystic vision which was akin to 'the sparks of fire in flints'" (93). Attar, therefore, raises the question: "Is it possible that the uncouth stranger in Wordsworth's poem, who is on mission to bury his 'twofold treasure', a stone and a shell that represent geometry and god, and science and imagination before 'the fleet waters of the drowning world' destroy them is none but Hayy

Ibn Yaqzan?" (93). Attar further argues that the very design of *The Prelude* is similar to that of *Hayy Ibn Yakzan*. *Hayy Ibn Yakzan* is considered an early example of *bildungsroman; The Prelude* is also a kind of *bildungsroman* that narrates the physical and psychological development of the poet from early childhood (89). There are other poems by Wordsworth where his debt to *Hayy Ibn Yakzan* can be traced. The "Lucy Poems" in particular seem to be indebted to *Hayy Ibn Yakzan*. Lucy grows up in the midst of nature without any human help and is educated by nature: "She shall be mine, and I will make/A lady of my own." Lucy seems to be the female counterpart of Hayy. She learns from the various activities and elements of nature: the "floating clouds," "the motions of the storm" "shall mould the maiden's form /By silent sympathy" (218).[20] Lucy, like Hayy, is taught by nature without human intervention. According to Attar, a similar relationship between man and nature is further developed in Wordsworth's "Intimations of Immortality from Recollection of Early Childhood" and "Tintern Abbey." Wordsworth's journey in the poems is from the "sensuous" enjoyment of nature to the "sublime," "the heavenly life of the hermit as seen in the natural and moral man Hayy Ibn Yaqzan" (87).

Even though Wordsworth was influenced by Eastern literature and Jones's discourse on Eastern poetry, he did not always endorse the East. Jones's celebration of the fertile Arabian landscape and climate as an inspiration for expressive poetry was rejected by Wordsworth. He primarily highlighted the arid deserts of the Middle East in his poems and the oasis landscape is presented with its association with the unnatural rather than a place of natural abundance. Further, Wordsworth's poetry of the desert wastes of the Middle East indicated the enormous destructive power of the despotic governments to lay waste nature (Haddad 105; Bewell, *Wordsworth and Enlightenment* 241). Emily Haddad contends that in poems like "Septimi Gades," "The Haunted Tree," and "The Solitary Reaper," Wordsworth foregrounds the contrast between nature in Europe and nature in the

Middle East. In "Septimi Gades," the landscapes from Rhone region in France and Grasmere in England is contrasted with pale Arabian desert:

> To him who faint and heartless stands
> On pale Arabia's thirsty sands,
> How fair that fountain seems
> Where last beneath the palmy shade
> In bowers of rose and jasmine laid,
> He quaffed the living streams. (258)

The speaker–traveler does not find the Arabian landscape pleasant or homely and the pleasant home is in the "quiet vale" of Grasmere. In "The Haunted Tree" Wordsworth links art and the Middle East:

> Couch beautiful as e'er for earthly use
> Was fashioned; whether, by the hand of Art
> That eastern Sultan, amid flowers enwrought
> On silken tissue, might diffuse his limbs
> In languor; or, by Nature, for repose
> Of panting Wood-nymph, wearied with the chase. (258)

Like Southey, Wordsworth associated Oriental art with artificiality. Haddad argues that Wordsworth associates art and the Middle East, but he dissociates it from nature. Both "art and the Middle East are defined ontologically in terms of their opposition to nature." The Middle Eastern landscape, therefore, cannot be the ideal aesthetic landscape for Wordsworth, though it has all the qualities of a typically Wordsworthian landscape (104–107; 155–157).

There are a number of other poems by Wordsworth that refer to the Middle East and some of these poems are marked by a sense of religious hostility, characteristic of medieval crusading romances. There are two verses in *Ecclesiastical Sonnets* entitled "Crusades" and "Crusaders."[21] In the first of these sonnets, Wordsworth represents Muslims as the fearful enemy of Christendom by raising the issue of Muslim occupation of Spain: "The crescent glitters on the towers of

Spain; / And soft Italia feels renewed alarms" (508). The 'scimitar' (which has been repeatedly used in Western literature as a symbol of Eastern cruelty) is not resistible:

> All Christendom: - they sweep along (was never
> So huge a host!) -to tear from the Unbeliever
> The Precious tomb, their haven of salvation. (508)

Surprisingly, Wordsworth refers to the hanging tomb of the prophet Muhammad, a misconception already rectified by the Western writers. The other sonnet is a meditation upon the sad fate of the crusaders. However, the crusader's life is glorified: "the romance / Of many-coloured life the Fortune pours / Round the Crusaders" (512). In the sonnet "Scene in Venice," Wordsworth describes the "Successor" of Caesar "whose strong arm the orient could not check/ He, who had held the Soldan at his beck" (509). The sonnet reminds us of an earlier sonnet, "On the Extinction of the Venetian Republic" where the poet meditates on the imperial glory of Venice and its subsequent decline: "Once did she hold the gorgeous east in fee; / And was safeguard of the west" but now these "glories fade" "titles vanish and that strength decay" (363).

Wordsworth represents the Islamic East as the Other in these poems. The first two sonnets are set in the medieval period and sentiments expressed in them can be attributed to the subjects that Wordsworth writes about. However, the third sonnet is on contemporary Venice. It laments that the city has lost its sway over the East. When Wordsworth wrote the sonnet, it was France and Austria who controlled Venice. The status of Venice saw a gradual decline after the discovery of the sea route to India (by the Portuguese) and other Eastern nations during the sixteenth century. The loss of prominence of the port of Venice was more the result of the infighting of the European superpowers, but Wordsworth does not concentrate on it. On the contrary, he looks back to the time when it commanded the Eastern nations.

Two other poems, "The Egyptian Lady or The Romance of the Water Lily" and "The Armenian Lady's Love" are also characterized by a sense of enmity between the non-Christian Middle East and the Christendom. Both the poems were composed late in his career and were published in 1835. They are written in imitation of the medieval romances and are set in medieval times. The poems can be interpreted as Wordsworth's 'conversion' poems. In the first poem, Wordsworth narrates how an Egyptian maiden is carried into the court of Arthur and is married to Galahad, one of the Knights of the Round Table. The maiden is a 'heathen' Egyptian woman whose father was indebted to Arthur for saving his Kingdom, and as Arthur narrates, the king "...plighted word/That he would turn to Christ our Lord,/And his dear daughter on a Knight bestow" (444). "Her birth was heathen" but she was meant to be converted like his father in recompense to the debt to Arthur. When "fair Izonda" reaches Arthur's court, her destiny is fulfilled. However, the journey of the Egyptian maid is not hazard-free. When "the ship to Christ devoted / From the land of Nile did go," Merlin, the magician wrecked the ship which was carrying her to Arthur's court. Merlin did this because he saw a 'heathen' symbol of the "Egyptian Goddess with a Lily" (the Goddess Nefertem or Nefertum). Merlin repents his action when the 'good' sorceress Nina tells him that the ship carried "the wished for bride" meant for Arthur's court. Nina and Merlin rescue Izonda, and Merlin carries her to Arthur's court in a chariot drawn by "two mute Swans." The poem contains several elements common to the Oriental Tale and Romantic verse narratives: an Eastern setting, a journey, an innocent heroine, a sorceress and a magician (both of whom turn out to be good), supernatural intervention, and some magical carriages. However, Wordsworth's narrative is rather short and he does not provide annotations as other writers of the verse narrative do.

Whereas Izonda is a pagan heroine, the lady in "The Armenian Lady's Love" is the "Daughter of the proud Soldan." She "loved a Christian slave," an imprisoned knight. In representing the lady,

Wordsworth follows the Western prejudice as she is characterized as a sensual and cunning woman. She approaches the Christian slave with some sensual intent but the refusal of the slave to indulge in sex turns her lust into respect and love for him. Wordsworth nurtures the misconceived notion that Islam encourages sexual profligacy: "[S]he shrunk from trust / In a sensual creed that trampled / Woman's birthright into dust." The lines at once transport us to the days of the Crusades. The "sensual creed" is compared to Christianity that celebrates wedded love: "Wedded love with loyal Christians, / Lady is a mystery rare" (163). The sultan's daughter escapes with the slave (the knight) and reaches the deck of Venice, where the knight's slave who waited long for his lord, welcomes him by falling on his knee. Surprisingly, Wordsworth does not find anything wrong with this slavery. The "Christian slave" (now turned Lord in his country) orders his servant to bring his wife and asks him to inform her of the Armenian lady, who is now described as "innocent and meek and good" (164). The Armenian lady might have been lustful and cunning but she will redeem herself by embracing Christianity: "with misbelievers bred; but the dark night / Will holy church disperse, by beams of gospel light" (164). Once converted, all the darkness of the previous faith is removed. The poem ends with a celebratory epitaph to the knight who lived a peaceful life with two wedded wives. The religious polemic is almost identical with the medieval romances where marriage and conversion were envisaged as a means to conquer the religious Other. This is also true of "The Egyptian Maid" where the Other is won over through marriage.

It is not easy to understand the reason behind the crusading spirit of these poems. There was no atmosphere of conflict between the Islamic East and Britain; on the contrary, Britain maintained a friendship with the Turkish rulers. The only cause of concern for some groups of Britons was the Turkish sway over Greece and the Greek War of Independence that started in the 1820s. Britain did not lend much support to the issue of Greek independence. Philhellenism was on the rise and accounts for the hostility of later Romantics like Byron and Shelley toward the Islamic Middle East. The Grecian war of independence against the Muslim rulers of Turkey was supported by Byron and Shelley and consequently, they nurtured a sort of hostility toward the Turkish rulers. They often censured the British government for not helping the Greek cause. Wordsworth, however, does not refer to Greece; rather he refers to Venice and Rome and sets them in opposition to the East. This shows the validity of Webb's argument that Wordsworth expressed the primacy of Christianity and Northern Christian European and English culture over the Eastern. The representation of Otherness in the non-Western pagan and the Islamic people and presentation of Christianity as the better religion in "The Armenian Lady's Love" and "The Egyptian Maid" can be attributed to the rise of Anglicanism and Anglo-centrism.

That Wordsworth gave primacy to Christianity and English culture can be seen in *The Prelude*. Forest Pyle in the chapter on Wordsworth in *The Ideology of Imagination: Subject and Society in the Discourse of Romanticism* tries to explain Wordsworth's Orientalism in *The Prelude* with reference to *Don Quixote,* which, according to Pyle is very important for understanding the representational politics in *The Prelude. Don Quixote* was written during the reign of Phillip II, which saw the expulsion of the Moors and the Muslims from Spain and it was a part of Catholic Spain's cultural politics that excluded the Arabs in an effort to consolidate Spanish identity. However, *Don Quixote* is presented to the readers as a translation from some Arabian manuscript. Pyle argues that there is a kind of duality in the novel—it appropriates an Arabian narrative, but the novel enacts enshrinement of the Spanish cultural identity. *The Prelude,* Forest contends, enacts a similar kind of cultural enshrinement by appropriating and expelling the Arab Other in Book V. He argues that the "interpretative instability and the representation of an internal Arab Otherness are intertwined and transferred through Wordsworth's reading of the novel in Book V of *The Prelude* and re-inscribed there in an apocalyptic dream." The "narrative instability" in both texts "is occasioned by the irruptions of the disturbing figure of Otherness" and it (Otherness) "serves ultimately to consolidate a sense of European cultural identity" (85). The process of consolidation of the European and British cultural identity is effected by gradual effacement and appropriation of the Arab Bedouin in the poem. Not only is the Bedouin equated to Don Quixote by Wordsworth, but the dream is also followed by an invocation to the tradition of English poetry that includes the names of British cultural icons like Milton and Shakespeare (Book V, 152–165). Pyle comments that the "logic of Wordsworth's dream text, the double movement of consolidation and dissolution that the poet calls imagination, reveals how figures of the Other are preserved in the structures of European monuments of cultural self-representation, such as *The Prelude*" (88). Regarding Hegel's *Aesthetics* and his theory of dialectics, Forest argues that "Romanticism is the consolidation of a European community predicated on the expulsion of the Oriental Other" (86). The "double movement of consolidation and dissolution" can be interpreted as an expression of Wordsworth's cultural anxiety—an anxiety that characterized the works of William Jones and Wordsworth's fellow Romantic poets. The superimposition of Quixote over the figure of the Bedouin is a marker of this anxiety.

Another aspect of Wordsworth's cultural and imperial anxiety in *The Prelude* is closely analyzed by Saree Makdisi by drawing our attention to Wordsworth's representation of the mob or the crowd in Book VIII. Makdisi notes that in *The Prelude* the crowd is nearly always an incipient mob, the embodiment of the dark side of Wordsworth's London, expressing the constant threat of disorder, and his fear of the city as an unknowable, unfathomable, and almost unmappable abyss. *The Prelude's* London crowd is, however, not only a crowd of Londoners or Britons. What makes the city and its constitutive crowd so infinitely complex, unfathomable, threatening, and even terrifying to Wordsworth, is that all of Britain's imperial relations and connections are also present and expressed in the teeming streets of London, and above all in the crowd scenes of Book VII. The crowd consists of all kinds of people: "all specimens of man / Through all the colours which the sun bestows, / And every character of form and face"; there are people of every nation and every climate (233–251). London is simultaneously the "center of empire and a condensed or miniature version of the entire space (of empire) of which it is the center" (*Romantic Imperialism* 33). Perhaps, most disturbing and threatening of all to a guilt-ridden William Wordsworth, is a stream of maimed, diseased, and crippled British soldiers and sailors— like the shadowy apparition in Book IV of *The Prelude*—now discharged and returned to haunt the island that sent them out to conquer (*Romantic Imperialism* 32). The metropole and the imperial periphery are not mutually exclusive—for the imperial periphery invade the metropole and destabilize the notion of order and purity. Wordsworth expresses his dislike for

> All moveables of wonder, from all parts
> Are here – Albinos, painted Indians, Dwarfs,
> The Horse of knowledge, and the learned Pig,
> The Stone-eater, the man that swallows fire,
> Giants, Ventriloquists, the Invisible Girl,
>
> ....
>
> All freaks of nature, all Promethean thoughts
> Of man, his dullness, madness, and their feats
> All jumbled up together to make up
> This Parliament of Monsters. (679–83, 688–91)

Wordsworth does not directly represent the East or the empire but the contemplation on London itself becomes a meditation on the empire. Thus, *The Prelude* is marked by imperial anxiety. The "Parliament of Monsters" is a site of infection. Wordsworth fears the infection of an imperial center by the periphery as it poses a challenge to the very notion of Englishness.

Apart from the general concern with Britain's growing empire, Wordsworth suffered a personal loss due to the greed that was fuelled by the growing trade with empires in the East. Wordsworth's brother, John Wordsworth (1772–1805) joined the East India Company in the capacity of a sailor and wanted to make a profit from the opium trade. Both Dorothy and William invested in the opium business of John. John's first voyage was to Barbados. When he made his first voyage to China in 1790, besides doing his job of midshipman, John wanted to make some private profit from the lucrative opium business to support Wordsworth in his poetic career. In his first voyage to China, he made some profit. After his return, he began collecting money for his second voyage to China and by this time, he became the captain of the ship, *Earl of Abergavenny*. Dorothy and William invested three hundred and fifty pounds in John's business hoping to gain profit which John boasted he would make (*Letters of John Wordsworth* 83, 93, 97–98). John, however, failed in his enterprise and he found himself in debt (*Letters of William and Dorothy* 517); but he could not rest at home and made another effort to raise money and about twenty thousand pounds were raised for his third voyage to Canton. This time the ship would sail via the profitable route of India and he was able to get his place in the ship with the help of Charles Grant and William Wilberforce. John was desperate for profit not only to repay his debt but also to help William. As William wrote: "[h]e encouraged me to persist in the plan which I had adopted: I would work for you and you attempt to do something for the world" (*Letters of William and Dorothy* 563). John died in this voyage and his death had a major impact upon Wordsworth's poetic career. Selincourt describes John's death as "the most terrible blow that either William or Dorothy ever suffered"; it "signals decline of Wordsworth's poetic power, his shift to Christianity, and his withdrawal into the isolation of Rydal mount" (187). To Selincourt's list, it may be added that this event also changed his attitude to the empire and the East and turned him not only to Christianity but also to the celebration of the local and the national as opposed to the global. Wordsworth mourned his brother's death in "Elegiac Verses in Memory of My Brother John Wordsworth." According to Stephen Gill, the course of *The Prelude* changed after his brother's death as Wordsworth began working with a greater zeal (242). Nigel Leak points to the poem "To the Daisy" to show how Wordsworth celebrates the imagined return of John. John is described quietly slumbering "Six weeks beneath the moving sea," a process, Wordsworth implies is that of the cleansing of John of his earthly cares and by implication of "eastern and commercial connections." He is then taken to the burial ground where John's loved flower the daisy grows. Kitson observes that although the poem "does not name China, India or the east in general, its emphatic stress on the 'native shore' that John now sleeps by and 'the English earth' the crew now stand on after returning from the voyage indicate that the orient must be the implied other . . ." ("The Wordsworths" 5).

Kitson also points to the representational politics and poetics of Wordsworth's Chinese gardens/landscapes. In contrast with his description of the metropolis ("the parliament of Monsters") in Book VII as a sort of pandemonium, Wordsworth presents the ideal "organic communal wholeness of the life at Grasmere Fair." According to Kitson, the communal life at Grasmere is privileged over the "commercial and tawdry business of the city" (*Forging Romantic China* 198). However, Wordsworth does not stop there as he compares his childhood home at the Lake District to the Qianlong Emperor's summer retreat of *Wanshu Yuan*. He describes the artificially created landscape of the garden in contrast to the Westmoreland countryside:

> Beauteous the domain
> Where to the sense of beauty first my heart
> Was open'd, tract more exquisitely fair
> Than is the paradise of Ten Thousand Trees,
> Chosen from the widest empire, for delight
> Or Gehol's famous Gardens, in a Clime

Of the Tartarian dynasty composed
(Beyond that mighty Wall, not fabulous
China's stupendous mound!) by patient skill
of myriads, and boon Nature's lavish help [. . .] (qtd. in Kitson 7)

Elizabeth Hope Chang observes that the eighteenth- and nineteenth-century descriptions of Chinese gardens, imaginary or real, "represent the first way that British literature came to conceive of China as space of visual difference in the post-chinoiserie century . . . the space of the Chinese garden . . . conveyed crucial meaning to the British viewers about a kind of geography encoded as despotic excessive, fantastic, incoherent, illogical and exotic"(23). Following Chang, Kitson observes that Wordsworth describes the famous pleasure garden as "a false paradise of artifice and excess antithetical to the natural beauty of the peopled Westmorland landscape." "Wordsworth reads into the Manchu landscape the orientalized forms of despotism, that are the origins of its existence, as opposed to the English landscape grounded in an untainted British liberty" ("The Wordsworths" 7). The representation of the Chinese landscape in *The Prelude,* therefore, bears similarity to the poetic use of the Middle Eastern desert or oasis in poems like "The Haunted Tree" and "Septemi Gedes." Oriental nature becomes artificial compared to the natural landscape of the English countryside. The heterogeneous East is, therefore, homogenized by Wordsworth as he employs the Chinese landscape and garden to the same purpose as the Middle Eastern desert or oasis.

In formulating his poetic principles, Wordsworth was undoubtedly influenced by Eastern poetry and poetic customs, chiefly via the works of William Jones and also by his reading of Oriental literature in translation. The fifth book of *The Prelude* bears proof of his enchantment with Eastern literature, but it is also demonstrative of Wordsworth's method of transforming the Eastern elements. Wordsworth uses the tale of the third Calender prince and his dream from the *Nights* but transforms the dream and the dreamer by superimposing the Western figure of Don Quixote and relating it to the Western poetic giants like Milton or Shakespeare. He overwrites the tale of the Calender prince. Similarly, Wordsworth superimposes the British landscape upon the Eastern ones to appropriate the 'expressive' poetry of the East, which Jones argued was inspired by the beautiful forms of nature found there. Wordsworth redefines Oriental nature as 'unnatural' and artificial while relocating the 'natural' in the English countryside. The relocation necessitated a redefinition of the East and this resulted in its hostile representation. The relocation was also fueled by an "anxiety of influence," a failure on part of Wordsworth to acknowledge his Eastern sources. This "anxiety of influence" might have been caused by more than literary considerations as there was accompanying imperial anxiety which became intense in Wordsworth after the death of his brother John. The insularity of Wordsworth might have had its roots in his dissatisfaction with continental politics and anxiety around Britain's growing empire. The public debate over proselytizing the non-Christians in India and other colonies of Britain which was supported and taken forward by his friends, Charles Grant and William Wilberforce also contributed to Wordsworth's hostility toward the East. Notwithstanding the insularity, it is undeniable that it was a "global village where Wordsworths lived and wrote" (Khosh, "The Wordsworths" 11).

Before concluding the discussion on Wordsworth, a brief note must be made on Wordsworth's pantheism and its possible link to the scholarly translations from India. It is customary to read Wordsworth's pantheism, which has also been termed as pan-deism or panentheism, with reference to Neoplatonism and the philosophy of Spinoza or Karl Krause (1781–1832). However, it is very difficult to ignore the impact of Upanishadic thoughts on Wordsworth that reached the Romantics embodied in Wilkin's translation of *The Bhagvat-Geeta*. The view that Wordsworth might be deriving his pantheistic belief from the Gita looks quite tenable when one considers the facts that his poetic principles are deeply linked to the writings of Jones, his close connections with Coleridge and Southey, who were deeply impacted by the ancient Indian philosophy, and especially when one finds recurring references in Wordsworth to India and Indian mythology in many places of his writings. References to India, Indian religion and customs and its people have been traced to several works of Wordsworth, but the most extensive reference is found in *The Excursion*.[22] In the third book of *The Excursions,* for instance, there is a passage describing the descent of Ganges according to the Hindu tradition:

> —then as the Hindus draw
> Their holy Ganges from a sky fount,
> Even so deduce the stream of human life
> From seats of power divine, and hope or trust
> That our existence winds her stately course
> Beneath the sun, like Ganges, to make part
> of living ocean. . . . (Book III, 254–260)

The passage is proof of Wordsworth's deep knowledge of the Hindu theological tradition. In "Tintern Abbey" Wordsworth speaks of an all-pervading spirit, a presence that runs through all living beings and non-living things:

> And I have felt
> A presence that disturbs me with the joy
> Of elevated thoughts; a sense sublime
> Of something far more deeply interfused,
> Whose dwelling is the light of setting suns,
> And the round ocean and the living air,
> And the blue sky, and in the mind of man:
> A motion and a spirit, that impels
> All thinking things, all objects of all thought,
> And rolls through all things. (ll. 93–101)

Read in the context of Wordsworth's knowledge of the ancient Indian theological/philosophical tradition, such passages where

Wordsworth speaks of God's presence in the universe, of an all-connecting force, can be identified as marked by the Upanishadic thoughts. One can easily locate the similarity of this passage, with what Krishna says in his argument with Arjuna in "Lecture VI: The Exercise of Soul." Krishna's speech reflects the Upanishadic belief that we all are emanations of Brahma, "He who beholdeth me in all things, and beholdeth all things in me" (Wilkins 65). It is not difficult to locate poems and passages by Wordsworth that reflect the idea of the one divine spirit running through all living beings.

Notes

1 Henceforth will be referred to as *Ancient Mariner.*

2 For discussion of slavery and *Ancient Mariner*, one may see William Empson's "The Ancient Mariner" and Patrick Keane's *Coleridge's Submerged Politics: The Ancient Mariner and Robinson Crusoe.*

3 See also, Julia Briggs's "The Ghost Story" in *A New Companion to the Gothic* (176–185).

4 In a note to Book III of *Thalaba, the Destroyer,* Southey refers to the story.

5 The issue of keeping the slaves as servants led to the ultimate failure of the friendship between Southey and Coleridge. Southey's aunt Miss Tyler had two African servants, Shad and Sally. Both the poets agreed to take them to America, but they differed on their precise position and role in their society. Southey wanted them to continue as servants, but Coleridge felt that there should be no servants in Pantisocracy. Coleridge wrote in a letter to Southey on September 18, 1794 and emphatically expressed his thoughts: "SHAD GOES WITH US. HE IS MY BROTHER!" (*LSTC*, Vol. 1, 77). In another letter to Southey (October 21, 1794), Coleridge expressed his vexation at Southey's proposal regarding Shad and Sally: "I was vexed too and alarmed by your letter concerning Mr. and Mrs. Roberts, Shad, and little Sally. I was wrong, very wrong, in the affair of Shad, and have given you reason to suppose that I should assent to the innovation" (*LSTC*, Vol. 1, 82).

6 A.R. Kidwai and Vincent Newy made some changes to Ober's version. See *Notes & Queries* (March 1993, Vol. 40 Issue 1, p. 38).

7 See *Coleridge: The Early Family Letters* (70–104).

8 All references to *Osorio* will be to the version of the text published in 1873 by Richard John Pearson, *Osorio: A Tragedy, as Originally Written in 1797*. Apart from act and scene number, the page number of this edition is also provided in the parentheses. The page number is followed by act and scene number e.g. 169, 5. 1. No line number could be provided because this edition does not have line numbers and no better edition of the play could be found.

9 See Jalaluddin Khan's article "Coleridge's 'Kubla Khan': A New Historicist Study."

10 The term 'Wujd' means the "mystic song and dance of dervishes" (Fulford, "Coleridge and the Oriental Tale" 229).

11 John Beer refers to Robert Southey's "snowy Ethiop" to explain the figure of the Abyssinian maid in "Kubla Khan" and comments that Coleridge must have conceived her as White (*Coleridge, the Visionary* 236–237). Southey's lines in the poem entitled "Romance" run like this:

> The holy prelate owns her power;
> In softening tale relates
> The snowy Ethiop's matchless charms
> The outlaw's den, the clang of arms,
> And love's too-varying fates; (Lovell and Southey 19).

12 See Beer's *Coleridge the Visionary* (223–253) and Heidi Thomson's "The Integral Significance of the 1816 Preface to 'Kubla Khan'" in *Coleridge, Romanticism and the Orient: Cultural Negotiations* (165–177).

13 See Elizabeth Schneider's *Coleridge, Opium, and Kubla Khan* (Chicago: University of Chicago Press, 1953).

14 See Chester Linn Shaver's *Wordsworth's Library: A Catalogue, Including a List of Books Housed by Wordsworth for Coleridge from C. 1810 to C. 1830.*

15 The italics in quotations of Jones are reproduced as it is in Pachori.

16 Unless otherwise stated, all citations of the Preface to *Lyrical Ballads* are from the text reprinted in *English Critical Texts* (162–189) edited by Enright and Chickera.

17 Captain Michel de Beaupuy was a late eighteenth-century French aristocrat. He was a supporter of the revolutionary cause and is said to have played a crucial role in shaping Wordsworth's early political views.

18 See T. Nishio, "A Bibliography of the *Arabian Nights* in the 18th Century" in *Bulletin of the National Museum of Ethnology*, vol. 36, no. 4, 2012, pp. 561–639. See also S. Wolfson's "Revision as Form: Wordsworth's Drowned Man", in William Wordsworth's *The Prelude: A Case Book*, edited by Stephen C. Gill (New York, Oxford University Press, 2006), 73–122. Wolfson traces the long history of publication of the four-volume edition in his essay (117).

19 *Arabian Nights Entertainments Consisting of One Thousand and One Stories, told by Sultanate of Indies, to Divert the Sultan from the Execution of a Bloody Vow... Tr. into French from the Arabian MMS by M. Galland... and now done into English* (London, T. Longman. 1789) I, 152–154.

20 Unless otherwise stated, all reference to Wordsworth's poems, except *The Prelude*, is to *The Collected Poems of William Wordsworth* (Ware: Wordsworth Editions Ltd, 1994). The page numbers are mentioned in the parentheses.

21 The *Ecclesiastical Sonnets* are supposed to trace the introduction and development of Christianity in Britain. The sonnets are divided in Part I and Part II, covering two different historical periods: Part I: "From the Introduction of Christianity into Britain, to the Consummation of the Papal Dominion and Part II: "To the Close of the Troubles in the Reign of Charles I."

22 For a quick look at the references to India or Hinduism, one may see Lane Cooper's *A Concordance to the Poems of William Wordsworth* (London: Smith Elder and Co., 1911). The book proved very helpful to this author with its compilation of an index to the "language of Wordsworth." See pages 438, 473–474 for keys to study the references to India. See also chapter 8 of Schwab's *The Oriental Renaissance*, pp. 195–196.

Conclusion

Said writes in the "Preface" to *Orientalism* that "nothing that goes in our world has ever been isolated and pure of any outside influence." However, the "disheartening part," Said notes, is the extent to which the "critical study of culture shows us that this is the case" (xxiii). This has been the case with the study of Romanticism also. Although, the Romantics lived, what Said designates as a "pluri-cultural life" ("Preface" xxiii), for long Romanticism has been defined as a purely European phenomenon. Thus, in charting Wordsworth's place in English poetic tradition, Seamus Heaney, as late as in 2001, wrote that Wordsworth's achievement "is most securely founded in the canon of native English poetry" (vii). However, the history of the cultural exchange between the East and Europe goes back to the Middle Ages and it saw a new high during the Romantic period. This is something Bertrand Russell in his 1946 book, *History of Western Philosophy* pointed to. In the chapter dedicated to the Romantic Movement, Russell observes: "The geography of the Romantics is interesting: from Xanadu to 'the lone Chorasamian shore', the places in which it is interested are remote, Asiatic, or Ancient."

The global nature of Romantic geography owed to an unforeseen growth of the knowledge of the East during the Romantic period and a daring use of this 'new' knowledge. The early Romantic poets appropriated the Eastern influence in their attempt to redefine English poetry. This process of redefinition started with William Jones, who introduced the Romantics to the Perso-Arabic poetic tradition as well as to the ancient literary tradition of India. Jones was the first English author who courageously spoke in favor of Oriental poetry and wrote about its potential power that could reinvigorate the British poetic tradition. With his translation of the Persian and Arabian poets, Jones introduced a new set of images, a simple direct manner of speaking, a description of the beautiful forms of nature and the poetry of expression, replacing the imitative poetry of the neoclassical poets. In his *Hindu Hymns,* he initiated the custom of using Hindu mythology in English poetry. As has been argued in the present study, Jones and his colleagues in Calcutta played a colossal role in giving shape to Romanticism. Similarly, the translation of the *Nights* and other collections of Oriental Tales also had a phenomenal role to play in the development of Romanticism. The *Nights* "altered" the course of English poetry (Fulford, "Coleridge and the Oriental Tale" 214). "It was Shaharzad, the storyteller of the *Arabian Nights,* that taught all of them the art of narration, the simple direct diction, the significance of imagination. Through her, the English Romantic poets found poetic freedom" (Attar 175).

The path laid down by Jones was adopted by the Romantic poets as they turned to the East in search of "new poetry and new poetics" (Fulford, "Coleridge and the Oriental Tale" 223). None of the early Romantics, however, did have a firsthand experience of the East, Eastern poetry or philosophy, because none of them had visited the East or had knowledge of Sanskrit, Arabic, or Persian, or any other Eastern language. They banked on the large body of Oriental Tales, travel narratives, scholarly treatises, translations, histories, and scientific and pseudo-scientific discourses for their knowledge of the East. There was also a large body of Oriental artefacts all around them giving them a glimpse of the life in the East. While forming his mythographic world, Blake turned to Indian mythology and Islamic theology and to Egypt, Africa, and the Americas. Landor sourced his narrative for the verse tale *Gebir* from the translation of the Arabian "The History of Ancient Egypt." Southey was inspired to compose *Thalaba* by his reading of the Arabian tale, "The History of Maugraby the Magician," and Sale's translation of the Qur'an. The Hindu mythology of *The Curse of Kehama* came from the numerous scholarly works from Calcutta. Coleridge assimilated his reading of the Oriental Tale, Islamic theology, and Hindu philosophy into most of the poems he wrote in the 1790s. It would have been impossible to have his "Kubla Khan," "Religious Musings," "Christabel," *Ancient Mariner*, "The Lewti," or the tragedy *Osorio* without the Oriental Renaissance. Similarly, Wordsworth's enchantment with the *Nights* and his reading of Perso-Arabic literature went to contribute to *The Prelude*. His Preface to *Lyrical Ballads* would not have been possible without the preceding works of Jones or his reading of Eastern literature available in translations.

The early Romantic poets borrowed the themes, stories, and formal elements from the Oriental Tales, the Gothic novels, the travelogues, and the translations of Eastern literary, philosophical and religious texts. The femme-fatale figures, the breed of female magicians, the villain-heroes, the despotic feudal lords or the despotic rulers of the East, the wanderer were adapted and transformed by the early Romantic poets; Oriental degeneration and decadence were often conveyed through the Gothic images of ruin and darkness. The technique of using frame tales, the use of the narratorial voice as having the power to change the world, an emphasis on simplicity of diction and form, imagination, and expressive poetry during the Romantic period developed under the influence of the Oriental Renaissance. Coleridge, Blake, and Southey made use of the Islamic monotheism for conveying their radical Unitarian principles. Hindu religious texts influenced the early Romantic poets' valorization of the principle of One Life and pantheism in a radical departure from Christian theology.

Although the early Romantic poets appropriated various Eastern elements in their poetry, they had reservations about the East that prevented them from embracing the East wholeheartedly. The initial fascination of the early Romantics with the East was followed by a late condemnation of it. Raymond Schwab explains the failure of the Oriental Renaissance in England by referring to the imperial politics of Britain: "The conquerors felt obliged to defend their conquest, which meant exalting their own race and religion" (43). In the effort to elevate the British and European self, the Eastern Other was relegated to a position of inferiority. Schwab argues:

> This resulted in political and spiritual unrest, which spread like an epidemic. The activities at Serampore, which provided many useful publications in the early days of Indic studies, seemed to coincide with the appearance of this 'missionary attitude', which wreaked havoc. . . . Later it would become clear how the episodes of colonial politics – the Sepoy Mutiny of 1857, the substitution of crown for company, and the proliferation of English personnel in India—came in gusts, reinforcing the English prejudice of Western superiority minimizing, for the parent state, the phenomena of the Oriental Renaissance. (43)

The complete shift in England's relationship with the East, that Schwab locates in the mid-nineteenth century, started to show its signs in the early years of the nineteenth century with the emergence of the missionary activities in India. 1780 to 1820s is roughly the period when British policy toward India took a definite shape. In the 1770s, British Orientalists started their scholarly discoveries of the ancient Indian religious, philosophical and literary texts for the European audience. It reached its peak under Hastings's patronage and Jones's curatorship; ancient Indian philosophy and religion were idealized. While it provided a great impetus to the development of Romanticism, it also challenged the superiority of Western civilization and Christianity as the primacy of the Bible came to be questioned. It was politically challenged by the evangelicals under the leadership of Wilberforce and Grant. The early Romantic poets had to re-negotiate with the situation. They were located in the imperial center and were discursively inside it; while they initially responded to the situation by adapting the syncretism of Jones, they ended up by regretting their early syncretism. Faced with the danger from outside, they turned insular and whatever intra-national radicalism they had, started vanishing. In other words, the creative use of Eastern resources was enmeshed in the geopolitical discourses of the time. Therefore, an *Osorio* could no longer be written, the only possibility was *The Curse of Kehama*. As they grew more insular and more nationalistic, Eastern art and literature came to be condemned as worthless. Jones could compare Ferdowsī with Homer in the 1770s, but for Southey in 1808–1809, Jones is a "barbarian," and Ferdowsī's poem, *Shahnameh* is but "the vilest copy of a picture" (*CPW* 318).

As England consolidated its hold over the Indian territories, there was a major policy makeover. "The moment called for a construction of Indian history that would *provide the future with a different empowerment*" (Rajan 90). James Mill became the spokesperson for the new policy in India and was followed by Macaulay. Mill wrote a "new text" in the form of *The History of British India* for India's past (and thus its future) rather than "amend[ing] an old one" (Rajan 90). Rather than cultivating syncretism, Mill advocated cultural assimilation. In this changed atmosphere, the opium that produced "Kubla Khan" would now produce the nightmares of Thomas De Quincey's "Oriental Dreams" in *Confessions of an English Opium Eater*. The latent anxiety of the early Romantics became manifest in De Quincey's Oriental dreams:

> The mere antiquity of Asiatic things, of their institutions, histories, modes of faith, etc., is so impressive, that to me the vast age of the race and name overpowers the sense of youth in the individual. A young Chinese seems to me an antediluvian man renewed. Even Englishmen, though not bred in any knowledge of such institutions, cannot but shudder at the mystic sublimity of castes that have flowed apart and refused to mix, through such immemorial tracts of time . . . Man is a weed in those regions. (81)

Faced with the ancient Asiatic civilizations, the early Romantics attempted to negotiate with it creatively, but such negotiations become difficult in an atmosphere of growing anxiety as seen in the case of De Quincey. Among the younger generation of Romantic poets, only Shelley could follow Jonesean syncretism. He wrote

Prometheus Unbound (1820) as late as in 1819–1820 and conceived of 'Asia' as the regenerator of Europe.

On the other front, the power struggle in the Middle East and the Greek War of Independence led to Romantic philhellenism, which resulted in a renewed hostility toward the Middle East. As Martin Bernal argues in *Black Athena*, European philhellenism indirectly sustained Eurocentrism and Orientalism. Throughout western Europe, the Greek War of Independence was seen as "a struggle between European youthful vigor, and Asiatic and African decadence, corruption and cruelty" (vol. 1, 291). Byron took up the Greek cause and fought for them. He wrote *Don Juan* (1819–1824) and many of the Turkish tales as a philhellene (Mc Gann, *Beauty of Inflections* 260). Similar hopes of the renewal of Greece led Shelley to produce *Hellas* (1822). Philhellenism does not color the works of the early Romantics the way it does the works of the younger generation of Romantic poets, but the hostility toward the Middle East in some of the later works of Wordsworth might have connections with the Greek War of Independence.

The early Romantic poets, therefore, wrote in a very tense intellectual atmosphere divided between men like Jones on the one hand and Grant, Macaulay and Mill on the other; where the desire for freedom engendered by the French Revolution co-existed with the bondage of slavery and racial classification; the imperial domination co-existed with the fear of being dominated and infected by the Empire. Romanticism was complicit in these developments. It was born in the borderline of these opposing forces. The Romantic poets turned to the Oriental Tale and the Gothic, to the Middle East and India, to Islam and Hinduism because these provided them with the opportunity to explore and inhabit the borderline, the "contact zone."

Therefore, the Orient played a crucial role in shaping the Romantic movement. Raymond Schwab argues that Romanticism would have been impossible without the Oriental Renaissance and defines

Romanticism as the "oriental irruption of the intellect" (482). Perhaps it is time to argue that the "Preface" to *Lyrical Ballads* of William Wordsworth would have been impossible without the Oriental Renaissance, without William Jones, without the translations of the Persian, Arabic, and Sanskrit literary texts into English in the late-eighteenth century, without the liberating discourses of the Gothic, without the invasion of the imaginative collections of Oriental Tales that disrupted the neoclassical creed with its liberal spirit. The creation of a new poetic idiom by the Romantics would have been impossible without these disruptions—the rupture created by these forms paved the way for the Romantic rapture.

Works Cited

Abbasi, Pyeaam, and Alireza Anushiravani. "Coleridge's Orientalist View of Mahomet." *k@ta*, vol. 13, no. 1, 2011, pp. 1–18, http://puslit2.petra.ac.id/ejournal/index.php/ing/article/view/18208. Accessed 12 June 2020.

Abrams, Meyer Howard. *The Mirror and the Lamp: Romantic Theory and the Critical Tradition*. Oxford: Oxford University Press, 1971.

Aeschylus. *Aeschylus I: The Persians, The Seven Against Thebes, The Suppliant Maidens, and Prometheus Bound* (*The Complete Greek Tragedies*), edited by David Grene, et al. 3rd ed., Chicago: University of Chicago Press, 2013.

Alatas, Syed Hussein. *The Myth of the Lazy Native: A Study of the Image of the Malays, Filipinos and Javanese from the 16th to the 20th Century and Its Function in the Ideology of Colonial Capitalism*. 1977. London: Routledge, 2010.

Ali, Muhsin Jassim. *Scheherazade in England: A Study of Nineteenth-Century English Criticism of the Arabian Nights*. Washington, D.C.: Three Continents, 1981.

Alighieri, Dante. *The Divine Comedy*. Translated by John Ciardi, New York, NAL Trade, 2003.

———. *The Inferno of Dante Alighieri*. Translated by Seth Zimmerman Lincoln, NE: 1 Universe, 2003.

Almeida, Hermione De, and George H. Gilpin. *Indian Renaissance: British Romantic Art and the Prospect of India*. Burlington, Ashgate Publishing Ltd., 2005.

Anderson, Ewan W. *The Middle East: Geography and Geopolitics*. 8th ed. London, Routledge, 2000.

Ankarsjo, Magnus. *William Blake and Gender*. Jefferson, N.C.: McFarland & Company, 2005.

Arabian Nights Entertainments Consisting of One Thousand and One Stories, told by Sultanate of Indies, to Divert the Sultan from the Execution of a Bloody Vow...Tr. into French from the Arabian MMS by M. Galland...and now done into English. Vol. I. London, T. Longman. 1778. Reprinted in 1789. https://books.google.co.in/books?id=khkHAAAAQAAJ. Accessed 12 August 2019.

Aravamudan, Srinivas. "Fiction/Translation/Transnation: The Secret History of the Eighteenth-Century Novel." A Companion to the Eighteenth-Century English Novel and Culture, edited by Paula R. Backscheider and Catherine. E-book, John Wiley & Sons, 2008, pp. 48–74.

——. *Tropicopolitans: Colonialism and Agency, 1688–1804*. Durham, N.C.: Duke University Press Books, 1999.

Attar, Samar. *Borrowed Imagination: The British Romantic Poets and Their Arabic-Islamic Sources*. Lanham: Lexington Books, 2014.

Backscheider, Paula R., and Catherine Ingrassia, editors. *A Companion to the Eighteenth-Century English Novel and Culture*. Chichester: Wiley-Blackwell, 2009.

Bahar-danush; or, Garden of Knowledge: An Oriental Romance. Translated by Jonathan Scott. E-book, J. Shrewsbury, and W. Eddowes, 1799. https://books.google.co.in/books?id=-nc-AAAAcAAJ. Accessed 12 June 2020.

Ballaster, Ross. "Narrative Transmigrations: The Oriental tale and the Novel in Eighteenth-Century Britain." Backscheider and Catherine, pp. 75–96.

Barbauld, Anna Laetitia, and John Aikin. "On the Pleasure Derived from Objects of Terror; with Sir Bertrand, A Fragment." *Gothic Documents: A Sourcebook 1700–1820*, edited by E.J. Clery and Robert Miles, Manchester: Manchester University Press, 2000, pp. 127–134.

Barfoot, C.C., and Theo D'haen. *Oriental Prospects: Western Literature and the Lure of the East*. Amsterdam: Rodopi Bv Editions, 1998.

Barfoot, C.C. "English Romantic Poets and the 'Free Floating Oreint'." Barfoot and D'haen, pp. 65–96.

Baugh, Albert C., editor. *Chaucer's Major Poetry*. London: Routlege & Kegan Paul, 1963.

Beckford, William. *Vathek*. 1786. London: Oxford University Press, 1998.

Beer, John B. *Blake's Visionary Universe*. Manchester: Barnes & Noble, 1969.

——. "The Languages of 'Kubla Khan'." Gravil, Lucy and Roe, pp. 218–262.

——. *Coleridge the Visionary*. London: Chatto and Windus, 1970.

Bentley, G.E. Jr. Introduction. *William Blake: The Critical Heritage*, edited by G.E. Bentley Jr., London: Routledge and Kegan Paul, 1975.

Berlin, Isaiah. *The Roots of Romanticism*. Princeton: Princeton University Press, 2001.

Bernal, Martin. "The Fabrication of Ancient Greece 1785–1985." *Black Athena: The Afro-Asian Roots of Classical Civilization*, vol. 1, London: Free Association Books, 1987.

Bernhardt-Kabisch, Ernest. "The Stone and the Shell: Wordsworth, Cataclysm, and the Myth of Glaucus." *Studies in Romanticism,* vol. 23, no. 4, 1984, pp. 455–490.

———. *Robert Southey*. Boston Twayne, 1977. "Sir Bevis of Hampton." *Middle English Text Series, Robbins Digital Project, University of Rochester*, edited by Ronald B. Herzman, Graham Drake and Eve Salisbury. https://d.lib.rochester.edu/teams/text/salisbury-four-romances-of-england-bevis-of-hampton. Accessed 13 June 2020.

Bewell, Alan. *Wordsworth and the Enlightenment: Nature, Man, and Society in the Experimental Poetry*. New Haven: Yale University Press, 1989.

Bignon, Jean Paul. *The Adventures of Abdalla: Son of Hanif.* E-book, London: T. Worrall at the Judge's Head, 1729. https://archive.org/stream/adventuresofabda00bign. Accessed 13 June 2020.

Birkhead, Edith. *The Tale of Terror: A Study of the Gothic Romance.* London: Constable Company Limited, 1921.

Blake, William. *Blake's Poetry and Designs*, edited by John E. Grant and Mary Lynn Johnson. 2nd ed. New York: W.W. Norton & Company, 2007.

Bolton, Carol. *Writing the Empire: Robert Southey and Romantic Colonialism.* London: Pickering & Chatto Limited, 2007.

———. "Thalaba the Destroyer. Southey's Nationalist 'Romance.'" *Romanticism on the Net*, issue 32–33, November 2003. *Érudit*, https://doi.org/10.7202/009260ar. Accessed 13 June 2020.

Boyle, Roger. *Parthenissa.* E-book, London: Herringman, 1676. https://books.google.co.in/books?id=To1LAAAAcAAJ. Accessed 13 June 2020.

Briggs, Julia. "The Ghost Story." *A New Companion to the Gothic*, edited by David Punter, Hoboken: John Wiley & Sons Ltd, 2012, pp. 176–185.

Brown, Norman O. "The Prophetic Tradition." *Studies in Romanticism*, vol. 21, no. 3, 1982, pp. 367–386. *JSTOR*, www.jstor.org/stable/25600364. Accessed 14 June 2020.

Brown, W.C. "The Popularity of English Travel Books about the Near East, 1775–1825." *Philological Quarterly*, vol. 15, 1936, pp. 70–80.

Burke, Edmund. "India: The Launching of the Hastings Impeachment, 1786–1788." *Writings and the Speeches of Edmund Burke, vol. VI,* edited by P.J. Marshall, Oxford: Oxford UP, 1991.

Burton, Richard F. *The Arabian Nights or The Book of Thousand and One Nights*. London: Blue Ribbon Books, 1941.

Butler, Marilyn. "Orientalism." *The Penguin History of Literature: The Romantic Period*, edited by David B. Pirie. New York: Penguin, 1994, pp. 395–446.

Butler, Marilyn. "Romanticism in England." *Romanticism in National Context*, edited by Roy Porter and Mikulas Teuch. Cambridge: Cambridge University Press, 1988, pp. 37–67.

Butlin, Martin. *The Paintings and Drawings of William Blake*, vol. 1, New Haven: Paul Mellon Centre BA, 1981.

Bygrave, Stephen. "Romantic Poems and Contexts." *Romantic Writings*, edited by Stephen Bygrave, London: Psychology Press, 1996, pp. 3–46.

Byron, George Gordon. "Hints from Horace." *The Works of Lord Byron*, vol. 9, London: J. Murray, 1832, pp. 93–94.

———. *Byron's Letters and Journals, Volume III: "Alas! the Love of Women," 1813–1814*, edited by Leslie A. Marchand. Cambridge, Mass.: Belknap Press, 1974.

———. *Byron's Poetical Works*, edited by Jerome J. Mc Gann, Oxford: Clarendon Press, 1980–1993. 7 vols.

Cannon, Garland Hampton. *Oriental Jones: A Biography of Sir William Jones, 1746–1794*. London: Asia Publishing House [for] Indian Council for Cultural Relations, 1964.

———. "Oriental Jones: Scholarship, literature, Multiculturalism and Humankind." *Objects of Enquiry: The Life, Contributions, and Influences of Sir William Jones, 1746–1794*, edited by Garland Hampton Cannon and Kevin R. Brine, New York: NYU Press, 1995, pp. 25–50.

Caracciolo, Peter L. *The Arabian Nights in English Literature: Studies in the Reception of the Thousand and One Nights into British Culture*. London: Macmillan, 1988.

Chambers, Sir William. *A Dissertation on Oriental Gardening*. London, W. Griffin, 1772. *Internet Archive*. https://archive.org/details/dissertation-onor00cham. Accessed 18 June 2020.

Chandler, David. "Robert Southey and *The Prelude*'s 'Arab Dream'." *The Review of English Studies*. Vol. 54, no. 214, 2003, pp. 203–219.

Chang, Elizabeth Hope. *Britain's Chinese Eye: Literature, Empire, and Aesthetics in Nineteenth-Century Britain*. Stanford, Calif.: Stanford University Press, 2010.

Chatterton, Thomas. *The Works of Thomas Chatterton*, edited by Robert Southey and Joseph Cottle, vol. 1. London, T.N. Longman & O. Rees, 1803. https://books.google.co.in/books?id=YOHQAAAAMAAJ. Accessed 18 June 2020.

Chatterton, Thomas. "A Burlesque Cantata." 1770. *A Supplement to the Miscellanies of Thomas Chatterton.* E-book, London, T. Becket, 1784. *Internet Archive.* 75-76, https://quod.lib.umich.edu/e/ecco/004902287.0001.000/1:26?rgn=div1;view=fulltext. Accessed 18 June 2020.

Christensen, Thomas. "A Horace Reading: An Introduction to the Mercury House edition of Horace Walpole's *Hieroglyphic Tales.*" *rightreading.com.* Thomas Christensen, n.d. N.pag. http://www.rightreading.com/writing/h_tales.htm. Accessed 18 June 2020.

Clark, J.C.D. *English Society, 1660-1832: Religion, Ideology and Politics during the Ancien Régime.* 2nd ed, Cambridge: Cambridge University Press, 2000.

Clark, S.H., and David Worrall, editors. *Blake, Nation, and Empire.* Houndmills: Palgrave Macmillan, 2006.

Clark, Steve and Masashi Suzuki, editors. *The Reception of Blake in the Orient.* London: Continuum, 2006.

Clyde, Paul H., and Burton F. Beers. *The Far East: A History of Western Impacts and Eastern Responses, 1830–1975.* New Delhi: Princeton Hall of Private Limited, 1988.

Cohen, Jeffrey J., editor. *The Postcolonial Middle Ages.* New York: Palgrave Macmillan, 2000.

Cohen-Vrignaud, Gerard. *Radical Orientalism: Rights, Reform, and Romanticism.* Cambridge: Cambridge University Press, 2015.

Coleridge, Samuel Taylor. Lectures, 1795: On Politics and Religion. *The Collected Works of Samuel Taylor Coleridge,* edited by Patton Lewis and Peter Mann, vol. 1, Princeton: Princeton University Press, 1971.

———. *Letters of Samuel Taylor Coleridge*, edited by Ernest Hartley Coleridge, London: William Heinemann, 1895, vol. 2.

———. *Biographia Literaria: Or Biographical Sketches of My Literary Life and Opinion.* London: Leavitt, Lord & Company, 1834. E-book, *Internet Archive,* https://archive.org/details/biographialiter13colegoog. Accessed 11 March 2014.

Coleridge, Samuel Taylor. *Anima Poetae: From the Unpublished Note-Books of Samuel Taylor Coleridge*, edited by Ernest Hartley Coleridge. London: William Heinemann, 1895. E-book, *Internet Archive*, https://archive.org/details/animapoetaefrom00colegoog. Accessed 11 October 2014.

———. *Coleridge: The Early Family Letters*, edited by Engel James, Oxford: Clarendon Press, 1994.

Coleridge, Samuel Taylor. *Coleridge's Poetry and Prose*, edited by Nicholas Halimi, Paul Magnuson, and Ramonda Madiano. New York: W.W. Norton, 2004.

———. *Osorio: A Tragedy, as Originally Written in 1797*. London: John Pearson, 1873. *Internet Archive*, https://archive.org/details/cu31924105501831/page/n7/mode/2up. Accessed 15 March 2014.

———. Poetical Works: Part 1. Poems. *The Collected Works of Samuel Taylor Coleridge,* edited by J.C.C. Mays, vol. 16, London: Princeton University Press, 2001.

———. *The Collected Works of Samuel Taylor Coleridge,* Volume 15: *Opus Maximum*, edited by Thomas McFarland and Nicholas Halmi, Princeton: Princeton University Press, 2002. 16 vols.

———. Essays on his Times: The Morning Post and the Courier. *The Collected Works of Samuel Taylor Coleridge,* edited by David V. Erdman, vol. 3, Princeton: Princeton University Press, 1978.

———. Lectures 1808–1819: On Literature I. *The Collected Works of Samuel Taylor Coleridge,* edited by R.A. Foakes, vol. 5, Princeton: Princeton University Press, 1987.

Collins, William. *Persian Eclogues. Written Originally for the Entertainment of the Ladies of Tauris*. London: J. Roberts, 1742. *Eighteenth Century Collections*. http://name.umdl.umich.edu/004897887.0001.000. Accessed 30 August 2010.

Coleman, Diedre. "The 'Dark Tide of Time': Coleridge and William Hodge's India." Vallins, Oishi, and Perry, pp. 39–54.

Connolly, Tristanne J. *William Blake and the Body*. Houndmills: Palgrave Macmillan, 2002.

———. "'The Authority of the Ancients': Blake and Wilkins' Translation of the *Bhagvat-Geeta*." Clark and Suzuki, pp. 145–160.

Cooper, Lane. *A Concordance to the Poems of William Wordsworth*. London: Smith Elder and Co., 1911.

Critical Essays on Some of the Poems, of Several English Poets: By John Scott ... With an Account of the Life and Writings of the Author; by Mr. Hoole. London, James Phillips, 1785. *Internet Archive*, Electronic reproduction. Farmington Hills, Mich.: Cengage Gale, 2009. https://archive.org/details/criticalessayson02scot/page/191/mode/2up. Accessed 30 August 2010.

Cunningham, Teresa L. "William Blake's artificial mythology and quotations from world mythos." *Graduate Theses, Dissertations, and Problem Reports*. https://researchrepository.wvu.edu/etd/806. Accessed 18 June 2020.

Curran, Stuart. *The Cambridge Companion to British Romanticism*. 2nd ed., Cambridge: Cambridge University Press, 2010.

Cuttings from the Annual Review, vol. I–VI, containing the contributions of Southey, edited by Arthur Aikin, London: T.N. Longman and Rees, 1805. *Internet Archive*, https://books.google.co.in/books?id=4uxZAAAAcAAJ. Accessed 12 June 2014.

Dalrymple, William. "The East India Company: The Original Corporate Raiders." *The Guardian*. 4 Mar 2015. https://www.theguardian.com/world/2015/mar/04/east-india-company-original-corporate-raiders. Accessed 9 March 2015.

Damon, S. Foster. *William Blake: His Philosophy and Symbols*. 1924. Whitefish, Mont.: Kessinger Publishing, LLC, 2010.

———. *A Blake Dictionary: Ideas and Symbols of William Blake*. New ed. Hanover, NH: Brown University Press, 1988.

Defoe, Daniel. *Robinson Crusoe*, edited by Michael Shinagel. 2nd ed., New York: W.W. Norton & Company, 1993.

Demata, Massimilliano. "Discovering Eastern Horrors: Beckford, Maturin and the Discourse of Travel Literature." *Empire and the Gothic: The Politics of Genre*, edited by Andrew Smith and William Hughes, Houndmills: Palgrave Macmillan, 2003, pp. 13–34.

De Quincey, Thomas. *Confessions of an English Opium Eater*. 1821. Edited by Barry Milligan, revised ed., London: Penguin Classics, 2003.

Drew, John. *India and the Romantic Imagination*. Delhi: Oxford University Press, 1987.

Empson, William. "The 'Ancient Mariner.'" *Critical Quarterly*, vol. 6, 1964, pp. 298–319.

Erdman, David V, editor. *The Complete Poetry and Prose of William Blake*. Electronic ed. Virginia, Institute for Advanced Technology in the Humanities, 2001. *William Blake Archive*, http://erdman.blakearchive.org/. Accessed 12 March 2019.

Fischer, Hermann. *Romantic Verse Narrative: The History of a Genre*. Translated by Sue Bollans, Cambridge: Cambridge University Press, 1991.

Floris and Blancheflour, edited by Erik Kooper. *Robbins Library Digital Projects. University of Rochester*. https://d.lib.rochester.edu/teams/text/kooper-sentimental-and-humorous-romances-floris-and-blancheflour. Accessed 21 August 2019.

Ford, Talissa J. "'Jerusalem Is Scattered Abroad': Blake's Ottoman Geographies." *Studies in Romanticism*, vol. 47, no. 4, pp. 529–548, 2008. *JSTOR*. https://www.jstor.org/stable/25602168. Accessed 31 December 2014.

Forster, John. *Walter Savage Landor: A Biography*. Boston: Fields, Osgood, & Company, 1869.

Frank, Frederick S. "The Gothic *Vathek*: The Problem of Genre Resolved." *Vathek and the Escape from Time: Bicentenary Revaluations*, edited by Kenneth Graham, New York: AMS Press, 1990, pp. 157–172.

Franklin, Michael J, editor. *Romantic Representations of British India*. London: Taylor & Francis, 2006. Routledge Studies in Romanticism.

———. "Accessing India: Orientalism, anti-'Indianism' and the Rhetoric of Jones and Burke." Fulford and Kitson, pp. 48–88.

———. "General introduction and [meta] historical background [re]presenting 'The palanquins of state; or, broken leaves in a Mughal garden,'" *Romantic Representations of British India* by Franklin, London: Taylor & Francis, 2006, pp. 1–44.

Friedman, J.B. *The Monstrous Races in Medieval Art and Thought*. Cambridge, Mass.: Harvard University Press, 1981.

Frye, Northrop. *Fearful Symmetry: A Study of William Blake*. Princeton: Princeton University Press, 1974.

Fulford, Tim. "Coleridge and Oriental Tale." *The Arabian Nights in Historical Context: Between East and West*, edited by Saree Makdisi and Felicity Nussbaum, Oxford: Oxford University Press, 2008, 213–234.

———. "Plants Pagodas and Penises: Southey's Oriental Imports." Pratt, pp. 188–201.

Fulford, Tim. "Poetic flowers/Indian Bowers." Franklin, pp. 113–130.

———. "Coleridge's Sequel to *Thalaba* and Southey's Prequel to *Christabel*." Vallins, Oishi and Perry, pp. 56–70.

Fulford, Timothy, and Peter J. Kitson, editors. *Romanticism and Colonialism: Writing and Empire, 1780–1830*. Cambridge: Cambridge University Press, 2005.

Fulford, Tim, and Maureen N. McLane. "Poetry, Peripheries and Empire." *The Cambridge Companion to British Romantic Poetry*, edited by James Chandler, Cambridge: Cambridge University Press, 2008, pp. 178–194.

Fuller, David. "Blake and Dante." *Art History*, vol. 11, no. 3, 1988, pp. 349–373. *Wiley Online Library*. https://doi.org/10.1111/j.1467-8365.1988.tb00309.x. Accessed 30 December 2012.

Galperin, William H. "Authority and Deconstruction in Book V of *The Prelude*." *Studies in English Literature, 1500–1900*, vol. 26, no. 4, 1986, pp. 613–631. *JSTOR*. https://www.jstor.org/stable/450615. Accessed 4 July 2014.

Gamer, Michael. "Gothic Fictions and the Romantic Writings in Britain." *Cambridge Companion to Gothic Fiction*, edited by Jerrold E. Hogle. Cambridge: Cambridge University Press, 2002, pp. 85–104.

Garcia, Humberto. "The Hermetic Tradition of Arabic Islam and the Colonial politics of Landor's 'Gebir.' *Studies in Romanticism*, vol. 46, no. 4, pp. 433–459, 2007.

———. "Holy Entrails and Schismatic Bodies: Esoteric Embodiments of Islam in William Blake's Art and Poetry." Presented at the Northeast Modern Language Association, Rochester, New York on 16 March, 2012.

———. *Islam and the English Enlightenment, 1670–1840*. Baltimore: Johns Hopkins University Press, 2012.

Genette, Gérard. *Paratexts: Thresholds of Interpretation*. Translated by Jane E. Lewin, Cambridge: Cambridge University Press, 1997.

Goldsmith, Oliver. *The Works of Oliver Goldsmith IV: Biographies; Reviews; Animated Nature; Cock Lane Ghost; Vida's Game of Chess; Letters*, edited by Peter Cunningham, London: 1854.

Grant, Charles. *Observations on the State of Society Among the Asiatic Subjects of Great Britain: Particularly with Respect to Morals: And on the Means of Improving It*. London: 1792. *Internet Archive*, https://archive.org/details/observationsonst00gran. Accessed 7 March 2014.

Gravil, Richard, Lucy Newlyn, and Nicholas Roe, editors. *Coleridge's Imagination: Essays in Memory of Pete Laver*. Cambridge: Cambridge University Press, 1985.

Haddad, Emily A. *Orientalist Poetics: The Islamic Middle East in Nineteenth-Century English and French Poetry*. Aldershot: Ashgate, 2002.

Hakluyt, Richard. *Voyages and Discoveries: Principal Navigations*. 1589. Reissue ed., Harmondsworth: Penguin Classics, 1972.

Hall, Edith. *Inventing the Barbarian: Greek Self-Definition through Tragedy*. Oxford: Oxford University Press, 1989.

Hamilton, Elizabeth. *Translations of the Letters of a Hindoo Rajah: Written Previous to, and During the Residence in England. To which is prefixed a Preliminary Dissertation on the History, Religion and Manners of the Hindus*. 1796. Edited by Pamela Perkins and Shannon Russell, Petsborough, Ontario: Broad View Press, 1998.

Harries, Natalie Tal. "'The One Life Within Us and Abroad': Coleridge and Hinduism." Vallins, Oishi and Perry, pp. 131–144.

Haskins, Charles H. *The Renaissance of the Twelfth Century*. New ed., Cambridge: Harvard University Press, 1971.

Heaney, Seamus. Introduction. *William Wordsworth: Poems Selected by Seamus Heaney*. New York: The Ecco Press: 1988; London: Faber and Faber 2001.

"History of Maugraby the Magician." *Tales of the East: Comprising the most Popular Romances of Oriental origin and the Best Imitations by European Authors with New Translations and Additional Tales never Before Published*. Vol. 2, pp. 219–234. Edinburgh: J. Ballantyne, 1812 *https://books.google.co.in/books?id=q3prMNDamvIC*. Accessed 23 May 2019.

Hodges, William. *Travels in India: During the Years 1780, 1781, 1782, & 1783*. London, 1783. *Internet Archive*. https://archive.org/details/travelsinindiad01hodggoog. Accessed 18 June 2020.

Hole, Roberts. *Pulpits, Politics and Public Order in England, 1760–1832*. Cambridge: Cambridge University Press, 1989.

Irwin, Robert. *The Arabian Nights: A Companion*. London: Allen Lane, 1994.

———. Preface. *The Arabian Nights and Orientalism: Perspectives from East & West*, edited by Yuriko Yamanaka and Tetsuo Nishio, London: I.B. Tauris, 2006, pp. vi–xiii.

Jackson, J.R. de J. *Samuel Taylor Coleridge: The Critical Heritage Volume 1 1794–1834*. Abingdon: Routledge, 2002.

Jarvis, Robin. *The Romantic Period; The Intellectual and Cultural Context of English Literature 1789–1830*. London: Routledge, 2014.

Johnson, Andrew Kurt. "Sir William Jones and Representation of Hinduism in British Romantic Poetry." University of York, Department of English and Related Literature, 2010, http//www. *etheses.whiterose.ac.uk/1236/*. Accessed 12 March 2014.

Johnson, Dr Samuel. *The History of Rasselas: Prince of Abissinia*, edited by J.P. Hardy, Oxford: Oxford University Press, 2009.

Kabir, Ananya Jahanara. "'Oriental Gothic': The Medieval Past in the Colonial Encounter." *Reorienting Orientalism*, edited by Chandreyee Niyogi, New Delhi: SAGE Publications, pp. 65–88.

Katsuyuma, Kuri. "Kubla Khan and the British Chinoiserie: The Geopolitics of Chinese Garden." Vallins, Oishi and Perry, pp. 191–207.

Keane, Patrick. *Coleridge's Submerged Politics: The Ancient Mariner and Robinson Crusoe*. Columbia and London: University of Missouri Press, 1994.

Kejariwal, O.P. *The Asiatic Society of Bengal and the Discovery of India's Past 1784-1838*. New Delhi: Oxford University Press, 1988.

Kelley, Theresa M. "Spirit and Geometric Form: The Stone and the Shell in Wordsworth's Arab Dream." *Studies in English Literature, 1500–1900*, vol. 22, no. 4, 1982, pp. 563–582. *JSTOR*. https://www.jstor.org/stable/450180. Accessed 7 July 2014.

Kelly, Gary. "Social Conflict, Nation and Empire: From Gothicism to Romantic Orientalism." *ARIEL: A Review of International English Literature*, vol. 20, no. 2, 1989, pp. 3–18, www.ariel.ucalgary.ca. Accessed 7 July 2014.

Kenneth, W. Gross. Introduction. *Hieroglyphic Tales, Horace Walpole*. Los Angeles: University of California Augustan Reprint Society, 1982, pp. i–xii.

Keri, Davies. "Mrs Bliss: A Blake Collector of 1794." *Blake in the Nineties*, edited by Steve Clark and David Worrall, Basingstoke: St. Martin's Press, 1999, pp. 212–230.

Keri, Davies. "Rebekah Bliss: Collector of William Blake and Oriental Books." Clark and Suzuki, pp. 38–62.

Khan, Jalal Uddin. "Coleridge's 'Kubla Khan': A New Historicist Study / قصيدة 'قبلاي خان' لكولريدج: دراسة من منظور التأريخانية الجديدة" *Alif: Journal of Comparative Poetics*, vol. 32, 2012, pp. 78–110.

Kidwai, A.R., and Vincent Newy. "The Outline of Coleridge and Southey's 'Mohammed.'" *Notes and Queries*, vol. 40, no. 1, 1993, p. 38.

Kitson, Peter J. "The 'Kowtow' Controversy and Representation of Asian Ceremonials in Romantic Poetry." Vallins, Oishi, and Perry, pp. 19–38.

———. "The Wordsworths, Opium and China." *Wordsworth Circle*, vol. 43, no. 1, 2012, pp. 2–12, www.questia.com. Accessed 27 December 2014.

———. *Forging Romantic China: Sino-British Cultural Exchange 1760–1840*. Cambridge: Cambridge University Press, 2013.

———. "Romanticism and Colonialism: Races, places peoples, 1785–1800." Fulford and Kitson, pp. 13–34.

Lamb, Charles. *Charles Lamb: Selected Writings*, edited by J.E. Morpurgo. New York: Routledge, 2003.

Landor, Walter Savage. *Count Julian: A Tragedy*. London: Printed for John Murray by James Moyes, 1812. *Internet Archive*, https://archive.org/details/countjulianatra00collgoog. Accessed 23 May 2013.

———. *Gebir: a Poem Seven Books*. 1798. London: Slatter and Munday; R.S. Kirby, 1803.

———. *Poems from the Arabic and Persian*. Warwick: Printed by H. Sharpe, 1800. https://lib.ugent.be/catalog/rug01:001119780. Accessed 23 May 2013.

Larrissy, Edward. "Blake's Orient." *Romanticism*, vol. 11, no. 1, 2005, pp. 1–13. *Edinburgh University Press Journals*. https://www.euppublishing.com/doi/abs/10.3366/rom.2005.11.1.1. Accessed 30 December 2014.

Leask, Nigel. "'Wandering through Eblis': absorption and containment in Romantic exoticism." Fulford and Kitson, pp. 165–188.

———. "Kubla Khan and Orientalism: The Road to Xanadu Revisited." *Romanticism*, vol. 4, no. 1, 1998, pp. 1–21. *Edinburgh University Press Journals*. https://www.euppublishing.com/doi/abs/10.3366/rom.1998.4.1.1. Accessed 25 August 2014.

———. *British Romantic Writers and the East: Anxieties of Empire*. Cambridge: Cambridge University Press, 2004.

———. Rev. of *Islam and Romantic Orientalism: Literary Encounters with the Orient*, by Momammed Sharafuddin. *BARS Bulletin & Review. no. 14.* n. pag. *British Association of Romantic Studies*. http://www.bars.ac.uk/main/wp-content/uploads/2017/07/14.pdf. Accessed 15 January 2015.

Lee, Debbie. "Forgeries." *Romanticism: An Oxford Guide*, edited by Nicholas Roe, Oxford: Oxford University Press, 2005, pp. 521–637.

Lessenich, Rolf. "The European Context." *Handbook of British Romanticism*, edited by Ralf Haekel, Berlin: Walter de Gruyter GmbH & Co KG, 2017, pp. 164–182.

Letters Writ by a Turkish Spy, who liv'd five and forty years...at Paris: Giving an Account...of the most remarkable transactions of Europe...from 1637 to 1682. Trans. From French, by W Bradshaw, and edited by Robert Midgley, MD. London, G. Strahan, 1637–1693. 8 vols. https://books.google.co.in/books/about/The_eight_volumes_of_letters_writ_by_a_T.html?id=UrU1AAAAMAAJ. Accessed 18 June 2020.

Letters of the Wordsworth Family, edited by Thomas De Quincey, New York: Haskel House Publishers Ltd., 1907.

Letters of John Wordsworth, edited by Carl H. Ketcham, Ithaca: Cornell University Press, 1969.

Levy, Michelle. "Discovery and Domestic Affection in Coleridge and Shelly." *SEL Studies of English Literature 1500–1900*, vol. 44, no. 4, 2004, pp. 693–713.

Lewis, Matthew Gregory. *The Castle Spectre, a Drama. In Five Acts. First Performed at the Theatre-Royal, Drury-Lane, on Thursday, December 14, 1797*. London: 1797. *Internet Archive*. https://archive.org/details/castlespectredra00lewiuoft. Accessed 8 March 2014

———. *The Monk: A Romance*, edited and introduced by E.A. Baker, London: Routledge and Sons LTD., 1907.

Libbrecht, Ulrich. *Within the Four Seas: Introduction to Comparative Philosophy*. Paris: Peeters Publishers, 2007.

Lonsdale, Roger, editor. *The Poems of Thomas Gray, William Collins, Oliver Goldsmith*. London: Longmans, 1969. Longmans' Annotated English Poets Series.

Lovell, Robert, and Robert Southey. *Poems: Containing the Retrospect, Odes, Elegies, Sonnets*. London: Printed by R. Cruttwell, 1795. *Internet Archive*. https://archive.org/details/poemscontaining00soutgoog. Accessed 9 March 2014.

Lowes, John Livingstone. *The Road to Xanadu: A Study in the Ways of the Imagination*. Boston: Houghton Mifflin, 1927.

Lussier, Mark S. *Romantic Dharma: The Emergence of Buddhism into Nineteenth-Century Europe*. New York: Palgrave Macmillan, 2011.

Macaulay, Thomas Babington. "Minutes on Education." 2 February 1835. *Internet Archive*. https://archive.org/details/Minutes_201311. Accessed 12 March 2014.

MacKenzie, John M. *Orientalism: History, Theory and the Arts*. Manchester: Manchester University Press, 1995.

Maclean, Gerald, editor. *Re-Orienting the Renaissance: Cultural Exchanges with the East*. New York: Palgrave Macmillan, 2005.

Madden, Lionel, editor. *Robert Southey: The Critical Heritage*. London: Taylor & Francis, 2002.

Majeed, Javed. *Ungoverned Imaginings: James Mill's The History of British India and Orientalism*. Oxford: Clarendon Press, 1992.

Mazumder, Aparajita. "Coleridge, Vishnu, and the Infinite." *Comparative Literature Studies* vol. 30, no. 1, 1993, pp. 32–52.

Makdisi, Saree. *Romantic Imperialism: Universal Empire and the Culture of Modernity.* Cambridge: Cambridge University Press, 1998.

——. *William Blake and the Impossible History of the 1790s*. Chicago: University of Chicago Press, 2003.

——. "Blake and the Ontology of Empire." Mee and Haggarty, pp. 204–259.

——. "Romantic Cultural Imperialism." *The Cambridge History of English Romantic Literature*, edited by James Chandler, Cambridge: Cambridge University Press, 2009, pp. 601–620.

Makdisi, Saree and Felicity Nussbaum, editors. *The Arabian Nights in Historical Context: Between East and West*. Oxford: Oxford University Press, 2008.

Marshall, P.J. "British-Indian connections c. 1780 to c. 1830: the empire of the officials." Franklin, pp. 45–64.

Marzolph, Ulrich, and Richard van Leeuwen. *The Arabian Nights: An Encyclopedia*. Vol. 1. Santa Barbara, CA: ABC-CLIO, 2004.

Mason, Michael, editor. *Lyrical Ballads*. New York: Routledge, 2013.

Maurice, Thomas. *The History of Hindostan: Its Arts, and Its Sciences, as Connected with the History of the Other Great Empires of Asia, During the Most Ancient Periods of the World, with Numerous Illustrated Engravings*. Vol. 1. 1795. London: W. Bulmer and W. Nicol, 1820. https://archive.org/details/thehistoryofhindostanthomasmauricevol1_284_T/page/n9/mode/2up. Accessed 7 January 2013.

Mc Gann, Jerome J. *The Beauty of Inflections: Literary Investigations in Historical Methods and Theory*. Oxford Oxfordshire: New York: Clarendon Press, 1985.

Macartney, George. *An Embassy to China: Being the Journal Kept by Lord Macartney during His Embassy to the Emperor Ch'ien-Lung, 1793–1794*. Hamden, Conn: Archon Books, 1963.

McKuisick, James C. "'Wisely Forgetful': Coleridge and the Politics of Pantisocracy." Fulford and Kitson, pp. 107–128.

Mee, Jon, and Sarah Haggarty, editors. *Blake and Conflict*. Basingstoke, England: Palgrave Macmillan, 2009.

Miles, Robert. "The 1790s: the effulgence of Gothic." *Cambridge Companion to Gothic Fiction*, edited by Jerrold E. Hogle, Cambridge: Cambridge University Press, 2002, pp. 41–62.

Mill, James. "The History of British India." Vols. 1–6, 4th ed., London: Madden and Co. 1840. *Internet Archive*, https://archive.org/details/historyofbritish01mill/page/n5/mode/2up. Accessed 7 July 2015.

Miller, J. Hillis. "The Stone and the Shell: The Problem of Poetic Form in Wordsworth's Dream of the Arab." *Mouvements Premiers: Etudes Critiques Offertes a Georges Poulet.* Paris: Librairie Jośe Corti, 1972, pp. 125–148.

Milton, John. *Paradise Lost*, edited by Alastair Fowler, London: Longman, 1998.

Miner, Paul. "The Polyp as a Symbol in the Poetry of William Blake." *Texas Studies in Literature and Language*, vol. 2, no. 2, 1960, pp. 198–205. *JSTOR*. https://www.jstor.org/stable/40753674. Accessed 5 March 2013.

Montesquieu, Charles de Secondat. *Persian Letters.* Trans. John Ozell. London: Garland, 1722. Volume 1, 3rd ed. https://books.google.co.in/books?id=jwE6AAAAcAAJ. Accessed 19 June 2020.

Moore, Thomas. *Lalla Rookh, an Oriental Romance.* 1817. 20th ed. E-book, London: Longman, Brown, Green, & Longmans, 1842. https://books.google.co.in/books?id=jwE6AAAAcAAJ. Accessed 19 June 2020.

Morris, Eaves, Robert Essick, and Joseph Viscomi, editors. *The William Blake Archive*. Lib. of Cong., 28 September 2007, http://www.blakearcive.org/blake/. Accessed 20 December 2019.

"nation, n.1." *OED Online*. Oxford University Press, December 2019. https://www.oed.com/view/Entry/125285?rskey=bjOJ3D&result=1&isAdvanced=false. Accessed 18 January 2020.

Nishio,Tetsuo. "A Bibliography of the Arabian Nights in the 18th Century" in Bulletin of the National Museum of Ethnology, 36.4: 561–639 (2012).

O'Gorman, Ned. "Longinus's Sublime Rhetoric, or How Rhetoric Came into Its Own". *Rhetoric Society Quarterly*, vol. 34, no. 2, 2004, pp. 71–89. *JSTOR*. https://www.jstor.org/stable/40232412. Accessed 20 December 2019.

Osmond, H. Percy. *The Mystical Poet of the English Church*. New York: The Macmillan Co., 1919.

Pachori, Satya Sheel, editor. *Sir William Jones: A Reader*. London: Oxford University Press, 1993.

Paine, Thomas. *The Rights of Man*. London, 1797.

Paley, Morton D. *The Continuing City: William Blake's Jerusalem*. Oxford: Clarendon Press, 1984.

———. *The Traveller in the Evening: The Last Works of William Blake*. Oxford: Oxford University Press, 2003.

Perry, Seamus, editor. *Coleridge's Notebook: A Selection*. Oxford: Oxford University Press, 2002.

Persian Tales: The Thousand and One Day. Translated by Ambrose Phillips. 3 vols. E-book, London: D. Graisberry, 1714–1715. https://books.google.co.in/books?id=6vJLPEnU4O0C. Accessed 19 June 2020.

Philmus, Robert M. "Wordsworth and the Interpretation of Dreams." *Papers on Language and Literature,* vol. 31, no. 2, 1995, pp. 184–195. *Questia.* https://www.questia.com/library/journal/1G1-16957567/wordsworth-and-the-interpretation-of-dreams. Accessed 12 March 2019.

Pike, Martha Conant. *The Oriental Tale in the Eighteenth Century*. New York: Columbia University Press, 1908.

Pinto, V. De Sola. "Sir William Jones and English Literature." *Bulletin of the School of Oriental and African Studies*, vol. 11, no. 04, 1946, pp. 686–694. *Cambridge Journals Online*. DOI: https://doi.org/10.1017/S0041977X00089758. Accessed 23 November 2014.

Pratt, Lynda. "'Where . . . success [is] certain'? Southey the literary East Indiaman." Franklin, pp. 131–153.

———. editor. *Robert Southey and the Context of English Romanticism*. Farnham, Surrey: Ashgate, 2007.

Pratt, Mary Louise. *Imperial Eyes: Travel Writing and Transculturation*. London: Routledge, 1992.

Price, Richard. *A Discourse on the Love of Our Country, delivered on Nov. 4, 1789, at the Meeting House in the Old Jewry, to the Society for Commemorating the Revolution in Britain. With an Appendix*. 2nd ed., London: T. Cadell, 1789.

Punter, David and Glennis Byron, editors. "The Gothic." *Blackwell Guides to Literature*, vol. 10, Malden: Wiley-Blackwell Publishing Ltd., 2004.

Punter, David. "The Gothic Tradition." *The Literature of Terror: A History of Gothic Fictions from 1765 to the Present Day,* vol. 1, 2nd ed., New York: Routledge, 1996.

Purchas, Samuel. *Purchas his Pilgrimage Or Relations of the World and the Religions Observed in All Ages and Places Discovered, from the Creation up to this Present*. London: William Stansby for Henry Fetherstone, 1613. *Internet Archive*, https://archive.org/details/purchashispilgri00purc. Accessed 9 March 2014.

Pyle, Forest. *The Ideology of Imagination: Subject and Society in the Discourse of Romanticism*. Stanford: Stanford University Press, 1997.

Raine, Cathleen. *Blake and Tradition: Volume II*. Princeton: Princeton University Press, 1968.

Rajan, Balachandra. *Under Western Eyes: India from Milton to Macaulay*. Durham, NC: Duke University Press Books, 1999.

Rana, Kabbani. *Europe's Myth of the Orient: Devise and Rule*. London: The Macmillan Press Ltd, 1986.

Randonis, Jennifer. "The Thunder of Thought and flames of fierce Desire: William Blake's transformations of the Gothic Tradition." *The Spirit of the Gothic*. Robert A. Douglas, n.d. N. pag. http://www.thatlineofdarkness.com/. Accessed 29 December 2013.

Reeve, Clara. *The Progress of Romance Through Times, Countries, and Manners*. 1785. London: Garland Pub., 1970.

Richard, Allen. "First Encounters Works by Sir William Jones and Others." *Literature and Nation: Britain and India 1800–1990*, edited by Richard Allen and Harish Trivedi. London: Routledge, 2000, pp. 28–42.

Richardson, Alan. "Epic Ambivalence: Imperial Politics and Romantic Deflections in William's Peru and Landor's *Gebir*." *Romanticism, Race, and Imperial Culture, 1780–1834*, edited by Alan Richardson and Sonia Hofkosh, Bloomington: Indiana UP, 1996, pp. 265–282.

Riley-Smith, Jonathan. *The Crusades, Christianity, and Islam*. New York: Columbia University Press, 2008.

Robinson, Henry Crabb et al. *Blake, Coleridge, Wordsworth, Lamb, etc.: Being Selections from the Remains of H.C. Robinson*, edited by Edith J. Morley, London: Longmans, Green & Co., 1922.

"Romantic Orientalism: Overview." Romantic Period. *Norton Anthology of English Literature. Norton Topics Online*, vol. D, 9th ed. Gen. ed. Stephen Greenblatt. Norton, 2011. http://www.wwnorton.com/college/english/nael/romantic/topic_4/welcome.htm. Accessed 20 March 2013.

Rousseau, Jean-Jacques. *Emile: Or On Education*. 1762. Translated by Allan Bloom, New York: Basic Books, 1979.

Ryan, Robert M. *The Romantic Reformation: Religious Politics in English Literature, 1789–1824*, Cambridge: Cambridge University Press, 1997.

Saglia, Diego "Orientalism." *A Companion to European Romanticism*, edited by Michael Ferber, Malden: Wiley-Blackwell, 2006, pp. 467–487.

———. "Words and Things: Southey's East and the Materiality of the Oriental Discourse." Pratt, pp. 167–186.

Said, Edward W. "Preface to Twenty- Fifth Anniversary Edition." *Orientalism*. Twenty-fifth Anniversary Edition, New York: Vintage, 2003, pp. xv–xxx.

———. *Orientalism*. 1978. New Delhi: Penguin Books, 2001.

Sale, George. *The Koran, Commonly Called the Alcoran of Mohammed*. London: Printed by C. Atkin 1734. *Internet Archive*, https://archive.org/details/Sale1734Koran. Accessed 19 June 2020.

Sato, Hikari. "Blake, Hayley and India: On Designs to a Series of Ballads." Clark and Suzuki, pp. 134–144.

Saurat, Denis. *Blake & Modern Thought*. New York: Russell & Russell, 1964.

Schmidt, Michael. *The Novel: A Biography*. Cambridge: Harvard University Press, 2014.

Schneider, Elizabeth. *Coleridge, Opium and Kubla Khan*. Chicago: University of Chicago Press, 1953.

Schwab, Raymond. *The Oriental Renaissance: Europe's Rediscovery of India and the East, 1680–1880*. Translated by Gene Patterson-Black and Victor Reinking. New York: Columbia University Press, 1984.

Scott, John. *The Poetical Works of John Scott Esq*. E-book, London: J. Buckland, 1782. https://books.google.co.in/books?id=XylDAQAAMAAJ. Accessed 30 August 2010.

Scott, Walter. *The Lay of the Last Minstrel*. London: Longman, 1808.

———. *Count Robert of Paris and Castle Dangerous*. Edinburgh, 1831.

———. *The Betrothed*. London, 1825.

———. *The Bridal of Triermain, or The Vale of St*. London, 1813.

———. *The Talisman*. London, 1825.

Sedgwick, Eve Kosofsky. *The Coherence of Gothic Conventions*. London: Methuen, 1986.

Select Poets of Great Britain: To Which Are Prefixed, Critical Notices of Each Author, edited by William Hazlitt, London: Thomas Davison, 1825.

Selincourt, Ernest De, editor. *The Prelude*. 2nd Revised ed., Oxford: Clarendon Press, 1926.

Sen, Amartya. *The Argumentative Indian: Writings on Indian History, Culture and Identity*. London: Penguin Books, 2005.

Serendipity and the Three Princes: From the Peregrinaggio of 1557, edited by Theodore G. Remer. Translated by G. Borselli Augusto and Theresa L. Borselli, University of Oklahoma Press, 1965.

Shaffer, E.S. *"Kubla Khan" and the Fall of Jerusalem: The Mythological School in Biblical Criticism and Secular Literature 1770–1880*. Cambridge: Cambridge University Press, 1980.

Sharafuddin, Mohammed. *Islam and Romantic Orientalism: Literary Encounters with the Orient*. London: I.B. Tauris & Co Ltd, 1994.

Shaver, Chester Linn. *Wordsworth's Library: A Catalogue, Including a List of Books Housed by Wordsworth for Coleridge from C. 1810 to C. 1830*. Garland Pub., 1979.

Shelley, Percy Bysshe. *Shelley's Poetry & Prose*, edited by Neil Fraistat and Donald H. Reiman. 2nd Revised ed., New York: W.W. Norton & Company, 2002.

———. *Prometheus Unbound*. 1820. Champaign, Ill.: Book Jungle, 2007.

Shore, John. *Memoirs of the Life, Writings and Correspondence of Sir William Jones*. Vol. 1 London: Brettell, 1806. https://books.google.co.in/books?id=Y-UEAAAAYAAJ. Accessed 19 June 2020.

Sicker, Martin. *The Islamic World in Decline: From the Treaty of Karlowitz to the Disintegration of the Ottoman Empire*. Westport, Conn: Praeger Publishers Inc, 2000.

Smith, Andrew, and William Hughes. *Empire and the Gothic: The Politics of Genre*. Houndmills: Palgrave Macmillan, 2003.

Smith, Andrew, and William Hughes. "Introduction: Enlightenment Gothic and Postcolonialism." Smith and Hughes, pp. 1–12.

Smollett, Tobias George, editor. *The Critical Review: Or, Annals of Literature*, vol. 54. E-book, London: W. Simpkin and R. Marshall, 1782. https://books.google.co.in/books?id=fnjQAAAAMAAJ. Accessed 12 May 2013.

Smylitopoulos, Christina. "Portrait of a Nabob: Graphic Satire, Portraiture, and the Anglo-Indian in the Late Eighteenth Century." *Revue d'art canadienne/Canadian Art Review*, vol. 37, no. 1, 2012, pp. 10–25.

Smyser, Jane Worthington. "Wordsworth's Dream of Poetry and Science: The Prelude, V." *PMLA* 7, vol. 1, no. 1, 1956, pp. 269–275. *JSTOR*. http://www.jstor.com/stable/460208. Accessed 3 July 2015.

Sonoi, Chine. "Southey's radicalism and the abolitionist movement." *Wordsworth Circle*, vol. 42, no. 1, Winter, 2011, pp. 22–26. https://doi.org/10.1086/TWC24043998. Accessed 16 August 2013.

Southey, Robert. *Southey's Commonplace Book: Second Series, Special Collections*, edited by John Wood Warter, London: Reeves and Turner, 1876. *Internet Archive*, https://archive.org/details/southeyscommonpl00soutuoft. Accessed 14 June 2014.

———. *The Collected Letters of Robert Southey Part One: 1791–1797*, edited by Lynda Pratt, 2009, Romantic Circle Electronic Edition, 2013.

———. *The Collected Letters of Robert Southey Part Two: 1798–1803*, edited by Ian Packer and Lynda Pratt, Romantic Circle Electronic Edition, 2011.

———. *The Collected Letters of Robert Southey Part Three: 1804–1809*, edited by Carol Bolton and Tim Fulford, Romantic Circle Electronic Edition, 2013.

———. *The Collected Letters of Robert Southey Part Four: 1810–1815*, edited by Lynda Pratt and Ian Packer, Romantic Circle Electronic Edition, 2013.

———. *The Complete poetical Works of Robert Southey.* New York: Appleton & Company, 1857.

———. *Wat Tyler: A Dramatic Poem by Robert Southey*. 1817. Edited by Matt Hill, 2004, Romantic Circle Electronic Edition, 2014.

Spivak, Gayatri Chakravorty. "The Rani of Sirmur: An Essay in Reading the Archives." *History and Theory*, vol. 24, no. 3, 1985, pp. 247–272. Rpt. in *Europe and Its Others*, vol. 1, edited by Francis Barker et al., Colchester: University of Essex Press, 1985, pp. 128–251.

Standard Dictionary of English Language. 2 vols. New York: 1895.

Steele, Richard. "Story of Santon Barsisa" *Guardian*. No. 148. 31 August 1713. Rpt. in Robert Lynn's *The British Essayists. Vol XI: Guardian*. London: J.F. Dove, 1827. pp. 194–197.

Staunton, Sir George. *An Authentic Account of an Embassy from the King of Great Britain to the Emperor of China*. London: G. Nicol, 1797.

Stevenson, W.H., editor. *Blake: The Complete Poems*. London: Longman, 1971.

Stubbe, Henry. *An Account of The Rise and Progress of Mahometanism: With the Life of Mahomet, and a Vindication of Him and his Religion from the Calumnies of the Christians*, edited by Hafiz Mahmud Khan Shairani, Whitefish, Mont.: Kessinger Publishing, LLC, 2010.

Sudan, Rajani. *Fair Exotics: Xenophobic Subjects in English Literature, 1720–1850*. Philadelphia: University of Pennsylvania Press, 2002.

Suleri, Sara. *The Rhetoric of English India*. Chicago: University of Chicago Press, 1992.

Sultana, Donald. *Samuel Taylor Coleridge in Malta and Italy*. Oxford: Blackwell, 1969.

Sung, Mei-Ying. "Blake and the Chinamen." Clark and Suzuki, pp. 63–76.

Susan J. "Revision as Form: Wordsworth's Drowned Man," in Stephen C. Gill (ed.) *William Wordsworth's The Prelude: A Case Book*. New York, Oxford University Press, 2006, pp. 73–122.

Symes, Michael. *An Account of an Embassy to the Kingdom of Ava, Sent by the Governor-General of India in the Year 1795*. Vol. 2 London: Printed for J Debrett, Piccadilly by Wilson and Co. 1800. *Internet Archive*. https://archive.org/details/account_of_an_embassy_to_the_kingdom_of_ava_vol2. Accessed on 19 June 2020.

Thomas, Gordon K. "Fact and Fiction, Stone and Shell: Wordsworth's Dream of the Poetic Paradox." *Neophilologus*, vol. 69, no. 3, 1985, pp. 446–451. *link.springer.com*. https://doi.org/10.1007/BF02001056. Accessed 7 July 2015.

Thomas, Helen. "Romanticism and the Slave Narratives: Transatlantic Testimonials." *Cambridge Studies in Romanticism*, vol. 38. Cambridge: Cambridge University Press, 2004.

Thomson, Heidi. "The Integral Significance of the 1816 Preface to 'Kubla Khan'." Vallins, Oishi and Perry, pp. 165–177.

Trautmann, Thomas R. *Aryans and British India: New Perspectives on Indian Pasts*. Berkeley, C.A.: University of California Press, 1997.

Tuchman, Barbara W. *Bible and Sword: England and Palestine from the Bronze Age to Balfour*. Reissue ed. New York: Random House Trade Paperbacks, 1984.

Tufyal, Ibn. *Hayy ibn-Yaqzan*. Translated by Simon Ockley, 1708. Revised with an Introduction by A.S. Fulton. E-book, London; Chapman Hall and Limited, 1929. https://archive.org/details/IbnTufailStoryOfHayy-BinYaqzanHistoryOckleyIntroFulton/page/n7/mode/2up. Accessed 20 June 2020.

Turkish Tales; Consisting of Several Extraordinary Adventures. With the History of the Sultaness of Persia, and the Visiers. Written originally in the

Turkish Language by Chec Zade, for the use of Amurath II, and now done into English translated by William King. London, J. Tonson 1708.

Vallins, David, Kaz Oishi, and Seamus Perry, editors. *Coleridge, Romanticism and the Orient: Cultural Negotiations*. E-book, London, Continuum Publishing Corporation, 2013. https://books.google.co.in/books?id=KyBFAAAAYAAJ. Accessed 20 June 2020.

Vallins, David. "Immanence and Transcendence in Coleridge's Orient." Vallins, Oishi, and Perry, pp. 119–130.

Viswanathan, Gouri. *The Mask of Conquest: Literary study and British rule in India*. 1989. Delhi: Oxford India Paperbacks, 1998.

Volney, Constantin-François. A New Translation of Volney's *Ruins: Or, Meditations on the Revolution of Empires*. 1791. E-book, London: Hood & Cuthell, 1811. https://books.google.co.in/books?id=d1wzAQAAMAAJ. Accessed 20 June 2020.

Voltaire. *Mahomet the Imposter: A Tragedy*. London: Printed for and sold by J. Watts and B. Dod, 1744.

Walpole, Horace. *The Castle of Otranto: A Gothic Story*. 1764. E-book, London: Bodoni, 1791. https://books.google.vu/books?id=e81ft0T0nIEC. Accessed 21 August 2009.

Warren, Andrew. "Coleridge, Orient and Philosophy." Vallins, Oishi, and Perry, pp. 103–118.

——. *The Orient and the Young Romantics*. Cambridge: Cambridge University Press, 2014.

Watt, W. Montgomery. *Muslim-Christian Encounters: Perceptions and Misperceptions*. London: Routledge, 1991.

Webb, Timothy. "Romantic Hellenism." Curran, pp. 149–176.

Weir, David. *Brahma in the West: William Blake and the Oriental Renaissance*. Albany: State University of New York Press, 2003.

White, Daniel E. "Idolatry, Evangelicalism, and the Intense Objectivism of Robert Southey," *Romanticism*, vol. 17, no. 1, 2011, pp. 39–51.

——. *Early Romanticism and Religious Dissent*. Cambridge, UK: Cambridge University Press, 2007.

Whitehead, Angus. "'A wise tale of the Mahometans': Blake and Islam, 1819–26." Mee and Haggarty, pp. 27–47.

Charles Wilkins. *The Bhagvat-Geeta, or Dialogues of Kreeshna and Arjoon; in Eighteen Lectures; with Notes. Translated from the Original, in the Sanskreet, or Ancient Language of the Brahmans, by Charles Wilkins, Senior*

Merchant in the service of the Honorable The East India Company, on their Bengal Establishment. London: C. Nourse, 1785. https://oll.libertyfund.org/titles/2369. Accessed 21 June 2020.

Williams, Dean, and Ananya Jahanara Kabir, editors. *Postcolonial Approaches to the Middle Ages*. Cambridge, Cambridge University Press, 2005.

Williams, Stanley T. "The Sources of Landor's Gebir." *Modern Language Notes*, vol. 36, no. 5, 1921, p. 315. *JSTOR*. https://www.jstor.org/stable/2915075. Accessed 28 August 2014.

Wood, Marcus, editor. *The Poetry of Slavery: An Anglo-American Anthology.* New York, Oxford University Press, 2003.

Works of the English Poets. With Prefaces, Biographical and Critical, by S. Johnson. London, 1790. Internet Archive. https://archive.org/details/worksenglishpoe05johngoog. Accessed 20 June 2020.

Wordsworth, William. *The Borderers*, edited by Robert Osborne, Ithaca, Cornell University Press, New York, 1982.

———. "Preface to *Lyrical Ballads*." *English Critical Texts: Sixteenth Century to Twentieth Century*, edited by D.J. Enright, and Ernst De Chickera, pp. 162–189. London: Oxford University Press, 1968 (paperback edition).

———. *The Collected Poems of William Wordsworth*. Wordsworth Editions Ltd, 1994.

———. *The Prelude: 1799, 1805, 1850*, edited by M.H. Abrams, Stephen Gill and Jonathan Wordsworth, New York, W.W. Norton & Company, 1979.

Wordsworth, William, and Dorothy. *The Letters of William and Dorothy Wordsworth: Volume I. The Early Years 1787–1805*, edited by L. Shaver Chester and Ernest de Selincourt. 2nd ed. Oxford, Oxford University Press, 2000.

Wright, Julia M. *Blake, Nationalism, and the Politics of Alienation.* Athens, Ohio University Press, 2004.

Wu, Duncan. "Wordsworth's Reading of Ahamad Ardabili." *N&Q*, vol. 37, 1990, p. 412.

———. *Wordsworth's Reading 1770–1799*, vol. 1, Cambridge, Cambridge University Press, 1993.

Yamanaka, Yuriko, and Tetsuo Nishio. *The Arabian Nights and Orientalism: Perspectives from East and West.* London, I.B. Tauris, 2006.

Zernatto, Guido, and Alfonso G. Mistretta. 'Nation: The History of a Word'. *The Review of Politics*, vol. 6, no. 3, 1944, pp. 351–366. *JSTOR*. https://www.jstor.org/stable/1404386. Accessed 20 June 2020.

Index

A

abolitionist movement, 27–28
Abrams, M.H., 195
Addison, Lancelot, 34
Adites, 109, 120, 185
The Adventures of Abdalla, son of Hanif, 50
aesthetic principle, 22, 31, 158
Aesthetics, 212
African Eclogues, (1770), 53
Aikin, John, 23
'Aladdin and the Wonderful Lamp' tale, 187
Alastor, 65
Alatas, Syed Hussain, 124
Alcoran of Mahomet (1649), 34
Alf Layla (*A Thousand Nights*), 46
Alf Layla wa Layla, 43
Ali, Haidar, 144. *See also* Tipu Sultan
Alinagar, battle of, 37
Allen, Richard, 69
America: A Prophecy, 98
American War of Independence (1775–1783), 28, 36
An Authentic Account of an Embassy from the King of Great Britain to the Emperor of China (1797), 191
The Analytical Review, 75, 78
anarchism, 30
Ancient Mariner (republishing 1817), 194
Ancient Mariner, 157–158, 160–164, 166–167, 177, 190, 193, 224
Anderson, 2–3
Anglican Church, 25, 194
  dominance of, 25
Anglican criticism of Hindu society, 16
Anglican-British imperialism, 113
Anglicanism, 151
  rise of, 211
Anglicism, 137, 173
Anglicist Clapham sect, 39
Anglicist-Orientalist debate, 38
Anglicists, 38, 81, 83, 131, 150
Anglo-centrism, 103, 151, 155, 211
  rise of, 211
Anglo-French war, 30
Anglo-Israel movement, 102
Anglo-Mysore wars, 144
Anima Poetae, 169
Annual Review on the *Periodical Accounts relative to the Baptist Missionary Society* (1802), 137
anti-authoritarian association, 169
anti-clerical violence, 63
anti-colonialist fable, 110
anti-imperial epic, 110
anti-imperial gesture, 96

anti-religious tendencies, 62
anti-slavery ideology, 162
anti-slavery sentiments, 54
anti-slavery trade agitation, 128
Arabian Nights Entertainments: Consisting of One Thousand and One Stories, 123, 202
The Arabian Nights, 24, 44, 47–48, 51, 57–58, 73, 120, 156, 165, 223
Arabian Romance, 119
Arberry, A.J., 74
Ardabili, Ahamad, 196
"The Armenian Lady's Love", 209
Arpenius, Thomas, 196
Asiatic Patriarchs, 84–85
Asiatic poetry, 22
    characteristic of, 22
Asiatic Society of Bengal, 37, 66–67, 75, 78, 81
Asiatick Researches, 67, 78
aspheterism, principles of, 28
Atheists, 25
Attar, Samar, 8–9, 159, 165, 205
Augustanism, 22, 24, 31
    aesthetic principles of, 31
    political and moral, 31
    principles of, 24
Austria, 33, 208
    stakes in decadent Ottoman Empire, 33

B

Bahar-Danush, 124, 186
Balkans, 11
Ballaster, Ross, 48, 57
Baptist Missionary Society, 131, 134, 137, 140
Baptists, 25
Barbauld, Anna, 128
Bard Bracy, 163, 167
Barfoot, C.C., 1, 31
Barlaam and Josaphat, 43
Barrow, Sir John, 37
Barsisa, 49, 62–63, 166
Bayle, Pierre, 35
Beauty of Inflections, 227
Beckford, William, 23, 48, 109
Bedford, Charles, 127–128
Bedouin, Arab, 53, 201, 212
Bentley, George, 96
Berlin, Isaiah, 9
Bernhardt-Kabisch, 117, 127, 205
The Betrothed (1825), 8
The Bhagvat-Geeta (translation of, 1785), 13, 69, 79–80, 140, 174, 177, 179, 175, 217, 219
Bible, as myth, 183
Bibliotheque Orientale (1697), 66
Biographia Literaria (1823), 140, 164
Birkhead, Edith, 58
Black Athena, 227
Black Sea, 33
Blake and the Impossible History of the 1790s, 89
A Blake Dictionary, 88
Blake, Garcia, 90–92, 95–96, 113–114, 122, 170, 194
Blake, William
    Anglo-centric, 101
    approach to India and Hinduism, 76, 85–86
    art forms in poetry and designs, 76
    Christo-centric outlook of, 101
    composite mythology, 75

cosmology, 86
criticism of the empire, 100
critics, 88
divine vision in writing, 83
early opposition to imperialism, 102
embodiment of "man-Britain", 101
engagement with Anglo–Israelites, 102
engagement with Islam, 15, 76, 87, 90–91, 95
familiarity with Wilkins's translation of *The Bhagvat-Geeta*, 80
four Zoas from the ancient Indian spiritual tradition, 73
Gothic terror in, 100
'Hindostan', 86
influenced by the Orientalism, 76
interest in phrenology, 95
knowledge of Hindu theology, 78
mythography, 73
placement of Muhammad, 92
polypus, 100–102
prejudice against Islam, 89
reference to Islamic beliefs, 98
reference to Qur'an, 89
relationship with East, 14, 74–76, 98, 106
representation of Egypt and Africa, 76
repression of humans, 99
thought and philosophy, 74
unironic utterances, 90
universalism, 83

Blake's Visionary Universe, 99
Blakean myth, 15, 74
Bolton, Carol, 119, 128, 136, 141, 144–145
Book of Ahania, 99–100
Book of Revelation, 26
Book of Urizen, 100
The Borderers (1796–1797), 65
Bradshaw, W., 51
Brahma, 78, 81, 87, 219
  "abstract philosophy" of, 98
Brahma in the West: William Blake and the Oriental Renaissance (2003), 74
Brahmin, 139, 143, 147
The Bramins (1809), 79
The Bridal of Trierman (1813), 8
Bristol riots, 145
Britain (British)
  Asiatic subjects of, 81
  anxiety of the trading class, 57
  colonial agency, 69
  colonial expansionism, 14
  colonial politics and policies, 31
  consolidation of identity, 33, 212
  cruelty and inhumanity of, 55
  cruelty of the British rulers in India, 56
  dominant European power, 11
  education system, 127
  fear of the Napoleonic power, 144
  freshness of spirit into poetry, 21
  imperial anxiety, 115
  imperial politics of, 224
  imperial relations and connections, 213

imperial strategy of, 38
imperialism, 100, 113, 144
knowledge formation about India, 37
nationalism, 1, 34
nationalistic ideals, 16
natural rights in, 27
Orientalism, 5
originary moments in India, 174
perception of India and Hinduism, 133
poetic standard, 136
policy toward India, 225
political dissidence, 13
post-French Revolution-period, 29
primacy of Christian cultural heritage, 150
print market, 1
radical critique of imperialism, 114
radicalism, 29
religious Nonconformity, 13
republicanism, 127
superiority of, 1

British Romantic Writers, 9, 115, 147
Brown, Norman O., 91
Brown, W.C., 35
Browne, William George, 35–36
Bruce, James, 35, 89, 185
Buddhism, 11
Burke, Edmund, 23, 29, 121, 140
critique of conservative defense, 27
trial speeches, 121
Burnet, George, 128
Butler, Marilyn, 83, 110, 118–119, 147
Buxar, Battle of, 174
Bygrave, S., 30
Byron, Lord 7, 18, 21, 64–65
Byron, Glennis, 58
Byron's Letters and Journals, 21
Byronic heroes, 65

C

cancerous crocodiles, 3
cannibalism, 191
Cannon, Garland, 9, 195
Canzade, Queen, 49
Cape of Good Hope, 39
Carlyle, J.D., 196
caste
caste division, 139
Christianization of lower-caste Hindus, 142
conversions, 139–140
lower-caste Hindus, 16
lower-caste pariah woman, 136
persecution of lower caste, 141
sati practice and, 138
sublimity of, 140
upper-caste Brahmins, 139
The Castle of Otranto (1764), *The Castle of Otranto*, 45, 61–62, 64, 121
The Castle Spectre, 165
Cathay Company, 32
Catholic Emancipation Act of 1829, 26
Catholic oppression, 178
Catholicism
evils of, 180

idolatrous tendency in, 182
Chambers, Sir William, 191
The Champion, 164
Chandler, David, 201
Charles II, 112
Charoba (1785), 44, 48
Charter Act of 1813, 38, 131
pious clause, 38
Chatterton, 53–54
Cherubim, 85
Childe Harold's Pilgrimage, 65
China
alternative space in Coleridge's poetry, 190
Buddhism and, 11
ceased to influence European art and philosophy, 39
contemporary geopolitics, 191
crucial location for Europe, 32
as a geopolitical space, 192
Chinese gardens, 191–192, 216
Chinese Tales or the Wonderful Adventures of Mandarin Fum-Hoam (1725), 50
"Christabel", 6–7, 49, 65, 155–156, 161, 163–168, 173, 193, 224
Christian monasticism, bondage of, 90
Christianity Consistent with a Love of Freedom (1791), 30
Christianity, 11–12, 14–15, 30–31, 34, 38, 76, 83–85, 89–91, 102, 107, 127, 137–138, 169–170, 172, 183, 210–211, 214, 221, 225
'arsenic', 154n18
agent of transformation, 138
British nationalism and, 34
Christianization of Hindus in India, 151
Christianization of lower-caste Hindus, 142
Christianization of the natives, 142
conflict with Islam, 107
fresh challenge for, 38
ideal of celibacy, 88
interpretations of Hinduism, 75
introduction of, 111, 141
laws of, 63
modernizing trends in, 30
monasticism, 90
pre-eminence of, 12
primacy of, 5, 77, 193, 211
republican order, 91
sacredness and primacy of, 5
spiritual Christianity, 172
superiority of, 14
sympathetic approach to other religions, 12
teaching of, 146
Christians, idolatrous Christians, 170
Chronicle of the Cid (1808), 106
Church Missionary Society, 131
The Citizen of the World, 44
civil and political rights, 27–28
Clapham Sect, 128
Clarke, Edward Daniel, 36
Clarke, J.J., 8
claustrophobic spaces, 59, 62, 120
Cockney School, 30
Cohen-Vrignaud, 31

The Coherence of the Gothic Conventions, 59
Coleridge, S.T.
  advocate of the anti-slavery movement, 173
  attitude toward Christianity, 172
  attitude toward India, 183, 175
  attitude toward the East, 194
  biblical root of Orientalism, 184
  celebrate Napoleon's Egyptian invasion, 171
  Christabel, 166
  Christian-centrism, 183
  compromise with conservatism, 194
  concept of 'One Life', 178, 181, 189
  confusion regarding the French Revolution, 171
  criticism of Hinduism, 182–183
  critique of despotism, 192
  critique of the trade, 156
  defender of Christianity, 169
  development as a poet and thinker, 169
  dream-vision of a paradise garden, 188
  enchantment with the Oriental Tale, 156
  evolution of ideas, 182
  experimentation with contemporary taste, 156
  exploration of religious syncretism, 155
  fears and anxieties, 160
  Gothic tragedy, 178
  incorporation of 'spirit', 158
  insularity, 163
  interest in Oriental Tale, 186
  involvement with Indian thoughts, 174
  nationalism and conservatism, 17
  opium-induced dream, 187
  Orientalism, 182
  pantheism of, 177
  pantheistic ideas, 181
  perspective on Islam, 173
  philosophical ideas, 182
  poetical schema, 162
  presentation of Geraldine, 164
  rejection of the Eastern and Indian philosophical ideas, 182
  relationship with Indian theology and philosophy, 174
  romantic sublimity, 189
  short lyrics, ballads, and narrative fragments, 155
  solution to the anxiety, 193
  Spinoza's materialism, 182
  sympathy with Hinduism, 182
  theological ideas of Hinduism and Islam, 16
  writing a tendency, 162
Coleridge's Poetry and Prose, 164, 166
Collins, 120
Collins, William, 23, 52
colonial policy, 70
colonial politics, 22, 133, 225
'colonial' organism, 87
colonialism, 3, 115, 128, 160, 194
Commentaries on Asiatic Poetry, 67

Commonplace Book, 3–4, 106, 116
A Comparison of the Institutions of Moses with those of the Hindoos and other Ancient Nations (1799), 75
Complete Poems, 170
Confessions of an English Opium Eater (1821), 3, 140, 226
Congregationalists, 25
Connolly, Tristanne J., 84
Constantinople, Ancient and Modern (1797), 35
The Continuing City, 100
conversion, 134–135, 139–140, 209–210
  caste-based, 139
  public opinion in favor of, 142
Corporations Act (1661), 25
Corsica (Napoleon's birthplace), 112
Cottle, Joseph, 116
Count Julian: A Tragedy (1812), 107
Count Robert of Paris (1831), 8
Cowper, William, 23
Critical Review, 134
cultural superiority, 5, 150
curatorial and exoticist approach, 151
The Curse of Kehama (1810), 5–7, 16, 56, 106, 123, 125, 129–131, 133–134, 136, 138–139, 142, 149, 151, 162, 223, 226

D

Dalica, Masarian, 108–115
Damon, S. Foster, 73, 88
Danvers, Charles, 131
Dârâ Shukoh, 66
"the darkness of Asia", description of, 80
Davies, John, 108
De Almeida, Hermione, 142
De Quincey, Thomas, 3, 7, 18, 140, 226
De sacra poesi Hebraeorum (1753), 24
de-Christianization campaign of 1793–1794, 30
Déclaration des droits de l'homme et du citoyen de 1789, 27
Declaration of the Rights of Man, 27
demonic female, 64
demonization, 147
Description de l'Égypte, 66
Description of the Character, Manners and Customs, of the People of India (1817), 174, 196
A Description of the East (1743–1745), 35
The Descriptive Catalogue (1809), 91
Devnagari, 79
Dias, Bartolomeu, 39
Discplina Clericalis, 43
Dissenting Protestants, 25
Dissertation on the Prototypes of Architecture, Hindu Moorish and Gothic, 189
Divine Comedy, 93
Domdaniel, 16, 118–121, 127, 129
Don Juan, 227
Don Quixote, 211–212, 217
Drew, John, 8, 188
Dubois, Jean Antoine, 196
Duperron, 41, 66, 130

E

Earl of Abergavenny, 214
Early Romanticism and Religious Dissent, 169
East India Company (EIC), 32, 36–38, 58, 69, 80–81, 132, 174, 214
East India Company Act, 36
Eastern fantasies, 167
Eastern tale of horror, 58
"East-Indianised English men", 132
East–West binary, 2, 12
Ecclesiastical Sonnets, 207
Edinburgh Review, 6
Egypt, 3, 11
  expedition of France, 171
  invasion of, 108
"The Egyptian Maid", 66, 210–211
eighteenth century literary market, 43
Elizabethan commerce, 32
Emile: or, On Education (1762), 50
Empire and Gothic: the Politics of Genre, 65
England, 9, 12, 23–33, 43, 47, 50, 79, 91, 100–103, 110, 115, 127, 131–132, 140, 150, 171, 183, 202, 207, 225–226
  adventures of exploration and trade, 32
  allegorical representation of, 110
  failure of the Oriental Renaissance, 224
  history of Oriental Tale, 47
  hostility toward China, 39
  imperial ambitions of, 100
  Jacobinism in, 29
  policy toward the Middle East, 33
  political and ideological divisions, 33
  radical politics and poetics in, 29
  relationship with the East, 225
  religious inequalities in, 25
  republicanism and radicalism in, 127
  revival of the Gothic in, 23
  rise of the evangelical lobby, 183
  stakes in decadent Ottoman Empire, 33
  'White' English poet, 96
  "white nabobs" in, 154n17
  See also Britain
English neoclassicism, 23
English novel, relation with Oriental Tale, 48
English radicalism, 26
English Revolution of 1688, 26
English-speaking Orientalists, 66, 98
Enlightenment period, 102
Enlightenment principles, 45
Enquiry Concerning Political Justice (1793), 28
Ethiopia, 3, 11
Eurocentrism, 122, 227
Europe
  Arabic poetry to, 67
  'Back to Nature' movement, 39
  civilizational mission of modernity, 140
  consolidation of cultural identity, 212
  discovery of ancient Hindu religious texts, 38
  enterprise of (slave) trade and commerce, 160

enthusiasm for Hindu theological texts, 38
era of appreciation of China in, 39
familiarity with Asia and Africa, 32
fascination with Islam, 34
incursion into India, 36
Islamic republicanism in, 34
metropolitan audience, 68
navigational enterprises, 32
notion of cultural superiority, 5
Oriental Renaissance in, 1
perception of China, 191
philhellenism, 227
poetry, 22
polite society in, 39
rationalism in, 205
Turkish incursions into, 32
evangelical and intolerant Orientalism, 79
evangelical lobby, 133, 183
The Evangelical Magazine (1793), 131
Evangelicals, 25
Evangelism, 137, 155
The Excursion, 218
exotic eroticism, 110

F

The Fableau of Dame Siriz, 43
The Fables of Bidpai, 43
The Fair Captive: A Tragedy (1721), 35
"fairy tale" foundation, 61
femme-fatale figures, 224
Ferdowsī, 151, 226
"feudal vices", 121
fictional symbolism, 147
Fischer, Herman, 7
The Flagellant (1788), 127
Flaxman, John, 79, 94
"The Flight and Return of Mohammed", 116, 118, 168
Foot, William, 128
Forbes, James, 37
Ford, Talisa J., 100
foreign factors, 1, 18n1
Forging Romantic China, 215
France, 9, 11, 24, 26, 28–30, 33, 36, 52, 101, 171–172, 178, 207–208
anticlericalism in, 30
anti-religious turn in, 30
defeat in the seven years war (1756–1763), 33
declaration of war with England (1793), 29
liberal policy, 26
Oriental Tales's popularity, 24
policy of religious tolerance, 26
stakes in decadent Ottoman Empire, 33
Franco-British war (1793–1815), 29
Frank, Fredrick S., 58
Franklin, Michael J., 8
French Revolution, 25–26, 28, 30, 33, 171, 227
aftermath of the, 13
Biblical prophecy, 26
moral threats and, 30
republicanism in England, 28
rise of Napoleon and, 33
Frye, Northrop, 74
Fulford and Attar, 186
Fuller, David, 95

G

Gaelic tradition, 24
Garcia, Humberto, 34, 95, 109, 168–169, 184
Garden of Knowledge, 186
Gebir, 6–7, 15–16, 64–66, 106–115, 119, 125, 162, 184, 223
Geddes, Alexander, 83
A General Dictionary, Historical and Critical (1737–1741), 35
George III, 112, 192
Gibbon, Edward, 89
Gilpin, George H., 142
Gita Govinda, 67
Glorious Revolution of 1688–1689, 25
Godwin, William, 27
Goldsmith, 52
Golgonooza, 86, 101
'good native' and 'bad native', 115
Gospel of Jesus, 83, 92, 170, 173
Gothic, 12–14, 23, 40, 45–46, 58–62, 64–65, 70, 98–100, 108–109, 120–122, 127, 146–148, 156, 161–162, 164–166, 178, 189, 224, 227–228
  advent of, 22
  architecture, 23
  darkness images, 147–148
  effulgence of, 58, 71n12
  images of horror, 121
  Imperial Gothic, 147
  influence of, 109
  narratives, 65
  otherness, 121, 127
  relation with the Oriental Tale, 12, 57
  role of Oriental Tale, 14
  tools, 98
  traditionalist features of, 98
  tragedy, 61
  villain-heroes, 65
  wandering motif, 100
Gothic novels, 23, 40, 58, 61–62, 64–65, 70, 108–109, 161, 164, 166, 224
  demonic women in, 110, 120
  elements from, 164
  features of, 60–61
  formula for, 62
  growth of, 23
  heroines of, 64
  images from, 121
  impact of, 109
  influence on Romanticism, 13
  motifs of, 61
  role molding Romanticism, 12
  sadistic patriarchs of, 166
  sensitive heroines of, 64
  villain-hero, 120
Gothic conventions, development of, 59
Gothic elements, theorization of, 121
Gothic horror, 121, 146
Gothic narratives, Oriental Tales and, 156
Gothic tale, alternative aesthetic principle, 14
Gothicism, 13, 23–24, 65
Gothicizing of culture, 147
Grammar of Persian Language, 67
Grant, Charles, 15, 39, 81, 111, 131, 138, 150, 214, 217
Grant, John E., 88

Gray, Thomas, 23
Grecian war of independence, 211
Greco-Roman heritage, 5, 66, 150
  cultural superiority of, 150
  superiority of, 14
Greco–Roman tradition, 84, 193
Greek War of Independence, 17, 210, 227
Gross, Kenneth, 61
Guardian Genius, 55
Gueullette, Thomas Simon, 50
guilt and shame, poisonous effects of, 60

H

habeas corpus, 29
Habed-il-Kalib, 119
Haddad, Emily, 8–10, 206
Halhed, N.B., 74
Hall, Robert, 30
Hamilton, Elizabeth, 45–46
Harries, Tal, 174, 176–177, 181
Hastings, Warren, 36–38, 58
Hastings trial, 15, 38, 81, 121, 131, 140, 150, 191
"The Haunted Tree", 206–207, 216
Haywood, Eliza, 35
Hayy Ibn Yakzan, 49, 181, 205–206
Hazar Afsanah (*A Thousand Legends*), (225 and 250 CE), 46
Heaney, Seamus, 222
Hegel, Regarding, 212
Heiroglyphic Tales, 61
Heliocentric model of Western European, 89
Hellas, 18, 227
Hellenism, 34, 182
Hermetic Tradition, 109, 113
The Hermit, 44, 96–97, 156
Hickathrift, Tom, 156
Hieroglyphic Tales (1785), 44–45
high-domed Mosques, 125
"Hindoo tale", 133
Hindoostanee, 134
Hindu Hymns, 223
"Hindu India", 10, 38
Hindu mythology, 67, 74, 129, 135, 223
The Hindu Pantheon (1810), 75, 79, 176
Hindu romance, 132
Hindu society, priest-ridden state of, 81
Hinduism, 2, 10–12, 14–17, 38, 70, 75, 77–78, 80–81, 83, 85–87, 130–131, 133–134, 136, 138, 143, 146, 182–183, 221, 227
  absurdity of, 143
  ancientness of, 77
  Christian interpretations of, 75
  Christianization of, 142, 151
  conceived as evil, priest-ridden and ritualistic, 80
  criticism of, 17
  denigration of, 16
  ethos of, 81
  idea of, 10, 83
  inception of, 78
  India and, 10–11, 14, 76, 85, 106, 173, 183
  monstrosities of, 134
  myths and theological ideas of, 12
  negative image of, 15

primitivism and degeneration of, 111
public paranoia, 16
as the 'sunny' religion, 83
sunny view of, 70
theological ideas of, 12, 16
valorization of, 38
Hindukush mountains, 104n8
The History of British India, 226
History of Hindostan (1795), 174
History of Hindostan (1796–98), 37, 75
History of Hindustan, 148
The History of the Decline and Fall of the Roman Empire, 167
The History of the Saracens, 196
History of the Saracens, 35, 196, 205
History of the Turks, 35
History of Western Philosophy (1946), 222
Hitopodesa, 67
Hodges, William, 37, 189
Holwell, J.H., 74
homogenization process, 11
Hoole, John, 56
horror, element of, 58, 62
Hughes, William, 65
human 'hypocrisy', 78
humanitarianism, 28

I

Ibrahim the Thirteenth Emperor of the Turks (1696), 35
idolatrous worship of authenticity and truth, 45
Imitation from the Persian (1828), 106
Imperial Gothic, genre of, 147
imperialism, 1, 9, 14, 54, 80, 102, 173, 192
Imr-al-Qais, 67
India
Blake's approach, 76, 85–86
British attention, 36
British knowledge formation, 37, 133
Christianization of Hindus, 139, 151
Coleridge's attitude, 174–175, 183
crucial location for Europe, 32
cruelty of the British rulers in, 56
curatorial policy in, 69
emergence of missionary activities, 225
England's policy, 33
Europe's incursion into, 36
Hindu India, 38
and Hinduism, 11, 14
Indianism, 151
literary tradition, 222
missionary activities in, 225
negative image of, 15
non-Christians in, 217
originary moments of the British empire, 174
perception of, 11
as "priest-ridden, cruel and despotic", 83
romantic imagination, 10
romantic reception and representation of, 9
Southey's engagement, 106, 131, 135

transfer of power, 38
Western approach to, 69
See also Hinduism
"Indian Bonaparte". *See* Kehama
Industrial Revolution, 25
infanticide, 137, 191
Institutes of Hindu Law, 196
Interesting Historical Events, Relative to the Provinces of Bengal (1765–1768), 37, 175
Irwin, Robert, 73, 120
Islam and English Enlightenment, 1670–1840, 34, 90, 92, 96, 168–170, 184, 194
Islam, 2–3, 8, 10–12, 15–17, 34–35, 63, 65, 76–77, 87–92, 94–97, 106–107, 116–119, 122–123, 127, 130, 142, 167–173, 178, 184, 194, 210, 227
conflict with Christianity, 107
criticism of, 17
as heroic religion, 178
laws of, 63
licentiousness of, 15
licentiousness, 88
Middle East and, 11, 33, 106
misconceptions about, 127
myths and theological ideas of, 12
religion of carnality and sacrilege, 89
sexual profligacy, 88, 210
theological ideas of, 12, 16
traditional views of, 15
Islamic liberty to Egypt, 169
Islamic monotheism, 15, 17, 117, 169, 224
Islamic Orient, 77, 118, 173
Islamic republicanism, 34, 91–92, 96, 169
Islamic theology, 35, 119, 223
"Islamicizing of a 'White' English poet", 96
Ivanhoe (1819), 8

J

Jacobinical School, 30
Jagannath festival, 145
Jahangir, 36
Jarvis, Robin, 25, 28, 30
Jayadeva, 67
Jeffrey, Francis, 6
Jerusalem (*A Blake Dictionary*), 86–87
Jerusalem, Fall of, 85, 169
Jerusalem: The Emanation of the Giant Albion, 15, 86, 101–102
Joan of Arc, 151
Johnson, A.K, 79, 82
Johnson, Joseph, 75
Johnson, Mary Lynn, 88
Jones, William, 10, 15, 17, 21, 37, 56, 58, 67, 74–75, 78, 130, 175, 184, 186, 189, 195, 212, 216, 222, 228
Journey to East Indies (1782), 140
Judaeo-Christian-Islamic idea, 92
Judaism, 91
Judeo-Christian and the Hindu framework, 190
Judeo-Christian machinery, 169
Judeo–Christian tradition, 83, 85

K

The Kalendar, 106
Kalidasa, 67
Kashmir, 48, 148, 188–189
  contemporary writings on, 188
  paradise image, 189
  popular narratives, 148
Keats, 48, 64
Kehama, 129–130, 137–138, 143
Kejariwal, O.P., 69, 80
Kelley, Theresa M., 205
Kelly, Gary, 121
Keri, Davies, 75
The Koran, Commonly Called the Alcoran of Mohammed (1734), 34
Krause, Karl, 217
"Kubla Khan", 6, 49, 66, 85, 148–149, 155–156, 163, 169, 173, 183–194, 224, 226
  impact of the 'holiness', 190
  interpretation of, 192
  landscape of, 191
Kubla Khan and the Fall of Jerusalem, 85

L

The Lady of the Lake (1810), 7
Lake School, 30
Lalla Rookh, 6–7, 65
Landor, W.S., 6–7, 13, 15–16, 64–66, 106–111, 113–116, 119, 125, 130–131, 133, 184, 223
  anti-colonial statement, 111
  characteristic of, 115
  oriental tale, 113
  'peopled' country, colonizing of, 110–111
  republican internationalism, 110
Lara, 64
Larrissy, E., 89–90
Lay of the Last Minstrel, 7
Leask, Nigel, 9, 115, 170, 192
Lectures on the Sacred Poetry of the Hebrews, 24
Lee, Debbie, 44
Lepanto, sea battle of, 32
Les Ruins (1791), 36, 82
Lessenich, 23, 25, 30
Letters from Xo-Ho (1757), 52
Letters of John Wordsworth, 214
Letters of William and Dorothy, 214
Letters Persanes or *The Persian Letters* (1721), 51
Letters Writ by a Turkish Spy, 43, 51
Levant Company, 32
Levy, Michelle, 166
Lewis, Gregory, 49
Lewis, M.G., 49, 161, 165
"The Lewti", 155, 190, 224
The Life and Death of Mahumed (1679), 34
lingchhi, 191
Linnell, John, 93
literary medievalism, 23–24
Literature of Terror, 98–99, 162
Locke, John, 27
lofty obelisks, 125
London Missionary Society, 131
London theatres, 1
Longman, T., 202, 221
Lonsdale, Roger, 22

"loose Bible", 89. *See also* Qur'an
The Lord of the Isles (1815), 8
Louis XIV, French court of, 51
Louis XVI, 112
love-diplomacy, 110
lower caste, persecution of, 141
Lowes, J.L., 9, 156, 183
Lowth, Robert, 24
"Lucy Poems", 206
lust, element of, 110
Lynda Pratt, 130, 132, 135
Lyrical Ballads (1798), 6–7, 13, 17, 155, 194–197, 224, 228
Lyttenton, Lord, 52

M

Mackintosh, Sir James, 174
Macpherson, 24, 44
magic, element of, 120
'magisterial' approaches, 151
magnificent palaces, 125
Mahan, Alfred, 2
"Mahomet", 155, 167–172
Mahomet the Impostor, 90, 92
Majid, Javed, 4–5, 135, 149–180, 192, 196, 198
Majumdar, Aparajita, 175
Makdisi, Saree, 9, 74, 89, 212
Malice of Woman, 49
Marie, Jean Louis, 196
Marmion (1808), 7
Maruth, Haruth, 120
Matthews, William, 197
Maugraby, 119–120, 223
Mazarin Library, 108
medievalism, 22, 24
Melmoth, the Wanderer, 59
metaphorical rubbish, 123
Middle East, 3, 8–9, 11, 33–36, 206–207, 209, 211
  cross-cultural negotiations, 34
  Islam and, 11, 33, 106
  Muslims in, 11
  power struggle in, 227
  rise of Islam in, 11
  romantic creativity, 8
  romantic reception and representation of, 9
Middle Eastern desert, poetic use of the, 216
Middle English romances, heroines of the, 64, 110
Midgley, Robert, 51
Mill, James, 4, 226
millenarian radicalism, 26
Miller, J. Hillis, 201
Milton, 84, 86–87, 151, 186, 212, 217
Mirandola, Pico della, 181
Missionary Tracts, 137
Mitchell Library, Sydney, 168
Miurtadi, Reverend Doctor, 108
mob imagery, 145–146
mob violence, 146
Modern Infidelity (1801), 30
Mogul Tales or The Dreams of Men Awake, 50
The Mollakat, 67
The Monk (1796), 49, 62–64, 110, 120–121, 162, 166
monolithic Christendom, 33
Montagu, Wortley, 37
Monthly Mirror, 134

Moor, Edward, 79, 176
Moore, Thomas, 6–7, 65
Morocco, 3
Mosaic religion, 38
The Most Material Points of the Mahometan Religion (1668), 34
motifs, 46, 61, 65, 74, 99, 110, 121
Mughal emperors, 'dark rules' of, 80
Murad the Unlucky, 44
Muscovy Company, 32
Mysore, third battle of, 144
The Mysterious Mother (1768), 61
The Mystical Poet of The English Church (1919), 89
Mystries of Udolpho, 58
The Myth of the Lazy Native, 124
mythological syncretism, 86

N

Nabokov, Vladimir, 73
Napoleon
  Egyptian expedition (1798–1801), 66, 169
  redemptive freedom, 115
Napoleonic imperialism, 192
narrative structures, 65
A Natural History of Aleppo (1756), 35
Nawab of Bengal, 36
necromancy, 59, 110
neo-classical critics, 23
neoclassicism, 22–24, 31, 40, 65
  literary dissent, 40
  norms of, 22
  rules of, 31
  spirit of, 22
neo-Platonism, 181
New Arabian Nights, 44
"Nilotic mud", 3
Nonconformity, rise of, 25
non-European culture, 77
non-Judeo-Christian culture, 77
Norton Anthology of English Literature, 65
'Noureddin and the Fair Persian' tale, 188
Nourjahad (1767), 48

O

O'Gorman, Ned, 23
Ober, Warren U., 168
"Observations on Egypt,", 173
Ockley, Simon, 35, 49, 196, 205
Ode on the Battle of Algiers (1818), 106
Old Testament prophecy, 170
Oneness, principle of, 178
Ordinances of Manu (1796), 174
The Orient and the Young Romantics, 8
Oriental artifice, 126
Oriental corruption, 5
Oriental Dreams, 3, 226
Oriental Eclogues (1782), 44, 54, 56
Oriental elements, theorization of, 121
Oriental Field Sports, 4
Oriental Gothic, 58
Oriental Homer, 126, 150–151
oriental idyll, 184
Oriental luxury, 110
Oriental Memoirs (1813), 37

Oriental Other, 13, 59, 121–122, 127, 212
The Oriental Renaissance, 1, 193, 221
Oriental Renaissance, 1, 5, 9, 13, 74, 107, 120, 149, 192–193, 200, 224–225, 227–228
  anxiety and fear of the poet, 193
  failure of, 224
  hearth of, 9
  influence of, 224
  new sources of creativity, 149
Oriental romances, 136
Oriental scholarship, 66–67
  political implications, 68
Oriental Tales, 1, 7, 24, 40, 43–45, 47, 51–52, 57–62, 64–65, 70, 107–108, 156, 163–165, 167, 223
  advent of, 65
  alternative aesthetic principle, 14
  collections of, 13, 43, 48, 223, 228
  common features of, 60
  economic ends, 57
  elements, 13, 16, 62, 156, 161, 165, 224
  features of, 12, 60, 120
  formal elements, 224
  genre of, 62
  Gothic narratives and, 156
  history of, 47, 57, 51
  images from, 121
  imaginative collections of, 228
  influence analysis, 109
  influence on Romanticism, 13
  lust and violence, 64
  major translations of, 50
  pleasure of, 57
  popularity of the, 24
  pre-Romantic period, 14
  presence in Europe, 43
  relation with English novel, 48
  relation with Gothic, 12, 57
  role in molding Romanticism, 12
  role in the development of Romanticism, 223
  of terror, 62
  unpredictable nature, 158
The Oriental Tales (1745), 45
Oriental verse romances, 106
Orientalism, 4, 7–9, 11, 14, 21–22, 24, 65–66, 68, 73, 76–77, 81, 83, 110–111, 118–119, 122, 147, 182, 184, 194, 211–222, 227
  biblical root of, 184
  component of eighteenth-century is, 77
  critical approaches to, 8
  history of, 69
  modern Orientalism, 66, 76
Orientalist poems, occidental core of, 32
Orientalist Poetics: The Islamic Middle East in the Nineteenth Century English and French Poetry, 8
Osmond, Lord, 165
Osmond, Percy H., 89
Osorio, 16, 155, 161, 178–180, 224, 226
Ossian poems, 24
Ossianism, 24
Otherness, 122, 211–212
  images of, 121
Ottoman Empire, 33

P

Pachori, Satya Sheel, 21–22, 67, 86, 185–186, 197–200
Paine, Thomas, 27
Paine, Tom, 83
Paley, Morton, 95
pan-European Christendom, 12
pantheism, 17, 177
Pantisocracy project, 152n5, 167
  failure of, 172
Paradise Lost, 186
pariah, 136, 139–140
Parnell, Thomas, 96
Patriarchs, 84–85
Peace Treaty of Karlowitz, 33
Peacocke, Richard, 35
Percy, Bishop, 24
Peregrinaggio, 50
Persia, 3
Persian Eclogues (1742), 44, 52, 120
'Persian epic', 130
The Persian Letters (1735), 52
The Persian Tales or Thousand and One Days (1714), 44, 48
Perso-Arabic poetic tradition, 222
Philhellenism, 210, 227
Phillips, Thomas, 96
Philmus, Robert, 202
Philosophical Enquiries into the Origin of the Ideas of Sublime and Beautiful (1757), 23
Pike, Martha Conant, 24, 43–44, 47
Pilgrimage, 196
Pinto, V. de Sola, 195
Pitt, William, 28
Pix, Mary, 35
Plassey, battle of, 36, 174
Poems Consisting Chiefly of Translations from the Asiatic Languages, 195
Poems from the Arabic and Persian (1800), 107
Poems on the Slave Trade, 29
Poeseos Asiaticae Commentariorum, 67
poetic genius, 82–83, 96
poetics and politics, 162
Poole, Thomas, 159, 174
post-Enlightenment notions of rationality, 65
Practical View (1797), 30
Pratt, Lynda, 130–132, 135
Pratt, Mary Louise, 9
The Prelude, 6–7, 17, 28, 53, 65, 146, 200–202, 204, 206, 211–213, 215–216, 221, 224
pre-Romantic medievalism, 22
Presbyterians, 25
The Present State of the Ottoman Empire Containing the Maximum of the Turkish Politic, 34
Price, Richard, 26
Prideaux, Humprey, 34
Priestly, Joseph, 26, 127
The Proces of Sevyn Sages, 43
Progress of Romance (1785), 108
Prometheus Unbound, 18, 65, 227
Prophet Muhammad, 17, 34, 116. *See also* Islam
Prophetic tradition, 91, 96
  interpretation of, 96
Protestant capitalism, 162
Protestant religion, 119

Protestantism, 162
pseudo-Oriental verse tales, 120
pseudo-translations
category of, 44, 51
imitations and, 46, 52
psychological curiosity, 193–194
Punter, David, 23, 58, 99, 161–162
Purchas His Pilgrimage, 187

Q

quakers, 25
Queene Mab, 65
Qur'an, 34
descriptions of paradise, 185
etymology of, 88
George Sale's translation of, 34, 94, 97, 109, 167, 184–185, 223
interpretation of Blake's, 89
paradise and paradisal landscapes references, 185

R

racial ideologies, 96
radical Protestants, 91, 113
radicalism, 26, 29, 31, 127, 129, 133, 156, 194, 225
Rana, Kabbani, 47, 188
Randonis, Jennifer, 99
Rasselas (1759), 44, 50, 57, 62, 133, 185
The Reception of Blake in the Orient (2006), 75–76
Reeve, Clara, 108
Reflections on the Revolutions in France, 27
Regulating Act of 1773. *See* East India Company Act, 36
reign of terror (1793–1794), 29
religio-mythological radicalism, 82
"Religious Musings", 161–162, 177, 224
religious proselytization, 102
religious syncretism, 12, 119
religious tolerance, 26
Reliques of Ancient English Poetry (1765), 24
Remorse, 155, 178. *See also* Osorio
Renaissance, Greco-Roman heritage, 66
representational politics, 122, 211, 215
republican internationalism, 110
republicanism, 28, 54, 127
The Retreat of Mirth, or *The Dangerous*, 60
The Revenge (1721), 35
reverse acculturation, 135
Revolt of Islam, 65, 142
The Rhetoric of English India, 121
"rich Bazars", 125
Richardson, Alan, 111
Rickman, John, 139
Rights of Man (1791–1792), 27
Riley-Smith, J., 8
The Rime of the Ancient Mariner, 6–7, 65, 155–156
The Rise and Progress of Mahometanism (1674), 34, 91
The Road to Xanadu: A Study in the Ways of the Imagination (1927), 156
Roberts, Daniel Sanjib, 10
Robinson Crusoe (1719), 50, 162

Robinson, Crabbe, 96
Rockby (1813), 7
Roderick, the Last of the Goths (1814), 106
Roe, Thomas, 36
"The Romance of the Water Lily", 7, 66, 209
Romantic genre, 162
Romantic Gothicism, 13
Romantic Hellenism, 34
Romantic heroes, 65
Romantic imagination, 1, 8, 10
Romantic Imperialism, 35, 70, 213
Romantic Orientalism, 6, 8, 13, 65
- categories of critical voices, 9
- characteristic of, 118
- connection with Romantic Gothicism, 13
- critique of, 9
- dimensions of, 8

Romantic period, 8, 10–11, 14–15, 21–22, 31, 33, 38, 44, 57, 107, 127, 186, 191, 193–194, 222, 224
Romantic philhellenism, 227
Romantic poetry,
- female magicians in, 64
- Orient in, 9
- Romantic theory of poetry, 28
- satanic villain-heroes, 65
- stereotypes of the East, 10

Romantic poets, 1–3, 5, 9–10, 12–15, 17–18, 31, 35, 37–38, 48, 64, 121, 142, 205, 212, 222–227
- first generation, 5, 12, 28, 70
- Unitarian sensibility, 35

Romantic Unitarianism, 169
Romantic verse narratives, 7, 45, 52–53, 111, 209
Romantic writers, sensibilities of, 1
Romanticism and the Slave Narratives, 162
Romanticism, 1, 8–9, 12–14, 48, 65, 68, 162, 169, 194, 211–212, 222–223, 227–228
- critical approaches to, 8
- defining moment for, 194
- definition, 9
- development of, 223, 225
- early phase of, 8
- early phase syncretism, 14
- Gothic novel role of, 12
- Hinduism, role of, 12
- Islam, role of, 12
- manifesto of, 200
- Oriental Tale role of, 12
- spirit of, 12
- strands of, 65

Ross, Alexander, 34. *See also* Qur'an
Rubaiyat, 67
The Ruins: or a Survey of the Revolutions of Empires (1791), 36, 75
Russell, Alexander, 35
Russell, Bertrand, 222
Russia, 32–33, 101
- stakes in decadent Ottoman Empire, 33

Rycaut, Paul, 34–35

S

"sacred wave", 55
Saglia, Diego, 126

Said, Edward, 20, 41, 66, 68, 76–77, 141, 222
Sale, George, 34
Sanskrit text, 66, 79, 189
satanic school, 30
satanic villain-heroes, 65
sati, 81, 138, 141–142, 145, 147, 191
    romantic artists' view, 142
    spectators of, 145
Saurat, Denis, 74
Schwab, Raymond, 1, 8–9, 66–68, 79, 221, 224–225, 227
scientific rationalism, 25
Scott, John, 54
Scott, Walter, 7
Sedgewick, Kosofsky, 59
Seditious Meetings Act, 29
Select Views of India, 189
Sendehar, Kalila and Dimna, 43
sentimental nature-worship, 39
September Massacres (1792), 29
Septimi Gades, 206–207
Serendipity and the Three Princes, from the Peregrinaggio, 50
A Series of Poems, Containing the Plaints of Consolations and Delights of Achmed Ardebeili, a Persian Exile (1797), 196
Seven Champions, 156
Seven Years War, 33, 36
sexual passion, 63
Shaffer, E.S., 85, 168
Shaftsbury, Earl of, 26
Shahnameh, 226
Shahrazad, 47–48, 163
Shakespeare, 212, 217
Shakuntala (1790), 67
Sharafuddin, Mohammad, 8, 108–110, 114, 120, 122
Shelley, P.B., 7, 18, 64–65, 142
Shorter Oxford English Dictionary, 3
Siege of Corinth, 164
Sierra Leone Company, 128
'Sindbad the Sailor' tale of, 159–160
Singh, Charu Sheel, 74
sin-punishment-redemption, 156, 162
Siraj-ud-Daulah, Nawab of Bengal, 37
The Sixth Voyage of Sindbad the Sailor, 187
slave-trade lobby, 173
Smart, Christopher, 23
Smith, Andrew, 65
Smith, Nathaniel, 80
Smyser, James Worthington, 201
Sobieski, John, 33
Sohrab and Rustom, 67
The Soirées Bretonnes (*Breton Nights* 1712), 50
'The Solitary Reaper', 206
The Song of Los: Africa (1795), 78, 81, 83, 87, 89, 98
The Song of Los: Asia, 98
The Song of Los II: Asia, 80, 83
Songs of Experience, 93–94
Sonnerat, Pierre, 140
Sonoi, Chene, 128
Southey, Robert
    anglo-centrism and, 155
    binary model, 148
    changing ideological, 150
    comment on Bristol riots (1833), 145

condemnation of the Oriental art, 150
conversion poem, 134
denigration of Hinduism, 16
depiction of the ritual, 141
descriptive phrases, 118
desire for material success, 134
engagement with India and Hinduism, 106
engagement with Islam, 106, 118, 122
engagement with Middle East, 106, 118, 124
evangelism and, 155
imaginative scheme, 146
implausible presentation of Hindu deities, 134
initial plans for the epic on Muhammad, 116
involvement in anti-slavery campaign, 127
oeuvre on the Orient, 106
opinion on Hinduism, 133
Oriental romances, 136
Orientalism, 122
Orientalist construction, 122
personal interest in an Indian career, 131
radicalism, 127, 129
republican sentiments, 129
scheme of things, 139
Thalaba, 7
valorization of Hinduism, 134
valorization of working-class, 127

Specimens of the Arabian Poetry, 196
Spinoza, 177, 181–182, 217
Spinozan materialism, 17
spiritual autobiography, 155–156, 161–162
Spivak, Gayatri, 115
The Squire's Tale, 43
Standard Dictionary of English Language, 3
Staunton, George, 191
Stevenson, W.H., 87–88
Stubbe, Henry, 34, 91
Sung, Mei-Ying, 76
Supreme Reality, 177
Surah Al-Khaf, 97
Sybilline Leaves, 156
syncretism, 12, 14, 16, 38, 79, 98, 119, 151, 155, 169, 189, 194, 225–226
Syria, 3, 36, 171
System of Magic, 44

T

"Tale of Maugraby", 120
The Tale of Terror: A Study of the Gothic Romance, 58
Taleb, Abu, death of, 168
The Tales of the Genii, 134, 196
The Talisman (1825), 8
Taylor, William, 107, 116, 119
Test and Corporation Acts, repeal of (1828), 26
Tests Acts (1673 and 1678), 25–27
Thalaba, the Destroyer (1801), 5–7, 15–16, 51, 53, 64–66, 106–107, 115–121, 123, 125–127, 129–130, 136, 145, 149, 162, 167, 173, 184, 201, 223
authentic document on Arabian life and Islam, 123

belief in Islamic monotheism, 117
celebration of the unfaltering faith, 127
central plot, 119
characterization of, 127
clear-cut division of characters in, 121
depiction of the Middle East in, 123
echoes of, 118
exoticism in, 126
exoticized image of the East, 127
Gothic features of, 120
images of fountains and rivers, 149
Islamic theology, 119
lasciviousness, 126
lust, 126
opulence, 126
pastiche patching, 119
representation of Islam in, 117–118, 173
representation of Islamic Orient, 118, 173
voluptuous vale, 123
working class' hero, 129

The Song of Los (1795), 78, 81, 89, 91
Thomas, Gordon K., 201
Thomas, Helen, 162
Thompson, James, 23
Thornton, Henry, 128
The Thousand and One Nights (1704), 43
Thousand-and-one Nights, 134
Tintern Abbey, 198, 206, 218
"Tipooing". *See* Tipu Sultan
Tipu Sultan, 144, 190
The Toleration Act of 1689, 25
Translations of the Letters of a Hindoo Rajah (1796), 45–46
Travels in Africa, Egypt and Syria from the Years 1792 to 1798 (1799), 36
Travels in China (1804), 37
Travels in India (1793), 37, 189
Travels in Syria and Egypt, During the Years 1783, 1784, & 1785 (1788), 36
Travels in Various Countries of Europe, Africa and Asia (1810), 36
Travels through Barbary, 196
Travels to Discover the Source of the Nile (1790), 185
Travels to Discover the Source of the Nile, (1768, 1769, 1770, 1771, 1772 and 1773), 35
Treason Trials, 30
Treasonable Practices Act of 1795, 29
Trinitarian Christianity, 172–173, 181, 194
'tropicopolitans', 105n17
The True Nature of Imposter fully displayed in the Life of Mahomet (1697), 34
Tufyal, Ibn, 49–50, 205
Turkey, 3, 32, 35, 211
Turkish Embassy Letters (1776), 35
Turkish power, decline of, 11
The Turkish Spy, 51
The Turkish Tales, 44

Two Treatises on Government (1689), 27

U

Ungoverned Imaginings: James Mill's The History of British India and Orientalism (1992), 4
Unitarian Jacobinism, 169
unitarian sensibility, 35
Unitarianism, 17, 169, 172–173
Unitarians, 25, 128, 169
Universal Histories, 167–168
Upanishadic golden age, 10
Upanishads, 66

V

Valentia, Lord, 37
Vallins, David, 182, 190
Vasco da Gama, 39
Vathek (1786), 44–45, 58–64, 107, 109–110, 120–121, 161
Vathek, Faustian, 61
Vattier, M. Pierre, 108
Vienna, siege of, 32–33
villain-hero, 64–65, 120, 224
A Vindication of the Rights of Men (1790), 27
A Vindication of the Rights of Woman (1792), 28
Vision of Mirza, 44
A Vision of the Last Judgment, 91–92
Viswanathan, Gouri, 135
Volney, 36
voluptuous vale, 123
Voyages and Travels to India (1809), 37

W

Walpole, Horace, 23, 44–45, 52, 60
Walter Savage Landor, 6, 106
wandering, element of, 64
Warren, Andrew, 1, 8, 182
Wat Tyler, 128–129
Waugh, Evelyn, 73
Webb, Timothy, 34
Weir, David, 74, 78
Western 'barbarian', 151
Western Orientalism, 3
Westminster School, 127
White, Daniel, 134, 169
whitewashing, 96
Wilberforce, William, 30, 39, 128, 131, 137, 150, 214, 217
Wilkins, Charles, 74, 79
William Blake and the Impossible History of the 1790s (2003), 74
William III, 112
Williamson, Thomas, 4
The Witch of Atlas, 65
witchery of Dalica, 108
Wollstonecraft, Mary, 27
Wordsworth and Enlightenment, 206
Wordsworth, John, 214–215
Wordsworth, William, 6–7, 12–13, 17, 28, 30, 34, 48, 65–66, 145–146, 155, 158, 174, 194–202, 204–219, 221–222, 224, 227–228
  account of the dream vision, 201
  'conversion' poems, 209
  crowd/mob imagery, 146, 212
  cultural anxiety, 212
  debt to the Oriental Renaissance, 200

decline of poetic power, 214
deep knowledge of the Hindu theological tradition, 218
dream sequence, 202
engagement with the East, 17
idea of poetry and poetic creation, 201
imperial anxiety, 212
manifesto of Romanticism, 200
pantheism, 217
poetic practice, 200
poetry of the desert, 206
primacy to Christianity, 211
represents the Islamic East, 208
Wordsworth's Reading 1770– 1799, 196, 202
Wordsworthian landscape, 207
'working class' hero, 129
The Works of Ossian (1765), 24
Wright, Julia, 102
Writing the Empire, 128, 136, 141, 144
Wu, Duncun, 202
Wat Tyler(1794), 29, 128–129

X

Xanadu, 156, 171, 185, 192, 222

Y

Young, Edward, 35

Z

Zadig, 50, 62
Zatani/Satan, evil disciples of, 119
Zend-Avesta, 66, 129–130
Zofanny, Johan, 142
Zoroaster, 130
Zoroastrianism, 12, 129

About the Author

Dr Md. Monirul Islam is Assistant Professor in the Department of English, Presidency University, Kolkata. His area of expertise is British Romantic poetry. He has been researching the Eastern connections of the first generation Romantic poets for a decade or so, and the present book gives a visible shape to his research. He is also keenly interested in posthumanist theories and is trying to locate the trans/posthumanist tendencies in the discursive practices of the British Romantics. In the essay, "'European Mind . . . engrafted upon the African constitution': Robert Southey's Theory of Miscegenation in the Tranhumanist Context," which forms the opening chapter of the book *Black Black Bodies and Transhuman Realities: Scientifically Modifying the Black Body in Posthuman Literature and Culture* (Lexington Books, 2019), he has effectively read Southey with reference to transhumanism.

Other areas of his interest are travel writing, pilgrimage as travel, and the philosophy of walking.